EMPIRICISM, EXPLANATION
AND
RATIONALITY

EMPIRICISM, EXPLANATION

AND

RATIONALITY

An Introduction to the Philosophy
of the Social Sciences

LEN DOYAL and ROGER HARRIS

ROUTLEDGE & KEGAN PAUL
London

First published in 1986 by
Routledge & Kegan Paul Ltd

11 New Fetter Lane, London EC4P 4EE

Set in Sabon 10/11pt.
by Falcon Graphic Art Ltd, Wallington, Surrey
and printed in Great Britain by
T J Press (Padstow) Ltd,
Padstow, Cornwall

British Library CIP Data
Doyal, Len
Empiricism, explanation and rationality:
an introduction to the philosophy of
the social sciences.
1. Social sciences — Philosophy
I. Title   II. Harris, Roger
300'.1   H61
ISBN 0–7100–9646–1 (c)
0–7102–0960–6 (p)

For our parents
and
in memory of Lin Layram

CONTENTS

Contents

PREFACE

For many years we have taught the philosophy of the social sciences on a variety of academic levels to students studying the entire spectrum of social scientific disciplines. The general problems from which we begin and to which we constantly return in this teaching are those which give this book its title – empiricism, explanation and rationality. Related questions which dominate most writing in the area concern the role of experience and evidence in the social sciences, the extent to which the explanation of human activity requires a different approach to that of the natural sciences and whether or not western science and culture have any greater purchase on truth and morality than the beliefs of other cultures. In our view, the educational importance of these questions cannot be overestimated. On the one hand, their analysis provides a conceptual map of what otherwise can become a labyrinth of contrasting traditions, confusing jargon and empirical detail. On the other hand, it enables students from an early stage to reflect critically on the 'big' issues confronting their respective disciplines. Unless they are in a position to do so, habits of thought can become established which seem natural but which are in fact specific to particular texts, lecturers or departments.

We have long been dissatisfied with existing 'introductions' to the philosophy of the social sciences for two reasons. First, some texts which purport to be introductory simply are not and presuppose too much background in both philosophy and social science. Second, many simpler texts reflect a sort of 'Plato to NATO' approach through summarizing a range of conflicting positions, partly presented through less than clear quotations from a variety of philosophers and social scientists. The former approach leads all but the best students to become even more mystified and frightened by philosophy than they were before beginning a formal study of it. The latter can just create confusion and disenchant-ment through suggesting that philosophical analysis is little more than a description of the arguments of other (often dead!) writers rather than something that offers the prospect of resolving the most important conceptual and explanatory problems confronting the social sciences.

This book is an attempt to provide an alternative. We have tried to simplify concepts and arguments as much as possible, each chapter building on those preceding. Yet we have also argued for quite specific theses concerning empiricism, explanation and rationality and hope to have introduced a coherent vision of the social sciences as a result. Our experience of teaching has suggested several conventions for achieving these aims and our text derives from material which has evolved in this context. Three of those conventions require justification as they may grate with more advanced readers.

First, we have kept references to specific writers to a minimum, deliberately avoiding quotations and offering instead expositions consistent with the development of our overall argument. Such a problem-oriented approach admittedly leads to oversimplification in some cases, especially where various 'isms' are discussed. Second, to counteract this danger while at the same time remaining as instructive as possible, we have included an annotated bibliography at the end of each chapter which reflects its argumentative structure. We have focused on what we consider the most accessible relevant literature, providing suggestions on how arguments might be pursued on more advanced levels. For both of these reasons, we felt it unnecessary to include footnotes in the text. And third, aware of how abstract and distant philosophical arguments can seem to many readers, we have consistently addressed them in the second person 'you' rather than the more usual 'we'. The latter is always employed only to refer to ourselves. This might strike some as patronizing but it is not meant to be. We hope it creates a sense of intimacy and involvement with the text that will accentuate both the excitement of philosophical debate and its relevance to everyday life. It invites *you* to agree or disagree with *us*.

The first chapter introduces the problem of empiricism through criticizing its most commonsense formulations. Since contemporary literature in this area invariably discusses or presupposes an understanding of the sophisticated empiricism of Popper and the anti-empiricism of Kuhn, their positions are contrasted and criticized in turn. Chapter 2 outlines the historical background of, and the conceptual components of explanation in, the natural sciences. Here the aim is to give the reader who is not a scientist or logician a feel for the logical structure of such explanation, along with why ideas like causality and natural necessity pose interesting philosophical problems. Chapter 3 argues that human actions require explanation of a different sort to that which operates in the natural sciences: that they have reference to reasons and not causes. Chapter 4 shows that reasons themselves are always formulated within the context of a social environment of rules. This point carries profound implications for the conceptualization of both individual actions and individual minds. Chapter 5 articulates a conception of freedom which is consistent with what has been demonstrated to be the social character of action and of mind, as well as with the reality of individual responsibility and the potential attainment of political liberty. It also presents the concept of ideology in order to explain how people can freely act against their interests. The spectre of relativism raised both by attacks on empiricism and by our analysis of ideology is explained in chapters 6 and 7. The former introduces aspects of the philosophy of language necessary to understand arguments for relativism at their strongest. The latter shows what is wrong with those arguments. Finally, chapter 8 draws together from previous chapters the conceptual requirements for the explanation of social structure. It ends with a proposal for the moral evaluation of societies, likewise consistent with preceding arguments.

This book has been the consequence of a long collaboration. Len Doyal wrote several of the chapters and either heavily edited or rewrote the others. For this reason, he is responsible for the style and presentation of the final text. Roger Harris has taken responsibility for the correctness of the annotated bibliography. As regards the latter, and because we have deliberately avoided footnotes in the text, tribute is due to the authors who developed the classic examples which we have sometimes employed to illustrate our arguments. We hope to have referred to everyone who falls into this category in the bibliography. However, many of these illustrations have become such an established part of philosophical lore that we may have unintentionally missed out someone. For this we apologize in advance.

ACKNOWLEDGMENTS

Because of personal tragedies and professional commitments this book has taken a long time to produce. Throughout it all, there has been one person without whom it would not have been completed. At great costs to herself from a variety of perspectives, Lesley Doyal carefully criticized, edited and sometimes re-edited every chapter. Her contributions have been invaluable both philosophically and pedagogically. Her labour and patience are greatly appreciated by us both and can never be adequately repaid.

Susan and Julian Pritchard have also helped enormously towards the book's completion. They worked together to type, check and even further edit the text with insight, competence and friendship which was always beyond the call of duty.

Hannah Doyal, Ellie Harris, Ivan Ridsdale and especially Daniel Wilsher contributed with the kind of support and love at home which only wonderful young people can provide.

We thank our students and colleagues who over the years have responded to earlier drafts and succeeded in convincing us that the book was worth both writing and finishing. In particular, Jeff Evans, John Farquahar, Grenville Wall, Peter Osborne, Jonathan Powers and Roger Waterhouse have all made important contributions in these and other ways. We also thank Robin Blackburn and *New Left Review* for permission to transcribe in chapter 7 parts of our article 'The practical foundations of human understanding', *New Left Review*, no. 139, May-June 1983, pp. 59-78.

Finally, although he has never met either of us, we owe a special debt to Anthony Giddens. The spirit of anti-sectarianism and synthesis which dominates his work – along with, of course, his substantial theoretical contributions – have greatly influenced and encouraged us. Indeed, we would like nothing better than for this book to be viewed as a comprehensive introduction to the philosophical background to Giddens's writing.

1
THE PROBLEMS OF EMPIRICISM

Traditional ideas about scientific method have been the target of much recent criticism. This has been directed particularly against empiricism – a doctrine which proclaims that all knowledge ultimately originates in experience. Empiricists argue that the final arbiter of any dispute in science must be the evidence of observation. Where observation is unable to play this role then dogma, speculation or superstition – anything but science – are said to be the result. All those who do not abide by the precepts of empiricism are thus threatened with excommunication from the bosom of science. This view of science has come under increasing attack in recent decades. The critics of empiricism claim that it never was and never could be the method of science and that conscious or even unconscious adherence to its principles can retard progressive scientific discovery. Indeed, there are some who argue that there is no such thing as scientific progress and that the importance of observation in scientific inquiry is minimal. Empiricism is therefore at the centre of fundamental disputes over the methods and, more important, the authority of natural and social science. This chapter will provide an introduction to these disputes. The first two sections argue that observation cannot be viewed as the foundation of scientific knowledge. However, the third section makes it clear that empirical research is still vital for scientific inquiry but that its importance cannot be understood by an empiricist theory of knowledge.

Crude empiricism and its problems

Social scientists, like everyone else, are philosophers of knowledge. In other words, they all have theories of knowledge – 'epistemologies' – of which they may not be clearly aware, but which nevertheless structure their attitudes about what is and is not 'scientific'. Such theories offer solutions to three key problems. What is the origin of scientific knowledge? How is the merit of such knowledge established once it has supposedly been created? What is meant by scientific progress and how

1

can it be identified? In future, we shall refer to these problems as those of scientific *creativity*, scientific *assessment* and scientific *progress* respectively. Epistemological theories are important because they are used to decide which sorts of explanations of the natural and social world to take seriously. They also influence criteria of good scientific practice and training.

Empiricism in its crudest form is probably the epistemology which is most generally accepted by people without philosophical training. It embodies the most common beliefs about successful science and scientists and is implicit in the images employed in the media to depict them. Crude empiricism assumes that the scientist is a sort of *spectator* of the object of inquiry. In other words, reality is presumed to exist externally to scientists and its structure and content are seen to be independent of their beliefs or desires. The problem scientists face is thought to be analogous to the popular conception of the problem facing the good journalist – how to make contact with reality which is not distorted by preconceived ideas about what it might or might not be like. The scientist is thus viewed as a *subject* who is attempting to understand an *object* and is trying to be objective by eliminating the bias that could lead to inaccuracy. The result of such understanding is said to be scientific knowledge which can be accepted as certain or at least very highly probable. If contact with reality is distorted by subjective preference the resulting understanding is relegated to the status of mere belief or opinion. It may be interesting, colourful or moving but it will not be science.

It is all fine and good to present the prospect of such undistorted contact but how is it to be achieved? For crude empiricists, scientific inquiry consists of the undistorted recording of particular observations. Such observations may be gained, for example, from experiments or surveys – both methods of collecting empirical data which have been devised to facilitate the process of discovery. This picture of the successful scientist with a passively receptive mind has been likened to a 'blank slate' on which nature writes its experiential message. Provided the data of such experiences are not literally misperceived, again through bias of some kind, the message can be securely relied upon. Reality will have been explained.

Thus if you want to be a good scientist it follows from crude empiricism that you must begin by ridding yourself of all preconceptions about what you are going to study. Indeed, this is one of the main things a good scientific education is thought to achieve. You will then be in a position to collect particular observations which you hope will reflect the regularities of nature or society relevant to the problem you wish to solve. When you have collected what you consider to be enough evidence, you may develop an explanation of the problem by generalizing from it. If your explanation is firmly grounded in such evidence, it can be assumed to be certain. The less firmly grounded, the less probable the explanation. This form of empirical reasoning is known as *induction*. It is the method proposed by crude empiricism to distinguish scientific inquiry from non-scientific speculation and until the 1960s was regarded in this way by most scientists and many professional philosophers.

For example, suppose you are interested in the causes of unemployment in inner cities. Crude empiricism dictates that you must begin your investigations without anticipating their results. In a variety of different ways you will systematically collect as much evidence about such unemployment as possible. You might start by observing those things which consistently seem to be correlated with it (e.g. poor investment, poor education, bad housing, certain types of psychological attitudes among the unemployed). But to arrive at a correlation which you believe to be *causal* rather than *accidental*, you will need to devise experimental ways of eliminating those factors which sometimes just happen to accompany unemployment but cannot be said to cause it. Much literature about research methods in the social sciences contains detailed descriptions of experimental designs which attempt to achieve this aim. After carrying out such experiments you might conclude that some factors (e.g. bad housing) do not cause unemployment since you have observed that they do not always accompany it. Or you might conclude that other factors (e.g. poor investment) are causal because on the evidence they and the employment trends are correlated.

Once a factor is identified which on the available evidence the researcher *believes* to be causally connected with the events to be explained, crude empiricists argue that the next stage of the inquiry involves a process of generalization. By inductive reasoning from particular evidence to general conclusions, an explanation is formulated which purports to apply to all instances of these events regardless of when or where they occur. This will not only facilitate understanding but also enable predictions to be made. Suppose, for example, you conclude that lack of investment is the primary cause of all unemployment in inner cities. It will thus be possible to *deduce* from this generalization that wherever there is a significant lack of urban investment, it will be followed in proportion by a rise in urban unemployment. Then you can check to see whether or not this is the case. If not, the crude empiricist would conclude that the inductive method of generating the hypothesis in question had not been properly followed. Much the same process goes on in everyday relationships. When you think that your beliefs about someone are justified by your past experiences of them, you predict their responses to new situations by deducing what follows from these beliefs. In short, for crude empiricism, induction is the method of consolidating the observational link between scientists viewed as inquiring subjects, and reality viewed as the separate object of their inquiry. By contrast, deduction embodies the method by which knowledge that has been inductively generated is applied and extended to other empirical situations not yet observed.

If scientific work is carried out in this mechanical fashion, then solutions to the epistemological problems of scientific assessment and progress are said to follow automatically. Proper use of the method of induction deals with assessment for it is taken to lead inevitably to scientific explanations which are either certain or probable to a degree which can be calculated with some certainty. For example, a crude empiricist might argue that the physical law which states that gases expand when heated is certain because it has been proved by the particular observational evidence from which it was induced. Or it might be argued that though absolute certainty is unobtainable, it is possible to calculate the probability of the law on the basis of all of the known evidence which confirms it. In any case, it is assumed that if the inductive method of theory construction is correctly applied, the problem of scientific assessment will take care of itself. And if this same method is followed by successive generations of scientists, then progress will also be inevitable. According to crude empiricism, the history of science is the ever-increasing accumulation of particular observations and of general theories systematically generalized from them. It also involves the accumulation of successful experimental methods developed to extend observational capacity and to ensure observational accuracy. Scientific progress is therefore portrayed as cumulative. The accretion of facts by induction takes place step by step, gradually yielding increasingly reliable knowledge.

The theory of crude empiricism is intuitively appealing because on first hearing it sounds like a sensible way for inquiry to proceed. Moreover, its conception of human beings and their place in nature seems to be supported by natural science. Humanity is believed to be part of nature and as subject to the same laws that govern every other part of the material world. Thus all the information that you or any other organism receives from the surrounding world must derive from some *physical process* to which you are subjected by your environment. The senses are located in and depend upon those organs of the body which are especially sensitive to particular effects of the environment impinging upon them (e.g. light, heat, sound, pressure, etc.). Two factors supposedly determine the capacity of an organism to learn from such stimuli. First, it is assumed to be sensitive enough to discriminate between small changes in its surroundings over a wide range of possible stimuli. Second, the organism is believed automatically to correct the flux of incoming data in a manner which corresponds with the regularities of nature. This is why, for example, someone who has suffered brain damage may lose the capacity to experience the world in the 'normal' way required for scientific investigation to proceed. Learning on this model must be inductive, it is argued, since all the organism learns from are particular sensory inputs. Therefore, the growth of science is assumed to be a natural causal process akin to the rudimentary learning processes that occur in simple animals. While humans may differ from them in degree, the basic inductive picture of the accumulation of knowledge remains the same for both.

How then does the crude empiricist explain what are now regarded as the mistakes of the scientific past? Previous errors are, again, basically to be understood as the result of the improper application of inductive method. The scientists involved simply distorted the reliable observational link between knower and known because of their prejudice, bias, superstition or whatever. It follows from crude empiricism that the book of nature or society is written in observational terms and can be correctly read by all who open their minds, reasoning carefully by induction from the particular to the general. Of course it would be granted that primitive experimental technology can also limit scientific achievement. However, bias or avoidable error is held responsible if scientists are blind to the experimental potential of existing technology or to the need for new and better instrumentation. For example, crude empiricists like to recount the oversimplistic tale of Galileo's opponents who refused to look through his telescope because their experiences might have conflicted with their prejudices. Similar tales and images dominate the presentation of science in school and in the media and their influence explains why crude empiricism is such a widespread doctrine. Yet it is now rejected by most natural and social scientists. Among philosophers of science it has long been regarded as foolish. Why?

There are four major problems with crude empiricism: *selectivity, certainty, error* and *interpretation*. We will begin with the problem of selectivity. You have seen the background to the argument that preconceived ideas — beliefs which are held prior to empirical inquiry — are anathema to any scientific process of discovery. They supposedly lead to error because it is argued that the truth will reveal itself only through perceptions undistorted by preconceptions. This is why crude empiricists claim that the scientific method entails reasoning from particular observations to general theoretical conclusions, and not vice versa. But it should be clear that any scientific investigation must begin by picking out observations which are relevant to the problem at hand from the infinite number of others which are irrelevant. Scientists do not collect evidence in a conceptual vacuum and they cannot observe everything. When a specific inquiry begins, much potential evidence has already been deemed inappropriate. Thus rigorous selection has already taken place, even though the inquirer might not be consciously aware of it.

To continue with our previous example, if you were attempting to explain urban unemployment it is unlikely that you would regard the number of bricks, manhole covers or pigeons in unemployed areas as relevant evidence. It is equally unlikely that the colour of hair, the number of pets or the type of toothpaste of the unemployed would strike you as important. Selection is inevitable and since it is particular observational evidence which must be chosen, scientists cannot simply be reasoning from the particular to the general when they select. Therefore, their general theories about what *might* be the case must lead them to look out for particular observations which they expect *to be* the case. Such theories constitute expectations both about what will happen in specific situations and about what should be defined as 'natural' and not worth attention. This is why scientists are surprised when they are mistaken. Yet since they are prior to observations deemed scientifically relevant, it is precisely these expectations that the crude empiricists must incorrectly reject as impeding the progress of science. So, contrary to their doctrine, order and understanding are not imposed on the passive inquirer by the data of observation. Rather, they are actively created by the inquirer selecting from the otherwise indiscriminate input of the senses.

The problem of *certainty* is intimately related to that of selectivity. It arises because when scientists develop explanations of events, their aim is to show why those events (rather than any others) occur when and where they do. But in all fields of science it is necessary to go beyond a simple recounting of the event to be explained. Any understanding of the expansion of a given volume of a gas when it is heated, the generation of electricity from a battery, the cognitive development of a child or the defeat of the Spanish Armada requires more than a description of what is already known! The more empirical situations there are to which explanations apply, i.e. the more universal their application, the more worth critical exploration they will seem. For example it is clearly more challenging theoretically to argue that all gases expand whenever and wherever they are heated than to suggest that such expansion only occurs in the labs of one university on Friday afternoons. If Karl Marx's theories of capitalism were restricted in their application to London during the period when he worked in the British Museum, they would have attracted little interest. And so on. Yet this need for explanatory generality poses a problem concerning assessment for crude empiricism. For the more the scientific attractiveness of an explanatory theory depends on its general applicability, the more difficult it will be to demonstrate the certainty or high probability on which the doctrine lays so much stress. Indeed, if any theory really does purport to be universal in its application, its proof will be impossible. There will always be the possibility of discussing conflicting empirical evidence which will not have been realized either for reasons of practicality (e.g. acquiring the funds to do all the necessary research) or of principle (e.g. there are parts of the universe which we shall never reach to do any research).

In the next chapter we shall look further at what more might be involved in explaining something, over and above merely recounting what happened. Suffice it to say at this point that the need always to go beyond a mere report of events in order to explain them means that the truth of explanations is always *underdetermined* by the evidence available. Everything a theory explains could be evidence for its truth, but in order to account for this evidence, the theory must go beyond it. Again, this is why a theory can never be fully supported or proved by the evidence of what it can explain. It is in this sense, for example, that even assuming that all of the available evidence supports Marx's theory of capitalism, it cannot be said to be certain – any more than the evidence that you have never been run over by a car proves that you never will be. Or to use a famous, though hackneyed, philosophical example, no matter how many white swans you may have observed, this does not prove the contention that 'All swans are white'. Ask any Australian! In short, although many interesting explanatory theories are taken to be universal in intent, it does not follow that they will be successfully universal in

application. Because of this problem of underdetermination, theories are
– like their originators – *fallible*. Accepting such fallibility does not mean
denying that some theoretical beliefs are better than others. It simply
means that it is necessary to find some other sense of 'better' than
'certain'.

The third problem with crude empiricism – *error* – concerns this
essential fallibility of scientific knowledge. You have seen how it is
argued that science proceeds through inductive reason from particular,
correct empirical data to general, correct theoretical explanations. That
is to say, crude empiricism claims that scientists learn through *not*
making mistakes from the very beginning of their inquiries. But can this
possibly be so? You already know that most of your own important
learning experiences have involved getting it wrong, making mistakes.
Learning occurs against the background of a variety of expectations
which are accepted as correct but are not necessarily recognized for what
they are. These expectations are analogous to theoretical beliefs in that
you use them to predict what will happen in specific circumstances in the
natural and social world. Recall what has already been said about
selectivity: when you have meaningful learning experiences, it is because
you discover that some of these expectations are false. This occurs when
what you predict to be the case turns out not to be so. Such mistakes
constitute the origin of most genuine motivation to learn and to attempt
to make new discoveries. You do not feel that you need to bother when
your experiences continue to confirm what you already believe to be
correct. Since the process of discovering empirical error involves reasoning from general expectations on the level of belief to particular
expectations on the level of observation, this must mean that learning
does not occur inductively as crude empiricism claims. To assert that one
learns through making mistakes may sound like a cliché. However, in
relation to the psychological and educational impact of crude empiricist
conceptions of learning, it is revolutionary. Think, for example, in
light of the extent to which a fear of making mistakes can often cripple
individual participation in education, of how liberating it would be to
recognize the importance and inevitability of error in the learning
process.

The fourth problem facing crude empiricism is that of *interpretation*.
We have shown how scientific knowledge is represented as the systematic
accumulation of the facts of experience. But the problem of interpretation arises precisely with the expression 'facts of experience'. Are these
facts just 'out there' waiting to be collected by the working scientist? Or
will the sense that is made of them depend upon some prior theory about
what sorts of things the world contains? A considerable body of
argument suggests the latter to be the case. We have already employed
the term 'data'. It means 'what are given' and its use embodies the key
assumption of crude empiricism – that science rests on a realm of given
facts, each admitting to only one correct interpretation. Indeed, crude
empiricists would altogether reject the use of the word 'interpretation' in
this context. They believe that facts are simply what they are, if they have

been scientifically observed. The problem of interpretation arises because this assumption can be challenged.

Of course, perception is often highly ambiguous. Consider the example of the Necker cube in this respect. Note that it may be seen as projecting up to the left or down to the right, more or less at will. The figure may also be seen flat, containing four trapezoids (ABCD), two triangles (EF) and a parallelogram (G). The grip of three-dimensional interpretation of pictures is so strong that this third interpretation is the most difficult to 'see'. Interestingly, too, this third, 'flat' interpretation which is 'neutral' with respect to the others cannot be used to decide which of the two alternative three-dimensional interpretations is 'correct'. What could it mean to ask which interpretation is correct? In this case nothing turns on which you accept, so it remains ambiguous. Yet even where ambiguity can be resolved, this gives the lie to the notion of self-sufficient observations. Other examples of 'gestalt switch' with which you will be familiar make the same point. Yet without the conception of *essentially* correct observational facts which all 'normal' people see in the same way, crude empiricism must founder.

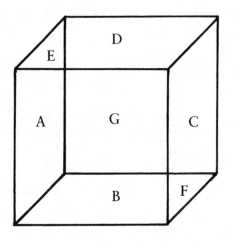

The Necker cube

For if simple pictures may exhibit such ambiguity, so too can those things which present themselves to the scientist as factual observations. For example, educated people before the Copernican revolution believed that the sun revolved around the earth. Later the very same perceptions were interpreted differently. Then it was argued that the perception of the sun's 'motion' was only an appearance produced by the *real* motion of the earth. In the context of the debate at that time, imagine that two astronomers go out to watch the dawn. One believes the sun goes round the earth each day while the other thinks that the earth revolves on its own axis in a day and goes round the sun each year. 'Look,' says one, 'the sun is rising.' 'No,' says the other, 'the horizon is going down, revealing the sun where it always is.' The same ambiguity is found in other types of scientific argument. For example, all things being equal, the consistent presence of idle adults occupying the street corners of particular urban neighbourhoods might be interpreted as confirming the very different theories that unemployment is due to laziness or that it is due to lack of jobs. The difficulty here is that as far as assessment is concerned observation cannot be regarded as self-validating. That is to say, when there is a dispute about the sense or meaning of a particular set of observations it obviously cannot be settled through continued reference to these data alone.

The preceding examples indicate the vital role that theory plays in leading scientists to construe what they see in one way rather than another. Theories dictate which observations are equated with reality and which are viewed as mere appearance so that experience takes on what has been called a 'theory-laden' character. In order to be understandable at all, reports of observations accumulated by those under the illusion of having a completely 'open mind' tacitly presuppose prior theoretical commitments. Hence, the implicit construction already placed *upon* what has been observed will inevitably prejudice the inductive conclusion drawn supposedly *from* what has been observed. No one, scientist or otherwise, can report an experience without using concepts to describe it. You cannot describe experiences without the use of language following specific linguistic rules. When scientists speak of making meaningful observations they are referring to experiences which they can *report*. An observation derives whatever intelligibility it possesses through the capacity of those who have it to give a coherent description to themselves and to others. What could an intelligible but indescribable experience be like? We shall devote more attention to these problems of language in chapter 6. For now, we may conclude that crude empiricism does not provide a coherent or practicable method for science. Nor does it appear capable of sustaining those claims it makes for the certainty or even the likely truth of scientific knowledge.

Alternatives to crude empiricism: Popper vs. Kuhn

If crude empiricism is an inadequate theory of knowledge, what are the alternatives and which of them is most acceptable? Other, more subtle forms of empiricism have evolved as responses to the preceding problems. In general terms, they have tried to resolve the central dilemma facing any epistemological doctrine which draws a sharp distinction between the subject and object of inquiry and then purports infallibly to bridge this gap with reference to a secure foundation of knowledge. Given this distinction, the spectator-as-inquirer of crude empiricism must somehow be able to make contact with reality, and experience is chosen as the link. Yet experience *per se* is inside the subject, and questions can always be raised about whether or not it really represents what is outside. This is why so much time is spent by crude empiricists railing against the dangers of subjectivity and discussing the proper method for observing reality without misrepresenting it. But the recognition that such misrepresentation is possible underlines the extent to which the view that experience really can accurately reflect the outside world is a belief in its own right. To be consistent the crude empiricist must therefore believe that this belief can be justified by experience. Yet to do so obviously begs the question of whether or not such a justification is possible in the first place. It is analogous to the problem faced by those who believe that all moral understanding must be justified by what they regard as the infallible foundation of all theological knowledge – the Bible. Nowhere is it written in the Bible that this is the source of all wisdom. Nor does it include instruction on how to go about using it to answer with certainty all of the moral questions that Christians face about how to conduct their lives. Similarly, nowhere does experience show that it is an infallible foundation to scientific knowledge or indicate in its own right how it should be employed for specific scientific purposes. In short, without arguing in a circle, *no* purported epistemological foundation – experience, reason, intuition, will, emotion, a particular set of cherished writings, etc. – can be self-validating.

In the mid-1930s, Karl Popper decided that the only way out of this circle was to give up the idea of justifying scientific knowledge on the basis of its inductive links with experience. With the problems of selection, certainty, error and interpretation in mind, he argued that the scientific method of induction envisaged by crude empiricism was a myth and that attempting empirically to refute rather than to prove theories was the driving force behind the progress of scientific inquiry. For however much evidence is amassed to confirm a theory, it goes no way towards demonstrating it to be true. The next observation might entirely refute it. So there is an asymmetry between empirical proof and disproof. No amount of evidence can prove an exciting, universal theory true, yet just one contrary instance can show that it is false. Thus evidence against a theory should always be of more interest to a scientist than evidence for it. There is no point in collecting a mountain of favourable evidence if all the time the molehill of negative evidence necessary for falsification is potentially at hand. Therefore, Popper makes *falsifiability* his criterion of demarcation for differentiating science from 'metaphysics' (i.e. those non-scientific claims about the world to which empirical evidence is critically irrelevant). It might look as though the statement 'God answers prayer' could be supported by evidence from experience. Popper argues that the crucial question, however, is whether a hypothesis may be refuted by observational evidence. Hence he would not accept that 'God answers prayer' is a scientific hypothesis since there is no evidence that could be inconsistent with it. 'No' is just as much an answer as 'Yes'. A truly scientific hypothesis must specifically forbid some phenomena. It must state that certain sorts of events will not happen or certain sorts of observations will not be found so that if they do or are, the theory may be rejected. The asymmetry between verification and falsification by empirical evidence can then be put to work, eliminating false hypotheses and aiding scientific progress.

Thus Popper argues that scientific inquiry does not begin with the open-minded collection of unambiguous data. Rather, observations are always made with some problem in mind and are selected and interpreted in relation to tentative solutions to that problem. Once these tentative solutions are clearly articulated as hypotheses, then it becomes possible to test them. As we have indicated, the hypothesis explains what had previously been puzzling; it will tell what is to be expected in other similar circumstances. A statement describing what empirically to expect is deduced and if it does not occur the hypothesis is seen to be refuted. Both the selection of empirical evidence and the terms in which it is to be described are dictated by the theory in question. For example, suppose you set out to test a theory that lack of investment is the primary cause of urban unemployment. If you discover consistently low levels of unemployment in some areas where high investment is predominant, you must revise your initial hypothesis. Clearly, any new theory you developed in this connection would have to be able to account for all of the correct empirical consequences of the old theory as well as the new information you have discovered which you believe to have refuted the old theory. On top of this, Popper argues that if your new theory is really worthwhile, it will also lead to new, unexpected discoveries when applied to a range of specific empirical problems beyond those it was initially invented to solve. For example, using the concept of gravity in his general theoretical system, Newton managed to explain not only what was understood about the empirical behaviour of the six planets known at the time; his theory was also later employed to predict the precise location of planets of which Newton was totally unaware.

With these views about both scientific creativity and assessment, Popper develops a different conception of the cumulative character of scientific progress from that of crude empiricism. However, at the same time he retains the notion (rejected by many sophisticated empiricists) of the inquiring subject making contact with objective reality. For he argues that through the non-inductive process of theoretical conjecture and experimental refutation, combined with a drive to explain and discover more and more at every stage of scientific inquiry, the 'explanatory power' of scientific theories is consistently increased. Through this increase, such theories approach ever closer to 'the truth'. If the quest for empirical refutation (rather than proof) seems hard – it seems more natural to try to find evidence to support rather than reject your beliefs – then no matter. Popper argues that it is the rewarding of such behaviour that has made good scientists successful and the scientific community effective in its essentially social pursuit of the truth.

Even on this very general account, Popper's conception of knowledge and science provides dramatic solutions to at least three of the four problems facing crude empirism. He accepts that the learning process is inevitably selective and that criteria determining which data are relevant for any specific inquiry are linked to preconceived theoretical beliefs. Far from being something to be avoided for the sake of objectivity, such beliefs are vitally necessary because observations achieve whatever significance they possess because of their critical relation to theories about the natural and social world. Further, Popper rejects certainty or even high probability as a possibility for science because its theories are so general and therefore so vastly underdetermined by particular experiences. Again, he argues that it is only the empirical fallibility of theoretical expectations that gives them whatever scientific status they possess. He points out, for example, that the most certain statements of all (i.e. statements which are true by definition) are the least scientific and the least capable of leading to fruitful empirical inquiry. It would make little sense to mount a research campaign to discover how many happily married bachelors live in London. Yet nothing could be more certain than 'All bachelors in London are unmarried'. There would be much more scientific point to the proposition that a large percentage of married people in London are unhappy. This hypothesis would be scientifically interesting to explore because, Popper argues, it is even more falsifiable and less certain than the preceding. Fallibility, not certainty, is the most important characteristic of scientific inquiry. This view also takes care of the problem of error since criticism becomes the dynamic principle of scientific progress.

Finally, Popper seems to handle the problem of interpretation as well – at least from one perspective. For reasons already described, he argues that neither observation, reason nor anything else can provide an infallible foundation for progressive scientific learning. As long as scientists keep their critical guns blazing, different theoretical interpretations of nature or society can abound. In the Darwinian competitive struggle between scientists, the weak will be rejected in favour of the strong; which is just another way of saying that it is through interpretations being efficiently appraised empirically that science progresses. In short, it is precisely because our experience is capable of sustaining many different interpretations that it is so vital to ensure that through rigorous criticism science winds up with the best one. The more rigorous the critical environment of scientific practice, the more rapidly will natural selection take place through the survival of the fittest theories.

On the face of it, Popper's approach to all of these problems is very plausible. Unfortunately, however, his solutions to the problems of error and interpretation run into difficulties when they are examined more closely, casting into doubt the overall coherence of his ideas about science. For all the advances his theory has made over earlier forms of empiricism, Popper remains an empiricist at heart. In the last analysis, when hypotheses are subjected to tests, the final authority is still said to lie with experience – it is empirical data alone which can say yea or nay. Popper tries to hedge his bets by denying it, but at the end of the day this must presumably mean that experience is in some sense neutral and unambiguous with respect to theoretical debate. And however it is philosophically packaged, this view will always founder since interpretations of experience differ in the most fundamental ways. These differences are made possible by the fact that interpretations are not derived from experience but rather *imposed* upon experience through the theoretical languages that scientists employ. Of course, this is not to suggest that scientists can adopt any interpretations, any language they like. The strength of Popper's position consists in his demonstration that experience can resist a theory by running counter to its predictions. His weakness, on the other hand, is evident when it is broad explanatory *approaches* rather than scientific hypotheses which are in dispute and when there is disagreement about the critical significance of any particular experience.

For example, a traditional healer might laugh at a western doctor who tried to convince her/him that just because their patient died, the supernatural basis of their medical practice had been refuted. They could always assert that whether or not 'death' was synonymous with 'failure' was a complicated question and that the westerner had not properly interpreted the particular instance of death. It might be argued that the patient died not because the traditional medicine was wrong but because the family of the patient did not properly follow the treatment prescribed, because the patient was incurable, because the patient in fact had a different ailment from the one for which treatment was given, etc. On top of these factors, the healer could also argue that the westerner should not forget all the patients who had recovered after the use of traditional medicine. Of course, when accused of failure by the traditional healer under similar circumstances, the western doctor could answer in similar terms. In short, in both cases, the death of the patient need not be interpreted as a theoretical failure – although of course it might be. Even if western medicine cured more patients on average than various traditional methods, the healers might simply claim that the spiritual and ritual disciplines associated with their practices make therapeutic instructions inherently more difficult for patients and their relatives to follow. However, they are just as effective – if not more so – when followed *properly*. After all, in western medicine the 'ritual' of hygiene is relatively easy to follow but even so it is still often inadequately observed and there is no reason why a similar argument should not hold in the case of rituals warding off evil spirits. Thus even an unfavourable comparison of actual numbers 'cured' does not *prove* the relative uselessness of traditional methods of healing.

All this suggests that experience cannot be employed by itself to decide between rival systems of belief which dispute its overall *meaning*. To maintain the opposite is either to fail to recognize the importance of the problem of interpretation or to endorse one particular historical and cultural world view without admitting it. Consequently, Popper's position still amounts to empiricism of a non-inductive variety if he is unambiguously to be able to claim that scientific progress is always the result of bold theoretical conjecture and rigorous empirical refutation – the central doctrine of his 'critical rationalism'. For on this view, either experience is regarded as epistemologically 'given' and not subject to

conflicting scientific interpretation or only one interpretation of experience – that of western science – is dogmatically endorsed as being
suitable for the purposes of empirical criticism. In either case, it is still
experience which is seen as the fundamental arbiter of truth and reason.
The most influential and overtly non-empiricist writer to explore the
problems and implications attending this view is Thomas Kuhn.

At the end of the 1950s Kuhn began to argue that successful scientists
do not behave in quite the way Popper suggests. At one level, learning
behaviour is much as Popper would have it; but only after the correctness
of a more general approach to research has been assumed. By 'approach'
– Kuhn most often uses the word 'paradigm' – he means that set of
conceptual commitments which dictate what is defined as a genuine
research problem, how scientists should try to solve it and what they will
accept as effective criticism of their solution. His argument is simply that
learning must occur *within* such commitments if it is to progress in the
way that Popper elaborates. It is possible to be critical within the
conceptual boundaries delineated by a paradigm. However, according to
Kuhn, one cannot at the same time be critical of those boundaries
themselves because it is acceptance of them which determines what is
actually meant by being critical. This was of course the thrust of the
preceding example of the debate between the western doctor and the
traditional healer.

To see further what Kuhn is getting at, consider the role of commitment in the way in which you go about developing a close relationship
with another person – important learning behaviour if ever there was
any. When you are just getting to know someone, as Popper suggests,
you formulate hypotheses about their interests, talents and sensitivities
which you then critically evaluate through interaction with them.
However, if you are at all serious about wanting a relationship you do
not give up your project at the first sign of a mistake. For you are engaged
in a programme of research concerning the essential characteristics of the
other person – traits which will inevitably seem ambiguous to you when
you first meet. By definition, your assumption that the programme is
worthwhile cannot be based on critical testing which has not yet taken
place. Rather, it must be related to preconceived commitments which you
have about what sort of person is in general worth getting to know and
why you feel the person in whom you are interested falls into this
category. Paradigms in Kuhn's sense embody similar conceptual commitments about the basic character of reality and thus are not open to
empirical criticism in the same way that specific hypotheses employing
the same concepts can be said to be. It is for this reason that Kuhn argues
ironically that dogma plays just as important a role as criticism in the
growth of scientific knowledge.

For example, it is not possible for someone to refute your commitment
to a research programme which presupposes that capitalism is a stable
economic system simply by pointing to unfavourable empirical evidence
(e.g. through producing evidence acceptable to you that the rate of profit
has decreased over the past twenty years). This might convince you that

your position is implausible. But you could also reply that such negative evidence did no more than pose an interesting problem which you were sure would be solved by sticking to your economic paradigm. Likewise, you cannot empirically refute a commitment to the view that capitalism by its very nature involves social conflict by simply pointing out empirical evidence which suggests social stability (e.g. data about the relatively low incidence of crime, strikes, etc.). In short, the mere existence of a problem does not in itself constitute a refutation of a set of conceptual commitments; getting someone to swap one set for another is as much a psychological as it is a logical/empirical matter. Experience can never *force* you to change your mind, for with imagination you can always find an interpretation which is consistent with your beliefs. Kuhn argues that it is precisely this imperviousness of paradigms to empirical refutation that makes successful science possible at all. How can he justify such a paradoxical claim?

New explanatory hypotheses are brought into being by the existence of problems regarded as in need of solutions. But to constitute a problem which motivates a search for new explanations an aspect of the natural or social world must fly in the face of scientists' expectations. If you accept a paradigm which embodies the assumption that long-term economic stability is not possible within the capitalist social and economic order, then it is an urgent problem for you to explain how apparent stability occurs. It will presumably surprise you that it does. On the other hand, if you employ a paradigm within which social order and economic stability are 'natural' occurrences, you will be most exercised by those conflicts which appear from time to time to disturb that stability. Again, you will not expect them to happen. In each case you work hardest to explain just what your opponents take to be their most pressing problem. Historically, the heliocentric cosmology was developed by thinkers who reasoned that its geocentric rival was problematic. This is not to say that the heliocentric paradigm has no problems of its own. Indeed, in order to generate a new cosmology from scratch to replace the one which was centuries old and fully developed, it was inevitable that the new view would initially encounter more problems and appear less plausible than the old. It should be clear, however, that if a large-scale explanatory strategy is rejected as soon as one hypothesis based on it encounters trouble, the strategy itself will never get off the ground. If you give up your commitment to get to know a person the first time that one of your hypotheses about them appears to be refuted, you will never get to know anyone. You will always be wrong about something. The problem is how and on what basis you interpret the mistakes which you will inevitably make. Just think of the early 'stormy days' of the relationships of couples who now seem totally devoted to each other!

Thus Kuhn argues that a paradigm is only successfully improved or 'articulated' once scientists are wholeheartedly committed to it as the *only* conceptual framework within which explanations can be formed. The failure of a particular hypothesis within the paradigm is not the failure of the paradigm itself. Quite the reverse. It is the failure of scientists to solve the problem for which they developed that hypothesis. The problem for which the failed hypothesis was formulated is a problem just because the paradigm is retained. You do not, for example, solve the problem of 'apparent economic stability' for the Marxist paradigm (according to which capitalism is an inherently unstable system) by switching your commitment to an alternative view according to which order and stability are natural to society. Within *that* paradigm, stability and order are not a problem to be solved. No more do you solve the problem set within this latter paradigm by 'apparent economic conflict' if you switch your commitment to a Marxist view which would claim such conflict to be endemic.

However, in 'mature sciences', two paradigms rarely co-exist. Hence the origin of expressions like 'Aristotelian', 'Newtonian' and 'Einstein-ian' science and their lengthy periods of separate historical development. Were too many paradigms to exist at any one time, it would detract from the rigorous investigations of any one of them – a state of affairs which Kuhn identifies with what he perceives to be the lack of any very dramatic explanatory success in the social sciences. More specifically, mature sciences are characterized by long periods of 'normal science' in which one paradigm alone dominates the particular discipline in question, alternating with short periods of 'revolutionary science' in which the old paradigm is quite rapidly abandoned and a new one adopted. In normal science, the task is one of problem-solving. To this extent, Kuhn argues, scientists do proceed by improving particular explanatory hypotheses much as Popper supposes they do. At the same time, their key textbooks and their vision of the best explanatory achievements embody precepts which are simply taken for granted. For example, modern medical science does not question the truth of the germ theory of disease or the experimental techniques employed to establish the presence of micro-organisms and measure their effects. Kuhn would maintain that medical scientists have plenty to do – and to argue about – without needlessly going back to first principles. If they did not have these principles to guide their research they would require others. For this reason periods of scientific revolution cannot be understood in the same terms as normal science since it follows that no criteria of adequacy exist for paradigms themselves. Thus Kuhn argues that the Popperian princi-ple of deciding between hypotheses according to their empirical ade-quacy – passing or failing empirical tests – applies within paradigms but not between them.

In his own illustrations of this point, as well as some of its interesting and unexpected consequences, Kuhn focuses attention on periods in the history of the natural sciences when programmes of research themselves undergo change – scientific revolutions. It follows from the preceding analysis that these changes must come about in ways which are consist-ent with the dogma supporting such programmes. So how is it possible to reconcile revolutionary change with dogmatism? Kuhn tries to answer this question by arguing that science cannot be understood without viewing it as a social activity involving a complex and co-operative division of labour. Some scientists are theoreticians while others are experimentalists researching the same conceptual commitments. This division of labour is necessitated by the variety of different ways in which a shared paradigm might be articulated and the need to be as critical as possible so as to eliminate those ways which are not empirically successful. The basic picture is of scientists working together as a team with the same explanatory goals. This, again, is something which Kuhn argues would be impossible if they were constantly at each others' throats about every single issue. Their co-operation is made possible by their collective acceptance of the explanatory potential of the same paradigm, whatever their differences about its precise specification and use.

Returning to our earlier example, to get to know someone better, you cannot recoil in horror the first time you fail to predict what they will do in particular circumstances, provided you do not judge this action as so damning as to be beyond the pale. It is precisely because of a prior commitment to the view that their actions must in some way be acceptable once they are properly understood that you have the confidence to try to find out the variety of ways in which they are acceptable. Even though you obviously do not think about it in these terms, you do this by assessing hypotheses about their actions which are relevant to your judging them to be an appropriate close companion. The more people, for example, who help you to formulate and test hypotheses about their appropriateness for a close relationship, the more quickly you will discover any explanatory anomalies between your conceptual commitments and the sort of person they are. If in time a larger number are discovered, you will have to decide whether or not you wish to give up on them as companions or to reject the commitments you share with your present groups of friends as to what, in principle, such companions should be like. If you make the latter decision, you will develop a new set of conceptual criteria for meaningful relationships (and a new set of friends!); you will have gone through a 'revolution' in your thinking about these matters. With similar points in mind, Kuhn claims that scientific revolutions result from the collective discovery of such explanatory defects which despite giving the paradigm every benefit of doubt, seem to 'revolutionary' scientists to be incapable of being put right. The programme of research historically exhausts itself and its supporters and is replaced. Kuhn explains the transition from the geocentric to the heliocentric and the Newtonian to the Einsteinian world view in these terms, as well as many other more minor but still dramatic shifts of belief in the history of science.

The spectre of relativism

The key problem with Kuhn's position can best be introduced by comparing his and Popper's conception of an epistemological spectator, an idea essential to crude empiricism. In summary, you will recall that according to this theory, the inquirer and the object of inquiry are completely separated and only brought together through the inductive method of observational discovery. Truth will be literally seen to be manifest provided that this method is not distorted by the preconceived ideas of the learner. Popper still employs the spectator metaphor but rejects the possibility of an inductive link between knower and known. Certainty about the truth will always elude scientists. But, according to Popper, they can still increasingly approximate to the truth through developing better and better tested theories which explain more and more. He thus retains a cumulative view of science progressing one step at a time, as it were, even if he discards its inductive trappings. Scientists progress not through getting more and more things right but by knowing that they are discarding more and more wrong hypotheses. Experimental error must still be viewed as a neutral arbiter if the concept of approximation to the truth is to retain any coherence. It is for related reasons that we have seen that, despite his denials, Popper too can be viewed as an empiricist, albeit of a much more refined kind than the crude empiricists we mentioned earlier. Kuhn throws out the epistemological spectator altogether. For him, the *meaning* of problems, theories, tests, experimental techniques and experience itself all depend on the conceptual tradition within which the scientists are working. If they are working in different traditions, because of the encompassing conceptual components associated with each tradition, they are literally working within what they conceive to be different worlds. The spectator is no longer making contact with a reality whose truth shows itself through either inductive experience or deductive/experimental tests. The 'reality' of scientists is presented as socially constructed by them through scientific practice linked to the language and rules of language use which make their practices conceptually possible and give it meaning.

The spectre thus presents itself of knowledge being relative to different conceptual commitments which, as far as their meaning and explanatory potential are concerned, are independent of each other. Therefore, if it comes to it, disputes between paradigms will have to be settled on the basis of who is the most powerful. For this reason, Kuhn argues that scientific revolutions like those of Copernicus, Newton and Einstein are radical changes of world view and have occurred in ways which have primarily to be understood in sociological and psychological rather than logical/empirical terms. Reason cannot dictate at which point a paradigm faced with anomalies will be overthrown in favour of a new conceptual approach. After all, it would never have appeared to be a fruitful paradigm if it had not been beset with interesting problems from the start. Proponents of an explanatory tradition can always continue to say that the scientists employing it are not clever enough rather than blame the paradigm itself for apparent difficulties. Indeed, Kuhn argues that the conceptual constraints of paradigms can be so systemic that opponents in different traditions can lose the ability even to understand one another's criticisms. Consequently, unlike Popper, he argues that the evolution of science is not cumulative. Scientific progress can only be said to occur *within* different scientific traditions of problem formulation and solution. Since traditions themselves cannot be rationally compared in the same sort of empirical way as the theories formulated within them, they are, according to Kuhn, 'incommensurable'.

Kuhn's analysis of the role of conceptual commitment in science and the difference between normal and revolutionary science is both correct and profound. It has changed the way an entire intellectual generation has thought and argued about science and its history. Because of this and also because his analysis incorporates many of Popper's equally correct insights about the scientific importance of empirical criticism, Kuhn's work can be viewed as a major philosophical advance. However, as its relativistic consequences suggest, his position is still very problematic and there is an extensive literature debating the consequences of his position. Some commentators positively revel in his relativism, arguing that it represents the only means to provide an adequate scientific basis for a study of other cultures which is undistorted by western values. Others argue that complex ways can be found to reconcile Kuhn's views with 'practical' methods of appraising rival explanatory approaches which, while not achieving Popper's rigorous critical goals, still enable meaningful critical communication between opponents. And still others claim that Kuhn's vision of science leads to epistemological anarchy of a sort which would quickly destroy the scientific advances of centuries and herald the dawn of a dark age of unreason. Again, we will concern ourselves here with the simplest and most unqualified version of Kuhn's work which has drawn the most well-known criticisms with it. In one way or another, most of these difficulties are related to Kuhn's conception of paradigms and their incommensurable status.

If programmes of research are not rationally comparable, that is if they do define autonomous spheres of inquiry which have nothing in common, it is difficult to see how there can be any critical relationship between them. But Kuhn – speaking as an historian of science – suggests that there is. For example, he does not think that the heliocentric world view succeeded the geocentric one by accident! As you have seen, he argues that new paradigms are created to solve problems that old programmes of research could not solve. Does this not mean in some sense then that there is a vital link between the old view of the world and the evolution of the new? The difficulty here is the claim that scientific problems mean different things when they are formulated in separate paradigms. To see what Kuhn is driving at, remember again the example of the debate between the western and non-western doctors. 'Illness' seemed just not to have the same meaning for them – they did not appear to be referring to the same thing when they employed their different languages of diagnosis and healing. Also think of how differently you perceive someone with whom you have fallen out of love. It is almost as if they are not the same person as they were. Yet if his claim is accepted, what would be the point of any argument between supporters of rival explanatory approaches?

For example, were conflicting paradigms totally incommensurable, one could not even say – as Kuhn at times suggests – that they are inconsistent with each other. Two programmes of research which presuppose completely different linguistic criteria for what constitutes *all* meaningful statements about the world could no more be said to be inconsistent than an apple can be said to be inconsistent with a pear or the language of art can be regarded as inconsistent with the language of science. All that can be said is that they are different and have followed each other historically in the specific form they have for no good reason. Something is clearly wrong somewhere. To assert that the new and old are connected through argument at all is to assume that there is some sort of rationality to conceptual change. Surely the problem is to figure out what kind, given Kuhn's correct observations about the difficulties posed for critical communication by radically different systems of belief. Some of his own excellent historical research has shown how scientists working within quite different explanatory traditions have certainly appeared to pursue arguments about matters of mutual interest. Through posing problems for each other, they aid the articulation of their respective positions – something which would be impossible if they were incapable of critical communication. Further, if it were assumed that communication could not be achieved between radically different modes of thought, much sociological and anthropological inquiry would become impossible. For the understanding yielded by such communication is precisely the object of such inquiries.

Of course, it might be argued that the success of such investigations, along with seeming communication between proponents of different explanatory traditions in science, is only apparent. However, it is then hard to see what could distinguish apparent communication from that which is real. You could always deny that you were communicating with someone even when you were absolutely convinced that you were. For how could you be sure that you did not just seem to be understanding each other? Despite appearances to the contrary, you could still hold a world view that was radically different from theirs without realizing it. Think of how profoundly wrong you can be about someone whom on first meeting you believe to share your basic values. In other words, there is nothing special about scientists who employ different paradigms running the risk of misunderstanding. In this respect, we are all in the same boat, even including those scientists who firmly believe that they agree on the same paradigm! There simply must be some intelligible difference between seeming to communicate and succeeding in doing so, both between those who profess conceptual agreement and those who do not. For all of its insights into the inner workings of the scientific community, the irrationality of some aspects of scientific change and the oversimplicity of theories of scientific method which emphasize logic at the expense of psychology, Kuhn's analysis of scientific revolutions inevitably tends to blur this distinction between disagreement and misunderstanding. Somehow, on the evidence available, such revolutions were the *practical* outcome of the debate and critical discourse that Kuhn both wants to question the efficacy of, and yet, in his more guarded moments, not dispense with altogether. It is this ambiguity that his critics have themselves articulated so keenly (as he would put it) and which he or his followers have not really succeeded in answering.

Paradoxically, then, Kuhn retains an implicit commitment to empiricism of a sort despite the severity and effectiveness of his criticisms of it. The pessimistic conclusion that the paradigm changes of revolutionary science do not constitute progress depends upon an assumption of empiricism, namely that if empirical evidence is insufficient to decide between paradigms then no rational decision can be made between them. Hence, the succession of paradigms becomes no more than 'one damn thing after another'. There is nothing left for Kuhn the historian or for other social scientists to do but observe this succession and to record its characteristics in as unbiased a way as possible. Since he cannot explain rationally why one paradigm should give way to the next he just has to accept that it does so contingently in the same sorts of reoccurring circumstances. Therefore, his historical method effectively returns to the level of crude empiricism: his conclusions about scientific revolutions are inductively generalized from the instances he has documented through 'objective' empirical research. Indeed, it is precisely on the basis of such historical 'facts' – for example, about the Copernican revolution – that he argues that Popper's model of conjectures and refutations is wrong!

Finally, a further, important difficulty which can only be mentioned here but which has been extensively explored elsewhere, is that Kuhn artificially abstracts scientific inquiry from the general social and economic context within which it occurs. He has interesting ideas about professional socialization in science, including the ways in which career incentives and specialized education help to perpetuate traditions within the scientific community. If scientists do not abide by the rules which their paradigms dictate, they do not become professionally qualified, retain recognition or even remain employed. But why are scientists employed at all? In other words, what is the relation between the scientific community and the community at large? Who pays for science and what do they expect in return? Why have specific kinds of explanatory traditions developed when they have? Given that it is possible to explore scientific traditions in innumerable different directions, why does the scientific community opt for some and not for others? Why is knowledge which is advertised as scientific publicly presented and packaged in the ways that it is? All of these questions point to the need to develop theories about the relations between science and society. In contemporary terms, this means theories about the relationship between capitalism and science; in historical (and anthropological) terms, it means, for example, theories about the relation between other modes of social and economic organization and what constitutes their 'science'. These questions will explicitly or implicitly be raised many times as our discussions in this book continue. You should already be formulating what you consider some of their provisional answers to be.

It would appear, then, that the problem of interpretation does not have quite the drastic consequences that Kuhn and others have supposed, at least at their most sceptical moments. We have shown that its most drastic formulation seems to call into question the very possibility of communication between supporters of rival paradigms. The belief that different concepts erect communicational barriers arises from the assumption of a particular theory of meaning. This theory attributes a spurious *determinacy* to the meaning of statements so that if you and we do not mean precisely the same thing by a given term, then we each mean something entirely different. We cannot go into detail now about why this theory of meaning and communication is wrong. This will be done in chapter 7. However, we can begin to undermine it. It has already been shown that absurd consequences follow from the most relativistic versions of Kuhn's views. Were they correct, people could never say with confidence that they were communicating critically with anyone, no matter how long or however consistently they might have appeared to be. With this in mind, it is appropriate to examine two examples of the way in which communication about empirical data certainly does appear to have occurred between conceptual opponents in the social sciences. This will be an important (though not conclusive) part of the argument developed later that there is no good reason to assume that such communication is inherently problematic. Of course, if critical communication between supporters of rival paradigms is possible, this underlines the importance of rejecting arguments which devalue the status of critical empirical research in science – arguments which ultimately claim that what is and is not the case is just a matter of opinion.

First, competing theorists often refer to the 'same' empirical data in the explanatory elaboration of their respective paradigms. That is to say, even though they are operating within quite different conceptual boundaries, there is sufficient overlap between them for certain kinds of information to be relevant to their explanatory purposes *without further analysis on their part*. For example, in this connection, Marxists and non-Marxists often employ the same information concerning income, wealth, employment, education and health, even though they explain it in different ways. Consider the explanatory use of figures concerning 'GNP'. Economic theorists from both paradigms accept that the 'developed countries' have higher gross national products than the 'underdeveloped' countries. There is also little disagreement about the basic correctness of the empirical data in both cases. Some argue that the low rates of economic activity result from, among other things, traditional attitudes in the Third World which if changed (e.g. through better education) would make increased growth and prosperity possible. Others explain the same data by referring to the way the developed countries exploit the Third World through, among other things, the use of cheap raw materials and cheap labour. They claim that while underdeveloped countries are dominated if not controlled by the developed ones, there is no real hope for increased prosperity. Therefore in the face of this kind of agreement what sense can be made of the claim that conceptual opponents are really deceiving themselves because the empirical data involved really mean something different for each? In particular, how can one account for the situations where opponents are indeed interpreting evidence in completely different ways, know it and understand why? Obviously, this is not to sugggest that the influence of systems of concepts on the selection and interpretation of empirical evidence is unproblematic. This would hark back to the crude empiricism with which we began. Rather, it is to argue that problems about the critical use of empirical data cannot always be reduced to problems about conceptual presupposition. It would be nonsense to claim, for example, that all data discovered by supporters of non-Marxist paradigms are useless to Marxist critics. In numerous instances, they are totally dependent on them and do not question their dependence.

Second, social scientists often generate sharp criticisms of the criteria employed within explanatory frameworks they oppose for the selection and interpretation of empirical findings. If you make use of 'official' statistics, you may or may not contest the definitions of 'social class', 'criminality', 'suicide', 'income', 'health', etc., that have been employed in their compilation. Likewise, you may or may not accept the basis for the decisions made by the compilers concerning what should and should not be documented. Debates of this sort are carried on in great detail and certainly belie the claim that the meaning of empirical data within one conceptual standpoint is totally different for those within an alternative conceptual framework. For example, Émile Durkheim, in his late nineteenth-century study of suicide, was subsequently criticized for taking suicide statistics at their face value regardless of the country of origin. It was noted that in Catholic countries authorities would be far more reluctant to conclude that any death was due to suicide, because of the religious stigma involved, than in Protestant or relatively non-religious states where no such reluctance would be shown. A consistent definition of suicide was thus not employed in the collection of the data which Durkheim used. This type of error is an illustration of the mistake of 'reification', which we discuss in chapter 5.

Similar arguments have been used concerning the question of which data are appropriate for collection under a given conceptual classification. For example, should the official estimates of losses to the exchequer through tax evasion be aggregated with criminal statistics such as shoplifting, pilfering from the workplace, vandalism, etc? Or, should the totals of tax exempt benefits be added to income distribution figures, rather than simply compiling them in terms of taxable income? These questions are so contentious just because, despite fundamental political disagreement, there is no essential lack of empirical understanding. Disputants can still agree that the data involved are informative (i.e. that the statistics are accurate in some respects). Further they can also agree why they disagree. To this extent, existing data on income distribution, for instance, will continue to be employed within rival explanatory frameworks (albeit in different ways) for their respective explanatory purposes. Think of debates about 'Thatcherism' in this connection. Indeed, even when empirical information is dismissed as useless because of its conceptual background, there are always recommendations for the generation of more useful data implicit in the arguments for its dismissal. When debates such as these have been going on for years and when participants themselves state that they have been persuaded by the arguments, it seems perverse to insist that all along those involved were really just misunderstanding each other.

In conclusion, in order for the kind of discovery and argumentative activity which is associated with science to make any sense it must be assumed that scientists can critically communicate with each other even though they may have profound conceptual disagreements. It should also be clear that the purpose that supporters of different programmes of research have in creating and articulating them is to describe, explain and discover more about the empirical world than they felt they knew to begin with. This is so even if empirical evidence is insufficient *on its own* to decide between different programmes or even different hypotheses. Because of the problems with empiricist theories of knowledge, there can be no doubt that the scientific importance of empirical evidence has been diminished. Observation in itself can no longer be viewed as the unambiguous arbiter of scientific dispute of whatever kind. Because of the problem of interpretation there are no exclusively observational foundations to scientific knowledge. Science is essentially conceptual, social and observational. The problem of interpretation may drastically affect the significance attributed within different paradigms to empirical evidence, but it seldom interferes with the identification of what requires explanation. If it systematically did so, it would be impossible coherently to identify the way in which one paradigm supplanted another in a scientific revolution. With reference to what did one lead to, or provide the background for, the other? The social drive for new discovery and the necessity for common empirical reference points in science will ensure the continuing importance of empirical research within scientific inquiry, no matter how much observations are dependent on the social use of concepts for their intelligibility.

Empiricism is dead. Long live empirical science!

Annotated bibliography

For reasons we gave in the introduction to the chapter, reading about crude empiricism is hard to find. Perhaps its most celebrated supporter was the early seventeenth-century author Francis Bacon. His influence is discussed in Losee 1980, chapter 7, and at greater length in Quinton 1980. A selection of his writings can be found in Kearney 1964. The nineteenth-century philosopher J.S. Mill comes closer than any other reputable modern writer to an enthusiastic espousal of an inductive method for science. His views are set out in Mill 1974, and a useful extract can be found in Brown *et al.* 1981, section 4. An excellent critical introduction to inductivism is to be found in Chalmers 1978, chapters 1 and 2, and an extended commentary on Mill's thought in Ryan 1970b.

Most empiricist philosophy is far less simplistic than the 'crude' version. The ideas of the seventeenth- and eighteenth-century British empiricists – Locke, Berkeley and Hume – are still profoundly influential, and an introductory account of their writings can be found in general histories of philosophy such as Coplestone 1975, vol. V, Jones 1969, vol. III, chapters 8-10, and Wedberg 1982, vol. II, chapters 4-6. For a critical but continuing influence, see Kolakowski 1972. Rorty 1980, chapters 3-5, analyses the general idea that human knowledge is a 'mirror of nature', and Dancy 1985 gives an account of the problems of empiricism in the context of a contemporary survey of epistemology.

The first three phases of our attack on crude empiricism – the problems of selectivity, certainty and error – derive from the work of K. Popper and are set out in detail in Popper 1980, an extract of which is contrasted with Mill in Brown *et al.* 1981, section 3. Popper has usefully summarized his views in the title essay of Popper 1972a, and most engagingly in his autobiography, Popper 1976. A good, though uncritical introduction to his views can be found in Magee 1985, while Ackerman 1976 and O'Hear 1980 provide more sustained and critical discussion.

Case histories of selectivity in action in natural science can be found in Koestler 1970, and in social science in Giddens 1971. The problem of certainty is an aspect of those problems concerning induction and causality classically raised by Hume. An introductory account of his ideas can be found in Ayer 1980b, and a lengthier treatment in Stroud 1977. A nice case history of the response of a scientist to the problem of error in developing his hypotheses is set out in Hempel 1966, chapter 2. A detailed treatment of the same problem in relation to mathematics is given in Lakatos 1976.

What we have termed 'the problem of interpretation' raises the controversy regarding the rationality of scientific progress. In its modern form this problem was first set out in Hanson 1965, an extract from which can be found in Brown *et al.* 1981. Its full impact on the conception of the history of scientific progress, in opposition to the fallibilist ideas of Popper, was made clear in Kuhn 1970 – the classic formulation of historical relativism in natural science. Relativism was taken to extremes by Feyerabend in a series of papers collected in Feyerabend 1985, vol. I, part I and vol. II, and in Feyerabend 1975 and 1979.This controversy has dominated the mainstream discussion of the philosophy of the natural sciences since the publication of Kuhn's views. An early collection of essays on this controversy is Lakatos and Mus-grave 1970. Lakatos's contribution to this volume and later papers in Lakatos 1980, vol. I and vol. II, chapters 6, 9 and 10, attempt to accommodate a Popperian model of scientific progress to Kuhn's arguments. In some respects the same can be said of Laudan 1977. Newton-Smith 1981 contains an interesting discussion of the difficulties with such an accommodation, including a devastating critique of Popper. The best introduction to these debates is Chalmers 1978, chapters 6-10. The opposed positions are also well summarized in the introduction to Suppe 1977. Kuhn 1977 follows up his original statement with more historical and 'metahistorical' arguments. The evolution of the debate between relativists and their opponents as regards natural science is documented in the collection of essays in Hacking 1981. This contains both early important contributions by Kuhn and Shapere and more recent retrospective essays by Hacking and Laudan. It also includes an amusing example of Feyerabend's methodological anarchism.

Our final aphorism regarding the death of empiricism is probably premature! That version of empiricism which appeared to justify an unswerving and exclusive confidence in its vision of science may, indeed, be dead. However, van Frassen 1980, for example, attacks from an avowedly empiricist standpoint the recent 'scientific realist' claim that the *success* of science in itself is sufficient to justify the confidence that empiricism, as a philosophy of science, can no longer sustain. As for the empirical content of social science itself, the essays in Irvine *et al.* 1979 address those questions of the origin, production and interpretation of data which are raised by the recognition that social science *needs* facts, even if facts do not 'speak for themselves'. For an excellent analysis of how this point relates to the use and abuse of official statistics, see Miles 1985.

2

EXPLANATION IN THE NATURAL SCIENCES

Our discussion of empiricism referred to the various ways in which different phenomena can be explained. We did not, however, differentiate between the natural and social sciences in this respect, and said only enough about the main characteristics of scientific explanation to enable us to deal with the tasks at hand. In this chapter, these issues will be shown to be more complex. We shall outline what it means scientifically to explain physical occurrences in nature. Understanding the structure and key assumptions of such explanations is crucial for a student of social science. Even for those without scientific education, it gives some idea of the sort of activity that natural science is. It also helps to avoid arguing incorrectly or accepting the arguments of others for the wrong reasons. Finally, it sets the stage for the discussion in the later chapters of the extent to which the explanatory approach of the natural sciences can be applied to the understanding of human beings. As you will see, your beliefs about the similarities and differences between natural and social phenomena have the most profound consequences for your understanding of yourself, your relationship with others, and your cultural heritage.

The historical background to explanation in modern physical science

The origins of modern natural science and of modern conceptions of scientific explanation are to be found in the Copernican revolution, the essence of which was the rejection of the geocentric view of the world which had dominated European thought for 1,500 years. The idea that the earth was at the centre of the world, and that everything in the heavens (i.e. the observable stars, sun, moon and planets) revolved around it, was replaced by the heliocentric view. Thus the sun became the centre of the universe, and the different objects in the celestial world, including the earth, were said to revolve around it. Yet, to a greater or lesser extent, as far as astronomy itself was concerned both explanatory systems were successful. Every time the expressions 'sunrise' and 'sunset' are employed it is testimony to the lingering explanatory power of the geocentric system. One of the reasons for the durability of this view was its simplicity. By and large it was supposed that reality was literally what it appeared to be. The heavenly bodies are observed to move and the earth is observed not to. Ask yourself why you believe, for example, that the earth moves. Without a background in science it is doubtful that you have any idea. Aside from its intuitive plausibility, there were additional reasons for the success of the geocentric theory. These stemmed from the conception of scientific explanation with which it was associated.

Aristotle, who lived in the third century BC, was the most influential classical proponent of the geocentric world view. He formulated *teleological* explanations of both the natural and social world. This type of explanation purports to make an event intelligible through ascribing a purpose to it. For example, if you explain the behaviour of your liver in terms of its role in maintaining your health, then the explanation is teleological. Explanations of human action are similarly framed in terms of purpose (e.g. 'She is dashing to that shed to take shelter from the rain'). Purposive explanations of this kind are commonsensical and easily comprehended, provided that you can already see how the behaviour or action serves the goal invoked to explain it. For example, the first of the above explanations presupposes a prior awareness that the body will die without the liver, while the second presupposes that you know that sheds give shelter from the rain. Thus, the Aristotelian conception of the world was simple and proved extremely powerful in helping people to feel that they successfully understood a wide variety of natural and social phenomena. It was further refined during the Middle Ages and, until the revolution in modern science in the seventeenth-century, was the foundation of European intellectual orthodoxy.

In Aristotle's formulation of geocentrism, the earth and its outer atmosphere consisted of four elements: earth, water, air and fire. In principle, each of these elements occupied its own 'natural place' – the earth in a sphere surrounding the centre of the world, water in a sphere surrounding earth, air in a sphere surrounding water, and fire in a sphere surrounding air. Each element also had its own 'natural motion' – the most direct path back to its natural place – and its own 'natural state' – rest. When an element was removed from its natural place and state, 'violent motion' was imparted to it. As soon as this ceased, natural motion once again took over, until the element achieved its natural state and was as close as it could get to its natural place. All of this – the earth and its atmosphere – was called the 'terrestrial sphere'. The 'celestial sphere' – inhabited by the stars, sun, planets and moon – was composed of one element: aether. Again, each object had its natural place (e.g. Mars was connected to a transparent celestial sphere) and its own natural, uniform and circular motion (e.g. the motion of the sphere to which Mars was connected).

Such a view of the world, so different from the modern one, may now seem strange. But as an attempt to make sense of nature, certain aspects of it had great merit. Clearly, Aristotle did not think that any of the four terrestrial elements could be observed in their purity. He conjectured that all observable substances consisted of different combinations of these elements. For example, a piece of wood would consist mostly of earth; but also, because of its porosity, of air; because of its need of nourishment for growth, of water; and because of its combustible qualities, of fire. Given this system of classification, the Greek conception of nature was closer to ordinary observation than modern atomic conceptions. You can see with your own eyes that watering makes plants grow, but have you ever seen, touched or felt a swarm of atoms? Provided that teleological explanation is accepted as scientifically legitimate, Aristotle's system is powerfully explanatory. Why does a stone fall when it is dropped, and why does it land at the feet of the person who dropped it? It follows from Aristotle's theory that stones consist primarily of the element earth and once removed ('violent motion') from their resting place (i.e. their closest physical proximity to their natural place) they will return at the first opportunity, eventually coming to rest in their 'natural state'. This is of course exactly what they do.

Generally, then, Aristotelians explained the physical behaviour of objects in terms of the purposes associated with their material constitution. When they moved purposively and unhindered, they did so 'naturally' and, therefore, no further explanation of their behaviour was required. Similar considerations were said to apply to the celestial world. The apparent circular and uniform motion of the stars around the earth was also explained as 'natural' in this sense. No further explanation was believed to be needed, in just the same way that explanations of human action are often brought to an end with the statement, 'That's just human nature!' A teleological explanatory approach was also employed to explain many other objects of physical change. Why does a boy grow into a man? Why does an acorn become an oak? Aristotle and his medieval followers answered with reference to future purpose or 'natural potential'. And note again how the capacity of such concepts to convey a sense of real understanding still lingers. For example, people often have something like the idea of natural potential in mind when they explain someone's success or failure in terms of natural talent or intellectual ability.

Thus, the geocentric-teleological conception of the world proved to be both empirically successful and conceptually unifying. Its empirical success did not depend on its leading to dramatic discoveries but it did prompt the development and application of schemes of empirical classification, the successful application of which appeared to confirm the natural order it proclaimed. For example, you can readily see how the ideas of purpose and design would have been of immense use in the classification of new plants and animals. In short, because its rationale was the conceptual unification of observational information about which there was little dispute, Aristotelian theory could not help but be empirically successful. Further, because the concepts of purpose and design are obviously so applicable to understanding and classifying various types of human activity, for centuries there seemed no end to the explanatory capacity of the Aristotelian world view. Why do people do the things they do? Because of their purposes, of course! Indeed, Aristotle argued that the key difference between animals and humans is that the latter are capable, through their use of reason, of selecting their own goals and the means for achieving them. However, if the wrong goals were selected – those not in conformity with natural potential as dictated by nature (e.g. slaves trying to become citizens, or, to give a modern example of the same idea, attempting by contraception to thwart the natural purpose of sexual intercourse), then the actions concerned would be morally wrong, and whatever success was achieved would be short-lived. The lingering feeling on the part of some that others 'have their natural place in society and should stick to it!' and, equally, that an action is wrong because it is 'unnatural' are obvious throwbacks to this belief. Hence, according to the Greek and medieval conception, neither nature nor society could escape its purposeful design, though humans in their wickedness or folly might make great efforts to do so.

Given the capacity of the geocentric system to account for such a wide variety of natural and social phenomena, why was it ultimately replaced by the heliocentric world view? The reasons are many and complex. Arguably the most important relate to the declining usefulness of teleological explanation in the light of the intellectual and social changes of the sixteenth and seventeenth centuries. Increasingly, the new aim of science became the *control* of nature – the attempt to use nature for human purposes rather than passively allowing it to continue to dominate so much of human existence. Thus, as nation states expanded through an increased volume of trade and commerce, the explanatory problems of the Aristotelian, medieval intelligentsia seemed unfruitful, if not downright vacuous. The solution to practical problems concerning the application of old knowledge (e.g. mathematics and astronomy) to new situations (e.g. the improvement of artillery or navigation), as well as the creation of useful ways of understanding newly discovered natural processes and materials (e.g. the physical behaviour of sound, light, magnetism, electricity, combustion, gases, etc.) both required a great deal more than mere speculation about teleological purposes.

To take an obvious example, if your armies are constantly being outgunned by an enemy and more effective weapons are needed, it is vital to have more knowledge than simply the purpose for which you will employ your new arsenal. What is required is an understanding of how to go about producing better guns of greater power and improved accuracy. Unlike teleological explanations, where present events are assumed to occur because of their relation to future purposes, this new type of understanding is essentially concerned with how what is done in the present affects the future, or how what was done in the past affects the present. Hence, it is possible to understand the explanatory principles of cannon manufacture only when past experience confirms what type of physical process will, when applied in specific ways, regularly and reoccurringly produce the kind of cannon desired. In short, if your aim is to make something or to make an existing thing better, you need information about causes and not about purposes. For example, if you are skilled at a particular craft, you produce things on the basis of your understanding of the regular and reoccurring characteristics of the materials with which you work. Thus it was increasingly argued during the seventeenth century that the general problem of 'natural philosophy' (as science was then called) was to discover the physical regularities which determined what nature did or would do in specific circumstances of human intervention. Nature came to be thought of as analogous to a huge machine – like a clock – and scientific activity was directed towards the discovery of its real inner workings as well as its outward observable manifestations. The scientist thus came to be concerned not with what natural phenomena were *for*, but with how they worked. On this latter basis one could predict how some process could be made to work better, or how to avoid the consequences of processes that would occur anyway.

The dramatic scientific and social consequences of this 'mechanization of nature' fall into three major categories. First, the discovery of observational regularities was viewed as a key to the discovery of the main characteristics of 'the reality behind appearance'. This motivated an explosion of experimental research, involving the development of new and more precise forms of instrumentation and more vigorous methods of experimental control. Through such experiments, nature was for the first time systematically manipulated – many dramatic new things were designed and made for scientific purposes. Second, the belief that a mechanistic reality existed behind appearances motivated an explosion of theoretical speculation as to what this mechanism might be like. The most influential hypothesis to emerge was that regular interactions between irreducible particles or atoms of matter caused the regularities of ordinary experience and of laboratory experiments. In short, material reality was regarded as purposeless 'stuff' determining the motion of other purposeless 'stuff'. This view still dominates modern science. Third, these assumptions came increasingly to be used not only for understanding nature, but for explanations of individual and social behaviour as well. Particularly after the major successes of natural philosophy in the seventeenth and eighteenth centuries, humans also came to be conceived by many as nothing but stuff interacting with other stuff – appearances to the contrary.

One outcome of the Copernican revolution was, therefore, a growing acceptance that nature should be explored both experimentally and theoretically with reference to its observed or conjectured regularities. Hence, the social aim of science became the discovery of *laws* of nature – descriptions of the essentially *purposeless* yet fundamental structure and patterns of the physical world. This search for laws which are presumed to determine the course of specific events has dominated the natural sciences ever since. A similar approach is often advocated for the social sciences and it is in order to assess this claim that we need to look in more detail at the use of laws as the basis of explanation in the physical sciences.

Deductive-nomological explanation

The concept of a causal law will occupy our attention in various ways throughout the rest of this book. As a starting point, it is important to understand that laws of this kind describe physical regularities presumed to be linked in a necessary, non-coincidental fashion. For this reason, such regularities are held to explain *why* particular events occur as and when they do. Although those who know only a little mathematics may have difficulty in understanding contemporary explanations in the physical sciences, the sort of explanation that physical scientists attempt to achieve is easy to understand. If you are trying to bake a sponge cake, put up shelves or grow flowers in your garden, you will obviously want to know what it is that makes the difference between success and failure. An explanation of your purpose which is equally compatible with success and failure will be useless, since in such circumstances you wish to control nature in specific ways. You will want to know what makes a sponge cake rise if you do not manage to get yours to do so, what keeps shelves up if yours fall down, and what conditions favour strong and healthy growth of flowers if yours wither and die. Thus, even if your formal knowledge of science is limited, you will nevertheless often look for and employ explanations which possess the same logical structure and conceptual properties as those in the natural sciences.

All such explanations rely on the existence of physical regularities which dictate that when one set of empirical conditions occurs, another set of empirical conditions *must* follow. For example, the recipe 'Mix two ounces of fat, four ounces of flour, two eggs, etc. and bake in the middle of the oven at 300°F for 20 minutes . . . ' gives the end result '. . . and you will have a fine sponge cake'. The recipe and the cooking instructions are universal: they do not refer to particular brands of ingredient, and are not restricted in their application to particular times and places. Moreover, the instructions and their supposed consequences are not assumed to be correlated through accident, say in the way in which people often believe bad weather is correlated with their desire for good weather. Belief in the existence of a law of nature distinguishes the resulting scientific prediction from a fanciful prophecy. If the recipe is correct in its description of a necessary and non-accidental regularity, and if it is applied correctly to a specific set of appropriate ingredients then you can confidently predict that a fine sponge cake will result. Conversely, you will not necessarily expect bad weather the next time you want a day at the seaside – no matter how many times the two have been correlated in the past. Whenever a new recipe is put to the test, it may be confirmed or refuted, provided that the instructions are properly followed and that no unknown factor (e.g. a faulty oven) ruins the cookery experiment. The laws of nature involved in the preparation of cakes may not be as general as some of the other laws in the natural sciences, but they are laws nonetheless. Factory production of cakes or beer is not unlike any other form of chemical engineering.

Natural scientists employ laws in similar ways. Even without having done a formal science course, there are physical regularities with which you are undoubtedly familiar. For instance, if you have ever played with a bicycle pump, you will know that if you block the outlet with your thumb you can compress the air inside. The harder you press, the smaller the volume of air becomes. This is an instance of an 'experimental' or 'observational' law of nature which relates together two variable properties of air (or any gas): volume and pressure. The law in question is one of the earliest and most famous experimental laws of physics – Boyle's law – and, simply stated, it says that at a constant temperature the volume of a given quantity of gas is inversely proportional to the pressure exerted upon it. This law may only be accurately tested in the context of an experimental situation where all but the relevant variable quantities are held constant, thus ensuring as much as possible that no other factors cause the event to be explained than those mentioned in the law itself. This said, it can then be observed (until very high pressures are reached) that volume does indeed vary in proportion to the pressure. The 'initial conditions' – the conditions of applicability of the law – follow from the law itself and dictate the form of experimental assessment. They constitute the values given to the variables of the law in the experimental situation in which it is to be tested. In the case of Boyle's law, the temperature and the quantity of the gas must be held constant and the variation in volume must be observed as the pressure exerted on the gas is varied. If the variation *is* inversely proportional then the law is confirmed.

Imagine constructing just such an experiment. You will need a gas-tight container whose volume may be varied and measured (e.g. a calibrated cylinder whose length may be varied with a plunger). The pressure exerted upon the gas within the container should be measurable (e.g. in pounds per square inch – the area of the plunger is known, and the weight pressing on the plunger is measured). Suppose you then fill the container with a gas and arrange to keep it at a constant temperature (e.g. in a thermostatically controlled bath of water). If Boyle's law is true, then through adding to the weight pressing in the plunger and producing a measurable increase of pressure you should observe a proportional decrease in the volume which you can measure. In short, the gas acts just like a *spring* which compresses in proportion to the weight pressing upon it. Indeed, when Boyle first proposed his law, he spoke of the 'spring of the air'. In logical terms, you will explain the preceding situation as follows:

General law: At constant temperature and at low pressure, the volume of a given quantity of *any* gas is inversely proportional to the pressure exerted upon it. (The qualification concerning pressure is due to the fact that at very high pressure, gases, liquefy and the law no longer holds true.)

Initial condition I:	The described experimental situation.
Initial condition II:	The pressure of the gas is increased by a measured amount.
Assumption:	All things else are equal. This means that there is no unknown factor (e.g. a leak in the container) which would unexpectedly affect the outcome of the experiment.
Conclusion:	The volume of the gas will be reduced proportionally to the exerted pressure.

In short, the premises of the above explanatory argument (i.e. the 'explanans') entail the conclusion (i.e. the 'explanandum') with 'logical necessity', a concept about which we shall say more in a moment. What should be intuitively clear at this point is that the conclusion 'follows from' the premises in such a way that the premises could not be true while the conclusion is false.

Yet to feel that your understanding was complete, you would presumably want to know more than just the information provided in the experimental law. As it stands, Boyle's law says no more than that, generally speaking, gases do in fact behave in the described way. If, as supposed, it is universally true throughout time and space, this justifies our deducing the prediction. Yet there is still no explanation of what *makes* gases behave in this way. To take a similar example from the social sciences, there is a sense in which you might explain why a particular family is poor by pointing out that they live in a neighbourhood where, so far as you know, all of the people are always poor. But, of course, to know that some people are always poor is not the same as understanding *why* they are. Indeed, without this information you will be unable to justify your belief that there is anything more to their collective poverty than coincidence: it is not living in that district that *makes* them poor. Similarly, despite the predictive success of Boyle's law not being restricted to time and place, there is still no further explanation of why it is successful or should continue to be so. What is required is some further understanding of what it is about those physical situations correlated by experimental laws which gives them whatever causal status they possess. Since the seventeenth century the dominant belief in modern science has been that observed regularities of nature are themselves necessitated by the fundamental nature of physical reality, one which is not directly observed but which was initially thought to be analogous to a hidden mechanism.

Those explanatory principles meant to describe this reality are usually termed 'theoretical laws' since they refer to universal correlations said to exist between non-observed physical entities (e.g. atoms, molecules, forces, etc.). They are thus contrasted with the more empirical character of experimental laws, and serve the function of explaining why experimental laws are true, if indeed they are. And like experimental laws their logical structure is deductive and nomological. This can be seen more clearly by examining the following simplified example:

General law I: *All gases consist of minute particles (atoms or molecules) in constant motion.* At relatively low pressures the average distance between these particles will be greatly in excess of their diameter.

General law II: *These particles obey Newton's laws of motion:*
(a) They continue at rest or in uniform motion in a straight line unless acted upon by some force.
(b) Force = mass × acceleration.
(c) Each force produces an equal and opposite reaction.

General law III: *These particles are perfectly elastic:* Two such identical particles moving at equal speeds in opposite directions towards one another along a straight line will, when they collide, each rebound at exactly the same speed in opposite directions along the same straight line. More generally, all such particles will leave any such collision with the same combined energy of motion as they had prior to the collision. This means intuitively that they may be likened to tiny billiard balls moving endlessly without friction in three dimensions.

General law IV: *These particles are neither destroyed nor altered by collison.*

General law V: *Time spent in collision is a negligible proportion of the time spent in motion.*

Initial condition I: *A quantity of such a gas at low pressure is enclosed in a sealed container whose volume may be altered by applying a force to it* (e.g. a cylinder with a movable plunger on which weights may be placed).

Initial condition II: *The sealed vessel and the gas it contains are maintained at a constant temperature.* This means that the sides of the vessel neither absorb nor impart energy to the particles moving within it and may also be assumed to be perfectly elastic.

Interim conclusion: *A gas composed of such particles enclosed within a sealed vessel will exert a force on the side of the container as a result of the continual collisions of the particles with the sides of the vessel.* The total force exerted on the sides of the vessel will be in proportion to the total energy of motion of the mass of moving particles enclosed within it.

Bridge principle: (A rule which enables translation of unobservable events to observable ones.) *The force exerted on the sides of the vessel in this way may be measured as the pressure exerted by the gas on the sides of the vessel.*

Initial condition III: *The pressure of the gas in the sealed vessel is doubled.*

Ceteris paribus
assumption *All else is assumed to be equal.*
Conclusions: (a) By the bridge principle, *twice the pressure implies twice as many impacts of particles* on the sides of the vessel in a given space of time.
(b) By general law IV and initial condition I, the number of particles remains constant because the quantity of gas is unchanged. Thus, *given general law V, twice as many impacts will occur in a given space of time when the volume within which the particles are confined is halved.*

This explanation clearly does more than merely relate specific observations of pressure and volume by means of a general law. It attempts to give an account of what makes the volume of gas decrease in proportion to the pressure. It provides a *model* of a mechanism which lies behind and explains appearances which may be expanded to explain many more experimental laws as well. Its capacity to do this obviously reinforces the belief that it is correct. For example, the same model can explain the phenomena observed when gases are heated as well as compressed. Experimentally it can be shown that gases at constant pressure expand in direct proportion to increases in temperature (i.e. Charles's law). Combining this with Boyle's law shows that pressure rises in proportion to temperature at constant volume. To see why this should be expected, try to picture what intuitively ought to happen if the model is correct. As we have pointed out, at very high temperatures, gases can become liquids. What happens to a liquid when it is heated and brought to the boil? Its overall *energy* apparently increases as a result. Assuming that the same sort of thing happens when a gas is heated – that the phenomenon of heat in a gas is a measure of the mean energy of its component parts – the result should be exactly the increase of pressure which is observed. Of course, the preceding account of the so-called *kinetic theory of gases* is an idealization and if you read about it in a chemistry textbook things will appear to be much more complicated. For example, gases behave and can be explained in the ways described only when pressures are low and temperatures well above their boiling points. Under these more complex, 'non-ideal' situations, additional hypotheses are required to explain such exceptions to the rule, though that need not be of concern.

The differentiation of experimental from theoretical laws is a useful way of distinguishing between scientific explanations which refer primarily to appearances and those which refer to a reality behind appearance. Hectic debate continues in the philosophy of science about whether or not the explanatory success of theoretical laws justifies belief in their associated conception of reality. Some have argued, for example, that the model presupposed by the kinetic theory is no more than a useful metaphor in ordering experience and making it intelligible; atoms do not really exist but are a helpful explanatory fiction. Suffice it to say for the moment that while in many ways helpful, a hard and fast distinction between observation and theory is extremely problematic. For example, a statement apparently as innocently observational as 'This balloon is full of helium' is already very far from a completely untheorized perception. No one has ever *seen* helium. It is an essentially theoretical concept which derives its meaning from an atomistic view of the world. If in any doubt, look up the meaning of 'helium' or of other specific gases in any chemistry textbook. Even the modern concept of a 'gas' as such is basically derived from the same conceptual foundations, although its usage can be much more varied than the quite specific claims of the kinetic theory. Indeed, it makes no sense to talk of 'filled balloons', as if the meaning of this phrase were dependent entirely on experiences which have not been conceptually interpreted. It is not *obvious* that a balloon contains gas. Distinct gases, as opposed to mere 'air', were not recognized before the end of the eighteenth century, and the idea that a container might be empty — contain nothing but a vacuum — was considered unintelligible before the late sixteenth century. Fill a balloon with helium and release it in front of people from a culture where western science is unknown. They will make a very different sense of what they see from what you do!

It is true that experimental laws have a more direct relation to measurement than do theoretical laws. This is because the value of each of the variables related by the law is usually itself some directly measurable quantity, at least in principle. On the face of it, this seems to make experimental laws more observational and less interpretative than theoretical laws where the value of some variables is not so straightforwardly empirical (e.g. force). However, once the theoretical significance of specific operations of measurement are considered, it again becomes obvious that theoretical and experimental laws conceptually overlap and are equally interpretative, albeit in different ways. For example, few things seem more straightforward in science than measuring the temperature of a gas. Though much more refined, this is essentially the same kind of operation as measuring a person's temperature with a thermometer. But what is a thermometer and how do you know that it measures temperature?

To answer such questions you must have ideas about what the thermometer is supposed to be measuring. When it is claimed that the mercury inside the thermometer rises because it gets warmer, and falls when it gets colder, this implies knowledge of at least a theory of heat which says, amongst other things, that heat and cold are not opposites, as they might appear, but are merely degrees of temperature. People with a fever feel hot to you but feel cold in themselves. In order to suppose that temperature can be measured independently of its subjective appearance, the assumption must be made that there is an objective magnitude to be measured. Although historically this was not always the case, the physical character of this magnitude is itself made sense of on the basis of the theory which we discussed above – the source of heat has mechanistically communicated and added its energy to that of the atomic constituents of the mercury. This in turn increases the volume of the mercury and makes it rise in its container. Of course, someone might reply that they can read a thermometer correctly without knowing anything about atomic physics and without being able to articulate the metaphysics of atomism. Up to a point, this is a correct observation. You do not need to be a theoretical chemist to use a thermometer to determine whether or not someone has a fever! However, natural scientists must have such information if they are to have any idea of what it is they are actually doing. In short, both the experimental *and* theoretical laws of modern science are linked to particular views of what the world is ultimately like.

Generally speaking, explanations in modern physical science are *deductive* in that their premises logically entail their conclusions, and they are *nomological* in that at least one of their *premises* is a law. If an explanation employs *universal* laws, the explanandum follows from the explanans with the same sort of logical necessity as the conclusion follows from the premises in this famous argument:

All men are mortal	Premises
Socrates is a man	
Therefore, Socrates is mortal	Conclusion

This kind of necessity is found in all valid arguments, a valid argument being one in which the accepted truth of the premises is necessarily transferred to the conclusion. For example, in the preceding examples of scientific explanation it was assumed that, if the explanans were true, the explanandum must necessarily be true. Once this characteristic of valid argument is made clear, it is easily seen why the link between explanans and explanandum feels so strong. Provided the logical argument embodied in the explanation is valid, there is no other possibility than for the one to follow from the other.

It is important to distinguish between the logical necessity which *deductions* derive from their validity, and the necessity with which *events* occur that fall under the laws of nature. For the logical necessity clearly remains even when the explanation is false and yields false conclusions – it is from these false conclusions that we deduce the falsity of the explanatory premises. The valid argument above, about Socrates, is valid because of the form of the statements it contains, which may be represented thus:

All Xs are Ys	Premises
A is an X	
Thus A is a Y	Conclusion

If we know that the premises are true, then we may only deny the conclusion on pain of contradicting one or other of the premises which we know to be true. We can contrast this with an invalid argument:

All devout Catholics are against birth control	(True)
Fidel Castro is against birth control	(True!)
Thus Fidel Castro is a devout Catholic	(False)

This has the following general form:

All Xs are Ys	Premises
A is a Y	
Thus A is an X	Conclusion

This form is invalid because all Xs can be Ys while not all Ys need be Xs. See if you can think of other specific examples.

Logical validity is independent of truth and must be so because it is just as important to use logic to deduce falsity as it is to deduce truth. In the argument about Fidel Castro the falsehood of the 'conclusion', because it is not validly deduced, has no impact on the truth of the premises. But in the following case you can see how the falsehood of the conclusion of a valid argument may be transferred back to one or other of the premises:

All swans are white	Premises
This is a swan from Australia	
This swan is white	Conclusion

The discovery of black swans in Australia *falsifies* the general premise 'All swans are white', and is an example of a valid deductive inference from falsehood to falsehood which is obviously crucial to the testing of scientific theories.

When a conclusion is deduced and turns out to be false, the falsehood of the conclusion is transferred back to one or other of the premises. When we validly deduce a true conclusion, on the other hand, that does not imply that the premises must be true. Truth is transferred in one direction only – from premises, if they are true, to conclusions. Equally, falsehood is transferred in one direction only – from conclusions, if they *are* false, back to at least one of the premises. Look at the possibilities which valid forms of argument allow (T for true, F for false). Of eight possible combinations, only one is disallowed.

	1	2	3	4	5	6	7		8
All Xs are Ys	F	T	T	F	F	F	T	F		T
A is an X	F	T	F	T	T	F	F	*But*	T
Thus A is a Y	T	T	T	T	F	F	F	*Not*	F

This may seem surprising, but it is not if you think about it. Take the cases in order, left to right, and consider the following examples of each:

(1)   The moon is made of green F
cheese
        Gorgonzola is not green cheese F
Thus Gorgonzola is not from the moon T (Pure luck.)

(2)   All men are mortal   T
        Socrates is a man   T
Thus Socrates is mortal   T

(3)   All men are mortal   T (Cats are mortal too
        Tibbles is a man   F but that was not one
Thus Tibbles is mortal   T of our premises.)

(4)   All swans are white   F (Some swans are
        This bird is a swan   T white of course, so we
Thus This bird is white   T were lucky.)

(5)   All swans are white   F
        This is a swan from Australia T
Thus The swan is white   F

(6)   All salt dissolves in water   T
        This typewriter is made of salt F
Thus This typwriter dissolves in water F

(7)   All swans are green   F
        Donald Duck is a swan   F
Thus Donald Duck is green   F

But not
(8)   All men are mortal   T
        Socrates is a man   T
Thus Socrates is not mortal   F

If you look back over (1)-(7) you will see that false conclusions are only compatible with one or other or both premises being false, but that true conclusions are compatible with any combination of truth or falsity in the premises.

This is why results which 'inductively confirm' a theory do not allow the deductively valid inference that it must be true, no matter how many times it happens. However many white swans you see, that does not imply that the next one cannot be black. The fact that only the combination of truth and falsity in (8) is ruled out shows why *establishing* the truth of the premises implies the truth of the conclusion and why *establishing* the falsehood of the conclusion implies the falsehood of at least one of the premises. Thus, all of the preceding examples illustrate how the *logical* necessity associated with valid argument has nothing to do with questions of truth and falsity and everything to do with the structural relations between the variables and constants in each argument. Scientists and non-scientists may both argue validly and yet differ completely about the truth or falsity of their explanatory theories.

It should now be clear why explanations conforming to the deductive nomological models were welcomed enthusiastically by the supporters of the new mechanistic science. Any application of an experimental or theoretical law to a new set of initial conditions leads to the deduction of a new conclusion and hence also a new prediction. If further experiments are then performed in order to confirm or refute the prediction, then whatever the experimental outcome, a new discovery will have been made. Predictions, discovery and explanations thus go hand in hand. Experimental criticism is effectively directed back towards the premises of the explanations and, if care has been taken experimentally to produce the relevant initial conditions, one of the physical laws in the explanans is usually at fault. Since the conclusion of a valid argument can be true although its premises are false, it makes sense to try to discover laws which are successfully applicable to more and more varied initial conditions, despite the fact that explanations which are vigorously believed at one point may be validly rejected at the next. Among other things, this helps to differentiate scientific from technological inquiry. For example, some physical theories with many correct consequences are now regarded as having been experimentally falsified. Yet their explanatory principles are so easy to understand that they continue to be employed to solve many technological problems. For example, even though Newtonian physics is now believed to have been falsified by experiments which in turn confirmed Einstein's theories, it continues to be confidently employed for many technological purposes where, among other things, its simplicity and familiarity are an advantage (e.g. launching earth satellites).

In our account of explanation in the natural sciences, the emphasis which thus far has been placed on falsifiability should sound very familiar. It clearly reflects Karl Popper's views about scientific inquiry which were discussed in the first chapter. Popper has been influential in his articulation of the logical and methodological principles inherent in deductive-nomological explanation. Indeed, his conception of explanation so complements his other views that he almost identifies it with the anatomy of scientific inquiry as a whole. Hence, it is not surprising that some of Popper's critics have chosen his emphasis on the deductive-nomological model as one of their targets. Their criticisms fall into three key categories.

First, in chapter 1, we showed how Kuhn demonstrates that too much emphasis on this model leads to many other dimensions of scientific inquiry being overlooked. These include the important role that socialization plays in teaching scientists how to employ the critical feedback gained from the application of the deductive-nomological model in the progressive 'articulation' of their explanatory traditions.

Without commitment to viewing such feedback as puzzles to be solved in specific ways rather than as refutations of the traditions themselves, no programme of research would get off the ground. Similarly, the transition from one tradition to another remains inexplicable on deductive-nomological grounds since in such situations, the interpretation of empirical data is itself in dispute. If there is no agreement on the meaning – much less the truth or falsity – of such data, their falsifying potential can obviously not be regarded as the key stimulus to revolutionary theoretical change.

The second difficulty concerns the ambiguity of empirical falsification – the problem of 'what's wrong'. When you accept that a consequence of a particular explanation is logically valid but empirically false, a purely logical analysis offers no basis for deciding which of the laws or initial conditions is the source of the error. In fact, because deductive-nomological explanations inevitably stipulate that 'all things are equal', they refer to an infinite number of possible unknown events as well as those which they specifically describe. So even when you *think* you know what is wrong – towards which component of the explanans to direct the falsifying force of an empirical counter-example – you can never be absolutely certain. Fortunately, as Popper is well aware, effective critical assessment of scientific explanations within the community of scientists does not require absolute certainty. But again, because of its potential complexity, such assessment does require agreement about what to try to blame in the face of empirical error and what to discount as beyond question. Agreement of this kind is essentially social in character and demands a different type of understanding to that provided by the deductive-nomological model. So to be scientific an inquiry must yield results which are empirically checkable. However, scientific inquiry as a mode of social action cannot be reduced to scientists formulating deductive-nomological explanations and empirically checking them.

The third problem is more complicated and concerns the role of analogy in science. If the aim of explanation is understanding, this can be achieved in a number of ways which do not immediately appeal to laws or to deduction in any rigorous sense. A clear analogy can be drawn between the behaviour of sound and light and the motion of waves, which enables us to 'explain' or understand the phenomena 'in terms of' such waves. It has been suggested that analogies such as these have played a crucial role in the history of theoretical science since they ground theoretical speculation about the unfamiliar (i.e. whatever reality is presumed to exist behind appearance) in a host of familiar natural processes. Recall, in this respect, the analogy with the behaviour of billiard balls implicit in our simplified formulation of the atomic theory of gases. Yet here the argument is not as strong as in the two preceding cases. If understanding is to be gained through analogy, what is to be understood must be assigned an analogical partner which is itself understood by means other than analogy. Carried to its conclusion, this implies that the use of explanatory analogies in the natural sciences is still ultimately based on explanations of a more general type. So to assess the extent to which a given analogy holds (i.e. to test the explanatory power of the analogy itself), one must formulate alternative explanatory laws about the analogical partner (e.g. about the motion of waves and of highly elastic bodies like billiard balls) and test them in accordance with the deductive patterns of assessment already examined. Consequently, while it may be true that many events and processes are understandable without direct reference to explanations of a deductive-nomological character, an examination of the basis of such understanding reveals that, in respect of the physical world, the deductive-nomological pattern remains a permanent and prominent conceptual feature of modern natural science. The same, however, cannot be said of the social world, as we shall shortly demonstrate.

Causality and natural necessity

Thus far in our discussion of explanation, we have simply assumed that the relationship between explanans and explanandum is causal in the sense that it is somehow non-coincidental and necessary. This is no more than an elaboration of the normal everyday use of the term 'cause', by which we mean an event or condition which 'makes' another event or condition – the effect – occur. In more detail, this means that the occurrence of the general and particular events described in the explanans (e.g. Boyle's law applied to relevant circumstances) comprises a *sufficient condition* for the occurrence of the events described in the explanandum. If one event is a sufficient condition for the occurrence of another event, then when the first occurs it is enough to ensure that the second will always follow. In this respect, sufficient conditions are different from *necessary conditions*. For example, in order to extinguish an electric fire, it is sufficient to turn it off. However, this is not the only thing which will lead to the same effect. A fuse may blow. Conversely, a necessary condition for lighting an electric fire is the presence of electric current. But again this is clearly not enough, not a sufficient condition. You can see from our preceding discussion of explanations that there is never just one cause sufficient for the occurrence of a particular effect but many causal conditions all working in conjunction. For example, it would be wrong to claim that it is *only* an increase in volume which leads to the decrease in pressure of a gas. Similarly, as those familiar with the difficulties of lighting coal fires will understand, it is an oversimplification to say that a fire is caused by the igniting match. The skill of lighting such fires involves getting all of the other conditions right as well. This being said, a serious problem is raised by viewing sets of events as causal in the sense of being sufficient for the production of other sets. For until the concept of causal necessity itself is made clearer, why this sufficiency amounts to more than surprisingly regular coincidence remains a mystery.

In the eighteenth century David Hume asked whether or not the concept of causal necessity could be derived from experience. He argued that when a causal relationship is supposedly experienced, the most that can be said is that there is a regular and reoccurring sequence of events. Consequently, no observational evidence exists for a sort of physical cement which bonds events necessarily together. Hume further argued that the physical existence of causal necessity was not demonstrable on purely rational or logical grounds. This is the case since no logical contradiction is involved in assuming that the relevant correlation will cease to occur. For example, it is not logically contradictory to deny that the pressure of a gas at constant temperature will increase if its volume is decreased – it had to be discovered empirically just because there is nothing contradictory about supposing that it might not be so. By contrast it is logically contradictory to deny that all bachelors are unmarried. Hume thus argued that beliefs about causal links are psychological in origin. They are no more than habitual expectations generated by past experience of undisturbed regularity (e.g. always observing that when the volume of a gas decreases, its pressure increases). Since there is nothing observationally nor logically necessary about the assumption that the future will resemble the past – indeed, you are familiar with the numerous cases where it does not – Hume suggested that causal relationships are within the believer and not actually in the physical world at all.

There are many problems with Hume's account, one of the most important being that his equation of causal beliefs with habit fails on his own terms. For, given an analysis, there is still no effective way of accounting for why some observational correlations are equated with causal relationships (e.g. Boyle's law) while others are not (e.g. night always follows day). Both causal and non-causal correlations should be psychologically reinforcing in Hume's sense. Those which are non-causal will be regarded as purely coincidental or as requiring further explanation in terms of other unobserved causes (e.g. again, night follows day). This is a particularly important point since it is clear that much argument within science is precisely about which observable correlations are and are not causal. For example, cigarette smoking is now generally regarded as a key causal factor in the production of lung cancer as well as a range of other diseases. But, as the tobacco industry and some committed smokers keep reminding us all, it is possible to interpret the existing correlational evidence in different ways. It is difficult to reconcile this possibility with Hume's psychological theory of causality. After all, are not both sets of disputants equally influenced by the same experiences? It is equally difficult to reconcile Hume's position with the fact that much of the causal understanding of modern science (e.g. the theoretical laws discussed in the previous section) consists of beliefs about a reality of regular and reoccurring sequences of events which exists behind appearance. For example, how do *you* explain why night follows day?

Much of the philosophy of Immanuel Kant, another famous eighteenth-century philosopher, was formulated in response to Hume's arguments. Kant begins by assuming as obvious that any intelligible experience of the world must be informed by a notion of causality. You unthinkingly possess a host of causal expectations about what will happen under certain circumstances, about what should and should not be understood as the result of coincidence or caprice. It is only on the basis of believing the world to be orderly and predictable that you can plan your day-to-day activities. Scientific inquiry is merely the refinement of such expectations through a rigorous system of empirical assessment. Indeed, without the assumption of a causally ordered world with detectable patterns of natural necessity, it would be impossible to remain sane, let alone have any motive for engaging in scientific activity.

So Kant reasoned that the capacity to make causal judgments could not be derived from experience. The intelligibility of experience and its use and control for human purposes presupposes that this capacity has already been exercised – that causal order of some kind has already been imposed. But this must mean that the ability to make causal judgments is in some way part of the structure of the human mind and that learning, among other things, involves the active projections of this structure on to uninterpreted sensations. Kant argued that for similar reasons the necessary structure of the human mind involved other basic conceptual abilities. For example, unless you have the capacity to make judgments about things and about relationships between things, you will not even be able to make sense of a simple experience like two cats resting on a mat. Thus, the human capacity to make causal judgments of the kind made scientifically explicit in experimental and theoretical laws must be presumed to exist prior to observation. Without this capacity (but with the other mentioned above) you would indeed be able to make some sense of the presence of two cats on a mat. Yet, unless you did so accidentally, you would never kick them off. It would simply never occur to you that you could!

In general, Kant's arguments reinforce Hume's view that any attempt to base beliefs about causal relationships solely on perception or logic must inevitably fail. Somehow, we actively *impute* causal necessity on to experience and vice versa. Yet, like Hume, Kant fails to provide any convincing explanation of why this capacity for imputation should be used in some cases and not in others. Just the reaffirmation that we do indeed have such a necessary capacity will not help. Nor will reference to those correlations within natural science which are already believed to possess causal status. This simply raises again the problem to be solved. It would be equally unsatisfactory to argue that such decisions are made on the basis of rigorous empirical assessment. Such assessment is employed to decide whether or not a given correlation is false. But the problem at hand is a wider one. What is there about a particular empirical correlation, even one with a high degree of empirical confirmation, that makes it a legitimate contender for causal rather than coincidental status? The decision to impute causal status – at least hypothetically – will clearly be made prior to any further empirical assessment. Otherwise, again, there would be no motivation for such assessment. Clearly, the most attractive solution would be one where the hypothesis that a correlation between events was causal implied some sort of essential characteristic which differentiated it from coincidence.

One criterion which might intuitively be used in this way concerns the universal character of correlations believed to be causal. This account is often termed 'Humean' because it is compatible with Hume's notion that cause is no more than constant conjunction or undisturbed regularity. The phrase 'causal relations' could then be retained solely for those empirically confirmed correlations which apply universally in space and time. Thus 'Everyone in this room is English' would not be attributed causal status because it is not universal. It contains specific reference to a particular place (i.e. this room) and an implicit reference to the present time. A rule of this kind would also, of course, ensure that the statement 'Every time I wash my car, it rains' was disbarred from causal status, irrespective of how many times it rained under such circumstances. On the other hand, statements like Boyle's law which are commonly regarded as causal universally relate their component variables. In this respect, they contain no reference to particulars. They may be false, but this in no way affects the legitimacy of their *claim* to causal status. So 'universal in space and time' appears to be a promising criterion for deciding the causal status of a correlation.

This decision procedure can only succeed, however, if there is no correlation which is both universal and obviously not causal. Unfortunately, these can be manufactured at will. For example, the fact that something is made of gold does not make it less than a given weight – say 1,000,000 tonnes. Somewhere there exists the largest piece of gold in the universe, but it is impossible to know whether or not it has yet been found. Whatever it weighs is a sheer accident and so, therefore, is the true universal generalization 'All pieces of gold in the universe weigh less than a given (unknown) amount'. On the other hand, the radioactive element plutonium has a 'critical mass' (i.e. a weight above which no piece of plutonium can exist because above that weight it would spontaneously explode). Consequently, it is a law of nature (employed in the design of the atomic bomb) and no coincidence that 'All pieces of plutonium in the universe weigh less than a given (known) amount'. As far as universality is concerned, both the statement about gold and the statement about plutonium are the same. Yet one is causal and the other is not. The logical possibility of a coincidence being universal in time and space shows that this cannot be sufficient condition for causal status which is being sought. But it does remain a *necessary* condition – a supposed law of nature which is broken never was a law of nature.

Another popular suggestion is that laws acquire their causal status, again assuming that the correlations in question are well confirmed and believed to be true, from their capacity to justify 'counter-factual conditionals'. These are statements which are conditional in that they state a hypothetical relationship between variables, but which refer to states which are known not to have existed in the past and/or which will not exist in the future. For example, it is accepted as true that 'If this typewriter were made of salt it would dissolve in water'. Being composed of salt *makes* an object soluble in water, and because in this case it is not soluble we can conclude that it is not made of salt. When counter-factuals of this kind are accepted as true it seems to be because of the inherent causal status of those physical laws to which they explicitly or implicitly refer (e.g. laws of solubility in water). General statements which are regarded as coincidentally true, and therefore as non-causal, will not justify counter-factuals in the same sense. 'All of the people in this room are English' may be true, but it does not justify the claim that if anyone else were to enter the room they too would be English – being in this room clearly does not make you English! Similarly, 'No piece of gold in the universe exceeds the weight of 1,000,000 tonnes' may be true, but it cannot be employed to support the statement that if, for instance, a piece of lead were gold then it too would necessarily weigh less than this amount. The fact of an object's being made of gold implies nothing about its weight in the way that an object's being plutonium does. Given the causal status of the laws of atomic physics, it makes perfectly good sense to assert that if this typewriter were a piece of plutonium then it would have to weigh less than a specific amount. Both cases, therefore, seem to confirm the view that only causal correlations can justify counter-factual conditionals. But again, like the criterion of universality, this rule also runs into difficulty.

The main problem is straightforward. The difference between causal and coincidental correlations is to be based on the capacity of the former to justify counter-factual conditionals believed to be correct. But the assumption that such conditionals are correct must not itself depend on the presumed causal status of related correlations. For if the truth or falsity of the conditional were itself a function of belief in the causal status of a particular law, then to justify the latter in terms of the former would be to beg the question at issue. Yet this is precisely what seems to happen. For example, 'If this typewriter were salt then it would dissolve in water' is accepted as a correct counter-factual. Why? The answer presumably depends in some way on the truth of the statement. But it has a funny sort of truth. It is counter-factual – contrary to fact. 'If this typewriter were made of salt (which it is not) then it would dissolve in water (which it does not).' Being contrary to fact, its truth is supported by no fact, so why else should its truth be accepted unless the law which it implicitly presupposes is already believed to be both true and causal (i.e. 'All salt dissolves in water'). The same point can be made about correlations which do not lend support to counter-factual conditions. 'All the people in this room are English' gains no causal status from 'If you were in this room then you would be English'. This is because it is believed that the latter is incorrect. But this belief itself depends on the prior belief that the former has no causal status, despite the fact that it may be true. So a completely confirmed correlation might or might not support a counter-factual conditional. Consequently, the causal status conferred on the correlation must depend on beliefs held prior to judging the correctness or incorrectness of the counter-factual. There is no purely *formal* decision procedure for awarding causal status to a correlation no matter how well it has withstood empirical scrutiny.

To be accepted as causal, a correlation must be universal (or statistical in a form subject to very rigorous constraints). Unless it is so, it will not suffice as the nomological component of the explanans in a deductive-nomological explanation. Also, the law must not already be believed to be false. As far as modern conceptions of natural necessity are concerned, these two characteristics are indeed necessary conditions for successful causal imputation. Yet more is required, for you now know that the concept of causation is not reducible to the universality of a correlation or to its empirical success. Similarly, more is required than the ability of laws to support counter-factual conditionals, although laws which have *already* been accorded causal status will have this potential. In the case of experimental laws, the conviction that they reveal causal relationships is increasingly strengthened the more accepted theoretical laws can account for them. Laws such as those of atomic physics which unify large numbers of experimental laws, in that they predict a coherent picture of the natural order, greatly reinforce belief in a reality behind appearance which *produces* the necessary relationship between their measurable variables. For example, the relationship between the pressure and volume of air in a balloon might well be regarded as coincidence within a system of belief that had no relevant conceptualization of its contents. Of course, when experimental laws can actually be deduced from theoretical laws, their causal status is even further reinforced. For example, when the relationship between the pressure and the volume of a given gas was itself explained in terms of atomic theory, the causal bond between these two variables was inestimably strengthened. It was shown to follow from, or be produced by, the presumed causal interaction of more fundamental physical realities. But what is the justification of imputing causal status to theoretical laws — to those descriptions of universal correlations which supposedly hold among unseen realities which determine the regularities of the appearances of things? Here the buck, as it were, has to stop. There seems no option but to assume that at this level of scientific analysis causal judgments are primarily expressions of conceptual commitment — mental projections about what the ultimate cement of the universe must be like.

This does not mean that conceptual commitments about the causal status of correlations are reducible to questions of individual whim. Causal commitments, and thus the modern belief in deterministic natural necessity, find their only significant expression in the social activity of science. This activity is rigorously constrained by sets of rules which, among other things, dictate the logical, experimental or theoretical circumstances under which some physical events or processes can legitimately be regarded as the cause of others. That is to say, while the capacity for causal imputation may be a part of everyone's mental make-up in Kant's sense, the particular form it will take in different social circumstances is something which must be understood in social terms. For example, for a correlation to be designated a causal law, it must conform to those necessary conditions which have already been introduced. No one is born with knowledge of these conditions or of how they are to be employed. In order to learn them, a long apprenticeship is necessary. Thus, by the end of their training, scientists cannot – as far as their scientific practice is concerned – be seen as autonomous individuals, free to do and believe what they like. They are part of a community with shared beliefs, motivations, risks, constraints, rewards and punishments. Their causes – in both senses of the word – are the causes of their colleagues. Yet the practical power, scope, detail, generality and, above all, logical and mathematical coherence of the products of scientific activity are hard even for scientists to appreciate, let alone non-scientists. This does not rest merely on social convention, any more than the force of social convention propels astronauts to the moon, despite the fact that it has required specific forms of institutions and social co-operation in order to be accomplished. In short, some causal imputations will work – thereby facilitating the accomplishment of practical goals – while others will not.

This does mean, however, that the criteria by which social decisions about causal status are made are by no means absolute, self-evident or immutable. As we showed at the beginning of this chapter, they have their own history. The western conception of nomological, deterministic causality emerged in the context of cultural purposes (e.g. to control nature by learning to manipulate and predict it) and cultural beliefs (e.g. that matter consists of a mechanized reality behind the appearance) which were quite foreign to Europe before the Renaissance, and which are still quite foreign to many other cultures. Moreover, even within western science, conceptions of precisely what constitutes a causal relationship have dramatically changed. The idea of nature as an unseen mechanized system, for example, still makes sense for contemporary science in so far as it states that changes in one part of the physical system determine changes in other parts. However, for a variety of reasons, it is also widely agreed that the commonsense notion of how a mechanism works is inapplicable at atomic and sub-atomic levels. Indeed, some writers now argue that traditional forms of determinism must be abandoned altogether ... and so the debate continues. Thus what is shown by these sorts of arguments is that causal imputation is not socially arbitrary any more than it is individually so.

As a concluding illustration, consider the fact that it would now be impossible to regard the law relating to pressure and volume of gases as anything other than causal without changing a great deal of scientific discourse (and a large part of ordinary language as well). Its status as a causal law is so embedded in assumptions about the causal status and meaning of other scientific concepts that to change one would entail changing all. More will be said about the philosophical import of this point in chapters 6 and 7. For now, it is important simply to emphasize that decisions about causal imputation are varieties of *social action* which have a history and are just as capable of evolution and redirection as other forms of social action. Therefore, we seem to have argued ourselves into the need for a type of explanation other than the variety which has so far been considered. We appear, for example, to require some way of explaining why the modern deductive-nomological approach to explanation itself emerged, but also why some cultures have still not adopted it. Would a deductive-nomological explanation of the cultural development of deductive-nomological explanation be tenable? Can western science as a form of social action – or indeed, social action generally – be explained in any other way? What is the relationship between the explanation of nature and the explanation of human action? These are the questions to which we must now turn.

Annotated bibliography

Losee 1980 gives an introductory historical discussion of modes of explanation in the natural sciences. Burtt 1980, Kuhn 1972, and Dijksterhuis 1961 are distinguished historical studies of the transition to the mode of explanation employed by modern natural science. In addition to some interesting historical essays, Kearney 1964 contains a number of extracts from writers of that period struggling to formulate new ways to understand the natural world, as does Hurd and Kipling 1964, vol. I.

C.E. Hempel is the writer who has probably contributed most to the development of the deductive-nomological analysis of explanations employing natural laws. Hempel 1966 contains a good introduction. His major contributions to this discussion are gathered in Hempel 1965, where in chapter 12 he argues for the overarching thesis that science is unified by the general applicability of the deductive-nomological pattern to all scientific explanation. A similar thesis is developed at greater length in Nagel 1961. For relationships between this thesis and the views of Popper concerning falsifiability as a criterion for the scientific status of an explanatory hypothesis, see Popper 1980, chapter 3. Our remarks on the nature of deduction are scanty. Lemmon 1965 is a clear introduction to the formal treatment of these topics. Copi 1982 is a widely used textbook introducing formal logic. Newton-Smith 1985 is the most recent introductory work which even contains a manual for a computer-assisted learning programme. Salmon 1963 introduces these issues in an informal fashion.

Hempel 1965, chapter 8, deals with the problem of the reality of the unobservable entities widely posited by theoretical laws in natural science. Harré 1975, Bhaskar 1978 and Hesse 1961 take a strongly 'realistic' line over such questions, while Cartwright 1983 reaffirms the 'instrumentalist' view that such entities as electrons are more akin to 'useful fictions' which enable predictions to be made about what scientists observe. The historical antecedents of the 'instrumentalist' view are traced in Kolakowski 1972. Popper sets out his 'realist' opposition to 'instrumentalism' in Popper 1972a, chapter 3. The issue is further discussed as regards the natural sciences in Newton-Smith 1981, chapter 2, and as regards social science in Keat and Urry 1982, chapters 2, 5 and 8.

The difficulty of discovering 'what is wrong' with a hypothesis, in order to falsify it, has been christened the 'Duhem-Quine problem' by

Popper. His discussion of this can be found in Popper 1972a, chapter 10. It was originally formulated in Duhem 1962, chapter 4. A similar position is reluctantly conceded in Hempel 1965, chapter 4, and is forcefully and radically propounded in the essay 'Two dogmas of empiricism' in Quine 1980. Further discussion of Quine's views is to be found in chapter 6 of this book, and references to his works in the bibliographical notes to that chapter. The importance of this problem, and the ineffectiveness of the Popperian rearguard action against it, can be judged from Lakatos's conclusion, in his essay in Hacking 1981, that scientists can only be 'wise after the event' regarding the falsification of their theories.

Losee 1980, chapter 9, has a brief historical introduction to the question of 'natural necessity' of natural laws. A far more detailed historical account is in Buchdahl 1969. Discussions of the contemporary analytical questions regarding laws and natural necessity from a variety of standpoints are to be found in Hempel 1965, chapter 12, Rescher 1970, part III, Achinstein 1971, chapter 3, and Armstrong 1983. Goodman 1983 presents a novel and challenging approach to laws, counter-factuals and induction. Sosa 1975 collects some recent contributions to this debate. The manner in which causal imputation takes place in the actual practice of natural science is discussed in Ravetz 1971, chapters 3-7. For an account of the strength of professional pressures socializing scientists into particular ways of explaining and investigating phenomena, see Mulkay 1980, chapters 3-4, and part II of Barnes and Edge 1982. This can be linked with the epistemological importance of the intervention of scientists stressed in Hacking 1983, part 2.

3
EXPLANATION IN THE SOCIAL SCIENCES

We have shown how explanation in modern natural science is conducted in terms of laws and initial conditions which between them are believed to constitute sufficient conditions for the occurrence of the event to be explained. This is why in the natural sciences there is generally a symmetry between explanation and prediction. If all of the components of the explanans – laws, initial conditions, the assumption that all things else are equal – are true then the explanadum must follow. This is just another way of saying that the event which it describes can be expected to occur and that if it does not, the explanans as a whole will be falsified. However, in the social sciences, a debate has been raging since the latter part of the nineteenth century about the suitability of this deterministic mode of explanation for the investigation of human action. Until quite recently it was argued by some that sociology was still awaiting its Newton, the implicit assumption being that until the correct laws of human action were discovered, the discipline would amount to little more than unscientific speculation. Many psychologists agree that – potentially at least – human action can be understood and predicted with reference to law-like regularities of past reward and punishment. In economics, the behaviour of both consumers and producers is apparently explained through the use of laws of market behaviour. Some anthropologists suggest that the structural features of society (e.g. kinship systems) are the prime determinants of how its members will act in specific situations – how they will raise their children, for example. Theorists of this kind believe that physical events and human actions are essentially the same sorts of things and that nomological explanatory principles are therefore applicable to such actions. We shall now introduce arguments to show that this assumption is false and that human activity requires an altogether different mode of scientific explanation.

Human action vs. physical behaviour

Suppose that you are a juror in a trial where the defendant has pleaded

52

not guilty to a charge of stealing a handbag from a woman unable to identify her assailant. The defendant, a well-known criminal, was caught running away from the scene of the crime with the handbag in his possession. The prosecution claims that his guilt is self-evident, but the defendant maintains that he found the handbag and was running to return it to another woman he thought had dropped it. Finally, assume that at the last minute and with all the odds against the defendant, the real culprit enters the courtroom, is recognized by the woman whose handbag was stolen and proceeds to confess all. Prior to the confession, the jury would be seeking to discover the correct explanation of the defendant's behaviour. Indeed, that is precisely what juries exist to decide. A closer look at how this is done and some of the issues that it raises will help to clarify what sort of thing human action is.

One thing is certain. In trying to decide upon the correct explanation of the defendant's action, you will not be interested in what his body was doing on a purely physiological level. For example, you know that he was apprehended while running, but the last thing you as a juror are concerned with is what the muscles, tendons and nerves in his legs were up to. A good physiologist might be capable of producing an excellent nomological explanation of the defendant's leg movements, as well as of what was occurring in his arms, his vital organs and even his brain. However, it goes without saying that a physiologist would not be called upon to give evidence, since such information would be irrelevant. What you, as a member of the jury, want to know is not what was going on in the defendant's body at the time of the crime, but what *he* was doing – why he was running and clutching the handbag to his presumably pounding heart. All the physiological theory and evidence in the world will not help you here. While taking it for granted that the defendant could not have been running away without a variety of causal determinants propelling his body, what you have to decide is whether or not he *was* running away. In order to discover an explanation which will answer this question you must, therefore, find out something about the defendant's reasons. In so doing, you will clearly distinguish between his behaviour – his physical movement – and his action. The latter derives its identity from the aims and beliefs presupposed by the way this movement is described.

Consider this distinction between behaviour and action in more detail. It is true that what is picked out as an action is generally a physical movement – or at least begins with one. But it is identified as an action because an intention can be attached to it and because it seems natural to attribute this intention to the actor who performs it. For example, to wink is to act in a way which cannot be identified solely with the physical eye movements which accompany a wink. Your eye does not wink: you do. If you wink then it is you and no one or nothing else determining that you will do so. Although a man with an uncontrollable tic in his eye might well *appear* to wink frantically at a woman, you would not describe his behaviour as 'winking', once you knew of his complaint. Indeed, you would not claim that he had *acted* in any way at all. Of course, you might make a mistake. You might either wrongly assume his physical behaviour to be evidence of an action and accuse him unfairly of sexual harassment; or wrongly assume that another man does suffer from such a complaint, thereby excusing him of what was in reality a harassing action. The point is that the description of the actual movement of the eyelid does not enable you to decide this question. The judgment you make will depend on whether or not the behaviour is considered to be 'purposeful' in the sense that it may be understood with reference to *intentions* rather than physiological causes.

Before going on to discuss what precisely an intention is, it should be noted that descriptions of behaviour are *indeterminate* with respect to the identification of the particular actions to which they correspond. It is not just that descriptions of behaviour lack the ingredient of intention which descriptions of action contain. Descriptions of actions display a similar indeterminacy with regard to the precise physical movement involved in the performance of the action. This means that human actions cannot be coherently identified and distinguished from one another just on the basis of the accompanying bodily motions. Human bodies are in a constant flux of motion. How do you divide this up into separate segments in order to classify it? One set of muscles contract, for example, and your arm extends, another contraction and your fingers clasp round an object, another and your arm retracts. You could describe this in terms of muscular contractions, angular movements of joints, forces acting on the skeleton – or you could say that you are picking up an object. Any single action may be accomplished by any one of an indefinite number of slight variations on the physical motions necessary to perform that action. Think of how many physically distinct ways there are of signing your name – they are all your signature, but each one is slightly different from all the others. Equally, any one specific bodily motion – behaviour – may be consistent with many different and possibly contradictory actions. Consider another example. Suppose you see someone just running along a pavement. The actor may have been doing all sorts of things – running for a bus, jogging, fleeing a thief, chasing a thief, etc. In trying to describe and explain this action, descriptions of actual bodily motions are hopelessly coarse-grained and/or ambiguous. Moreover, they do not allow the identification of two actions which have been performed for the same purpose but which have been accomplished in physically different ways. To set about the identification and explanation of an action, it seems natural that you should inquire what is 'going on in the mind' of the actor. But this is not as simple a task as it might seem and there has been a long history of philosophical dispute about what the mind actually is and how it is related to the body. For the time being, we will inquire no further into these debates but will look at the question of how agents would describe their actions themselves – what they would say about their *reasons* for the intentions that inform their actions.

Consider what sort of thing a reason is. First and foremost, a reason justifies an action – an action is done for that particular reason. In the examples examined thus far, stating the reasons for an action entails describing the purposes of the action and/or the beliefs by which it is assumed these purposes can best be achieved. So, someone might say as they were running down a pavement 'I'm after that bus!' In so doing they would reveal their reason with reference to one set of aims. On the other hand, they might say 'I'm keeping fit', emphasizing their belief that what they are doing will achieve another purpose or goal. In either case, both aims and beliefs are integral to the description of reasons. See what happens when you try to imagine an activity – any activity – which can be described without reference to aims and beliefs of some kind. Think of studying, shaking hands, buying groceries, going on holiday, having a bath, driving a car, participating in a political demonstration, doing any job you name, and so on. In all of these cases, the descriptions of the actions will name either a purpose or a belief or both. Even for activities which on the face of it appear either to be biological (e.g. 'making love', 'going to the toilet') or simply aimless (e.g. 'taking a walk', 'twiddling your thumbs'), you will still discover beliefs about acceptable ways in which to achieve given aims. Consider, for example, the cultural variability of sexual practices. What would be identified as love-making in our culture might be dismissed as evil deviance in another. Similarly, someone taking a walk might not seem to have any apparent aims or beliefs but it is possible to take a walk in the wrong way – for example through just pacing back and forth!

The link between acting and having aims and beliefs suggests a close relationship between action and consciousness. To be conscious as opposed to being unconscious means in part to have a range of sensory experiences which are the by-product of your physiological relationship with your environment. For example, the purely physiological dimension of pain links your experience when, say, hit by a whip to what is experienced by an animal under the same circumstances. What distinguishes human consciousness, however, is not susceptibility to the immediate sensation of the pain, but the *reflective awareness* of it. Doctors should have an easier job than vets because their patients can describe their pain – animals cannot. Only humans classify different types of pain, describe where they are felt, and recognize them in others in the same way. More generally, the reflective consciousness or self-awareness of human beings is related ultimately to language, which they use to try to make sense of their physical and social surroundings and to formulate goals and beliefs about ways of achieving them. Without the use of language, what would it mean to attempt any of these things? Try it! Hence, when you are trying to discover which actions are to be identified with which physiological behaviour, the first place to turn is apparently to actors' consciousness – the particular way in which they intentionally describe what they are doing. It is in this way that any actions may be recognized as initiated by, and the responsibility of, specific persons. So the determination of who is responsible for what activity will evidently depend on what actors think when they choose to act in specific ways.

To see the force of this more clearly, consider the following problem.

Would it make any sense to convict a robot of a crime? Suppose a robot ran amok and killed someone. It would obviously be silly to bring it to trial for murder and to sentence it as if it were human. But why? Presumably because it makes no sense to say that the robot is responsible for its behaviour. It did not *choose* to kill and therefore should not be blamed. Its behaviour – as opposed to action – is understandable in a purely deterministic sense. Through discovering what went wrong in the robot's circuitry, with hindsight and appropriate nomological principles of electronics the malfunction could have been predicted. In this respect, it would make as little sense to blame the robot as it would to blame your car for having carburettor trouble. The murder in question cannot be attributed to the robot because it did not choose to act on the aims and beliefs appropriate to identifying it as the murderer. Indeed, to this extent it is a misnomer to identify the relevant killing as a murder at all. Even if afterwards, the robot uttered 'I did it and it was fun', you would still not blame it for what had occurred. Rather, you would probably begin to suspect that someone had programmed it to kill and confess, and that it was this *person* who was the real killer. But again, why?

There is at first sight a clear and straightforward answer. A machine, unlike a human being, has no mind. Humans can consciously plan to act in particular ways, and choose both the ends they will pursue and the means they will use to do so. When one interprets what a person does as murder, but refuses to interpret a machine's behaviour in the same way, it seems to be accepted that the person possesses intentions and beliefs and makes choices quite differently from the way in which the machine 'possesses' a programme. The person seems to be the exclusive *author* of purposes. It appears to be the mental existence of purposes – leaving aside for the moment what 'mental existence' might be – that justifies the attribution of the subsequent action of the person in whose mind those purposes are to be found. This is the most obvious way to account for the link between the allocation of responsibility and the conscious freedom of action of an individual. You are responsible for your action, it is commonly supposed, because you made up your mind to do it, when you could have changed your mind and refrained.

So action and choice go hand in hand. This seems to suggest that all actions are preceded by a period of deliberation where alternative aims and beliefs are rationally appraised. No doubt in many activities (e.g. those specifically involved with planning for the future) such deliberation is present. Indeed, many ideas about maturity and what it means – accepting *responsibility* for choosing particular courses of action – rest on the belief that such deliberation is both possible and advisable. However, in many other circumstances, actors may not even be aware of the reasons for their actions and certainly do not consciously deliberate their merits or demerits. For example, you probably seldom work out the reasons why you are dressing in one way or another, yet you do not class your action as purposeless. Moreover, you would find it distinctly odd if someone said 'The physiological behaviour of your brain certainly determined a weird get-up for you today, didn't it?' This is because you believe that *you* determined it and to the extent that others believe the same thing, they will hold you responsible for your attire. So even though you may not be conscious of your choice, with hindsight you will probably be able to specify the aims and beliefs behind it. Another way of saying the same thing is that even though your reasons for acting may be unconscious, to the extent that you accept that an action is yours, you will be willing to identify yourself with aims and beliefs which are rationally reconstructed as being appropriate. In this way you clarify the deliberation which led to the choice of your clothes. 'Although I must confess that I really didn't think about it, I must have worn those trousers because they are the only ones I have which seem appropriate for this kind of gathering.'

Of course, there will be some situations where an action has occurred but where the reasons for it resist clarification. Actors may be unable to formulate convincing explanations of what they do, even with the help of others, and understanding such opaque actions through an intentional explanatory approach seems fundamentally problematic. So far, it has been assumed that actions are identified by what is in the mind of the individual actor. Presumably actors either know what they are doing or they don't! In this century, Sigmund Freud attempted to resolve this tension through arguing that choices are still being made even when it is not possible to create a purposive description of an action that is consistent with the beliefs and desires of a person, and/or when the actor's own account of the action and the reason for it are clearly wrong. The reasons for these choices may be unconscious and lie way back in the actor's past and be completely forgotten. Thus, hysteria with no apparent reason might serve the purpose of enabling the actor to avoid facing an experience which unconsciously reminds him of others which were extremely painful and 'repressed' when he was a child. Such actors are choosing not to remember the traumatic past, even though they may not be consciously aware of doing so. Indeed, when this kind of repression occurs, actors may be unaware that they are doing anything at all (e.g. those significant slips of the tongue called 'Freudian slips').

Although we cannot go into any detail about Freud's thought here, there is no reason to believe that this concept of the unconscious contradicts anything about the purposive understanding of actions outlined thus far. We have shown that activity can be unconscious in the sense that actors are unaware of the reasons for its execution. In our preceding example of choice of dress, the relevant aims and beliefs were easy to reconstruct in a way both the actor and anyone else would be happy to accept. In the case of more opaque actions, such a reconstruction is problematic. For example, activities typically associated with Freudian analysis are sometimes so opaque that the discovery of their reasons may take many years. Yet there is no problem identifying such actions as *actions* – each is described in such a way that an intention 'is attributed to it'. The problem is in reconciling the conscious aims, beliefs and desires of the patient with such unconscious intentions so that they will be able to understand and gain rational control over them. This does

not mean that the unconsciousness is anything like a computer programme in a robot which determines activity in the same sense in which
the cue ball determines the behaviour of the eight ball. Were this the case,
patients involved in Freudian analysis – or in any other form of
psychotherapy – would be foolish to think that they could alter their
activity when its real reasons became clear. The eight ball – like the robot
– has no choice. In short, to the extent that you dressed yourself this
morning, you are responsible for your attire even if you have to think for
a minute why you chose as you did. Similarly to the extent that a
particular form of neurotic behaviour – compulsive washing for instance
– is yours then you are responsible for it even if you have to work
therapeutically for years to discover your reasons. Such discovery may
not be *sufficient* for neurosis to be overcome but the theory is that it is at
least a necessary condition for success. In both these cases the explanatory problem is the same – the identification of the more or less deeply
unconscious aims and beliefs which informed your choice of an action.

The need to be taught how to explain actions which would otherwise
be opaque has profound consequences for understanding both human
consciousness and individuality. We shall introduce some of these in the
next chapter. For now it is important to recognize some of the equally
profound ethical consequences of believing that actors can possess the
kind of freedom and responsibility for which we have argued thus far.
For the degree of freedom you accord actors will in turn profoundly
affect what you will define as acceptable moral activity on either an
individual or collective basis. So, returning to our robot, if you believe
that human activity is so determined by nomological regularity – of
positive or negative reinforcement, of genes or of socialization – that
actors cannot be held responsible for what they do, then you will be
unable either to allocate blame or to believe that they will be able to act
differently through their own volition. In such circumstances, crime and
punishment will be conceived in much the same way as the inconvenience
and repair of a broken motor car. If the machine is not functioning
properly you take it out of service and either 'fix' it or throw it on the
scrapheap. Similarly, without a belief in the freedom and responsibility of
the actor, criminal justice is reduced to the problem of how to cause a
change in criminal behaviour (e.g. through suitable programmes of
negative conditioning – punishment). As with your old banger, if the
behaviour becomes too much of a burden and you believe that it cannot
be fixed, the problem of justice is no more than the problem of effective
disposal.

With these points in mind, it should come as no surprise that one of the
leading exponents of determinism in the social sciences has written an
influential book called *Beyond Freedom and Dignity*. B.F. Skinner
believes that actions are caused by past histories of positive and negative
reinforcement and that they can be deterministically altered by new
causes of behavioural conditioning. The only thing in the way of human
happiness, he concludes, is the right training. Since individual choice is an
illusion, bad training is responsible for bad behaviour and good training

for good behaviour. According to Skinner, one of the things that keeps people from submitting themselves to what he conceives as good training is their conception of individual freedom and dignity. Get rid of these myths and you can tailormake society to your liking. We may all be animals, as it were, but there is no reason why society should not be planned to maximize pleasure and minimize pain – so that we will at least be well fed and smiling animals! Social planning on this view quite literally becomes social training of a sort that is perfectly analogous with animal training. Similarly, the aims of such training become equally analogous with the scientific study of the physical needs – nutritional, sexual, etc. – of any other animal species.

Skinner's ethical opponents would argue that the members of a society can only be said to be happy when their freedom and dignity are not just recognized, but maximized. This is just another way of saying that it is by your opportunity to implement your own initiative and to take responsibility for your actions that the quality of your life can be measured. It is for this reason, they would argue, that so many have suffered so much – have willingly endured pain and even death – in fighting for a sense of human dignity which itself presupposes belief in freedom and responsibility. It is also for this reason that so many find the kind of society described in Aldous Huxley's *Brave New World* so repugnant. For here he portrays a behaviouristic social paradise – plenty of food, drugs and sex, all used to produce and control a range of conforming human activity. To the extent that its members revel in all three, do not complain and make no attempt to change their situation, then in some purely physiological sense they might well be defined as 'happy' and would certainly be 'beyond freedom and dignity'. If you are repulsed by such a sea of drugged social complacency, it is presumably because you believe that lack of choice and responsibility is tantamount to lack of humanity as such. In short, if you believe that part of what it means to be a person – rather than an animal or a robot – is the freedom to explore your creativity and the dignity to admit your mistakes, then your vision of morality requires that you approach the explanation of human action in terms of reasons, beliefs and choices.

Returning to our initial example of the jury, in attempting to decide whether or not to convict the defendant, you will be concerned with his reasons and not with the nomological explanation of whatever physiological events might accompany them. More specifically, you will wish to know which description of his intents and beliefs is true: his, or that of the police. This is just another way of saying that you want to know what the defendant really did, already accepting that there is no dispute about his bodily behaviour. No doubt you will listen carefully to his defence and cross-examination in order to try to detect whether or not the explanation he offers can be substantiated by himself or others. His actual behaviour will always be consistent with different possible intentional descriptions, as we have already shown, and it is precisely this difference that the trial is all about. His behaviour will, of course, also be consistent with different possible non-intentional descriptions. Perhaps the defendant had been hypnotized, given the bag and told to run. Perhaps he was drugged and behaving (literally) aimlessly. In either case, it would be inappropriate to classify his behaviour as an action. If the defendant had no choice in the matter, it would be as silly to blame him as it would be to hold him responsible for the behaviour of his heart or his nervous system. On the basis of the available evidence (excluding that of our surprise, last-minute witness) you might consider him guilty of a criminal action. Were you to do so, it would be because you had decided that he had chosen to act in a criminal way and hence could be held responsible for what you take him to have done.

The types of action considered so far have been linked to fairly substantial instances of physical behaviour (e.g. running, winking, changing clothes, etc.). However, the strength of the link between actual thought and language becomes even more apparent when the parallel is noted between understanding an action in terms of the 'thought behind it' and doing the same for a verbal utterance – both are dependent for their intelligibility on the same explanatory framework of purposes and beliefs. For example, you are acting – as opposed to merely behaving – when you do no more than speak to each other. Think of how happy or furious you can be made simply by what someone says! Consider also how many actions in social life are performed merely by saying some- thing: 'I declare you man and wife', 'Ready, Steady, Go!', 'I arrest you in the name of the law', etc. Again, you may not be aware of your reasons while having a conversation – you just have it. But if anyone asked why the conversation was taking place or why you were making specific state- ments in it, then you would probably be able convincingly to reconstruct your reasons. Indeed, someone might be engaged in frantic activity of a purely deliberative nature without their saying anything at all and with very little physical movement. For example, when playing a board game, you may be exhausting yourself with deliberation and decision-making (e.g. 'I'll do this rather than that when it is my turn') without appearing to do anything at all. The fact that some of the most complex and momentous actions in human history have been identified with some of the most feeble bodily processes underlines this point very well. Think of how little physical effort – the movement of a thumb, a wrist? – it took to drop the atomic bomb on Hiroshima.

Reasons and causes

As we have indicated, ordinary discourse – the 'folk psychology' of everyday language – makes it natural to assume that action is distinct from behaviour because of the 'possession' of reasons, intentions, motives, or purposes by the performing agent. This could lead to the view that the explanation of action is not, after all, so different from the explanation of nature. Despite the differences between behaviour and action, surely there must be some way in which the regular and reoccurring possession of reasons – the habit, so to speak, of thinking about specific actions in specific ways – causes agents to do the things they do? If this is so, two sets of causal laws should be available for the explanation of each action – one concerning physiology and the other consciousness. Yet the conception of such a parallel is fundamentally misconceived. To show why, we must begin by referring back to our discussion of the deductive-nomological pattern of explanation in the natural sciences.

If a physical event is explained in deductive-nomological terms, then the natural laws and initial conditions describing the circumstances which are supposed to have *produced* it should always be applicable whenever these circumstances are repeated. This accounts for the symmetry between explanation and prediction in the natural sciences. It is also why the premises of the explanatory deduction – the explanans – may be assessed with reference to the accuracy of such predictions. It is in this sense that an adequate deductive-nomological explanation lists the sufficient conditions for the occurrence that it explains. If the explanation is correct, nature declares that the conditions listed are by themselves enough to lead to the occurrence that is explained. The general form of such explanations is: 'These laws . . . and these circumstances . . . made this . . . happen.' In principle, explanations of this type can, for example, explain the motion of people's bodies just as they can the circulation of their blood. Yet as we showed in the previous section, specific deductions/predictions about either bodies or blood can only be made if there is at least one general law in the premises of related explanans. However, if what people do is explained in terms of their reasons, then it turns out to be the case that there is no such requirement. For what is then described is the state of affairs which justifies rather than determines the action in question. This will state: (a) the result that the action is meant to bring about; and (b) the means by which it is believed that this result may be achieved. 'Why have you taken the wheel off your car?' Explanation: 'It has a flat tyre, and I need to replace it with the spare in order to continue my journey.' As you can see, agents explain their actions in the very same terms that they justify them to themselves.

Contrast the following two examples in a little more detail:

A   Problem: Why does the copper expand?
       Deductive-nomological explanation:
       (1)   All metals expand when heated.
       (2)   Copper is a metal.
       (3)   This piece of copper has been heated.
     Therefore:
       (4)   This piece of copper expands.

B   Problem: Why is the worker running towards the hut?
       Intentional explanation:
       (1)   It is raining.
       (2)   The worker labouring outside wishes to keep as dry as
              possible.
       (3)   The worker believes that shelter will keep her/him dry.

(4)   Shelter is available, i.e. the hut.
Therefore:
(5)   The worker runs to the hut to shelter from the rain.

These two explanations appear similar. Both have premises and a conclusion. Both, it seems, enable predictions to be made about what would happen in similar circumstances, provided of course that some other factor does not interfere with the outcome. There are, however, crucial differences between A and B. We shall first note some which are fairly straightforward and then move on to consider the difficulties with a range of strategies for maintaining the thesis that an intentional explanation is really a causal explanation 'in disguise'.

First, notice that the second example includes no statement of a general law. Each statement of B is particular, not universal. In A, however, the explanandum – the expansion of the heated copper – does not follow logically from the explanans without the statement of the law of nature, A(1). This is because in A, you and not the copper have to make the appropriate deduction. You must do so in accordance with those rules which dictate that the logical form of A is a valid one. This can be seen through considering your reaction to changing A(1) to the particular statement 'Some metals expand when heated'. Even though you may not consciously go through each stage of the deduction, you immediately sense that the argument is invalid. In explanation B, however, the situation changes. Here a universal statement does not seem to be required for the conclusion to follow from the premises. This is because, unlike the copper, the worker has to make the appropriate deduction and if she makes a mistake it is her fault and not the logic of the explanation. It is her capacity to act rationally – to understand what action follows from holding particular aims and beliefs in specific empirical circumstances – that the validity of B depends upon. Again, ask yourself if the conclusion of B would follow if it were assumed that the worker could not inferentially link running for shelter with her desire to stay dry. So, universal statements are not required in the premises of B because the subject matter of the explanation is itself a process of cognitive deliberation rather than one of natural necessity. This does not mean that actors inwardly go through each step of an intentional explanation before they act. How much they do is debatable, as we shall later show. For now it will suffice to note that, on the one hand, such considered forethought would not facilitate the worker's professed aim in B of staying as dry as possible! However, on the other hand, the explanation would be false if the worker could not possibly have engaged in such deliberation – for example, if the hut was hidden by a wall. Again, the reason justifies the action and the hypothesis is that this is why the worker thought running to the shelter an appropriate thing to do.

The attribution of the reason, and so the reasoning, to the person whose action is to be explained is tied up with the removal of ambiguity from their physical movements. As was indicated in the previous section, not only may the same movements be implicated in different actions, but the same action may be accomplished by different movements. For example, the same action may be unproblematically performed by left- or right-handed people. Conversely, a given description of physical behaviour – say in the preceding example of the worker – is compatible with the attribution of any one of many different actions. Perhaps she usually enjoys working in the rain but is going to the shelter for a cigarette. If so, then 'taking shelter from the rain' will have to be redescribed as 'taking a break for a cigarette'. If the action was not performed for the reason one supposed, then the initial identification will be incorrect. The action is different even though the associated bits of observed behaviour are the same. This means that imputing a reason to a person and attributing an action to that person are not logically distinct. You may be sure that the copper expands, *even if you do not know why it does.* Having independently identified the effect, you may then go on to look for the cause. But in the case of the worker, you cannot understand what is being done until you understand the reasons. Generally speaking, therefore, natural laws describe how the purposeless stuff of nature works – how one set of events produces the next, like the depression of the piston causing the crankshaft to rotate. Here the question 'Why does that happen?' is interpreted to mean 'How do things work so that it happens?' and is answered with reference to the regularities of nature. By contrast, intentional explanations seek to explain, 'Why does he/she do that? . . . What for?' Here the answer – a reason – does not in itself describe or determine how anything works. Rather, it identifies what someone does by identifying what it is that they have chosen to try to bring about.

So intentional explanations require no general statements in their premises. Nothing need be known of past regularities in the actions, purposes and beliefs of particular people; yet their actions may still be easily understood by reference to their present reasons. You can find an action perfectly intelligible – for example, climbing Mount Everest – without any appeal to law-like generalizations concerning the actor's past. If an intentional description of an action is accepted, it is at the same time understood and therefore explained – at least in principle. After all, it is possible to attempt something that has never been done before – climbing a particular face of Everest, for example. So past knowledge will not necessarily be relevant to the immediate explanatory task at hand. Moreover, you can perform actions that you have never even thought of before. Pause, use your imagination and act *now* in a manner in which you have never acted before. Your explanation of the action that you have just performed will clearly mention no generalization about the past and in the case of each reader, might be different. One of you might have stood on his head, another could have tried to touch her toe with her nose, while a third attempted to whistle Beethoven's Fifth, and so forth.

Yet it still might be argued that even if nomological generalizations are not explicitly contained in the premises of an intentional explanation, they are still implicitly presupposed. For example, consider the concept of rationality which we have argued is behind the validity of such explanations. Does not the belief that all actions must be explained with reference to reasons not amount to the same thing as claiming that, in some sense, all actions are rational? And is not such a principle of rationality itself a nomological generalization? With the worker sheltering from the rain, the explanation seems to rely on the assumption that anyone who really wishes to stay dry and really knows how to do so will *always* take shelter when it is available and it is raining. If professed purposes are real purposes, and a person knows how to pursue them, then reason determines what actions will follow much as the laws of mechanics and appropriate initial conditions determine when the eight ball goes into the side pocket. What it means to say that an action is rational will be further discussed in later chapters. For now it will suffice to argue that a deterministic conception of rationality or reason is either obviously false or entirely lacking in explanatory power. It is not a nomological regularity and does not play its role in the explanation of human activity by analogy with that of a natural law in the physical sciences. Why is this the case?

Ordinarily, when people speak of the rationality or otherwise of actions, they refer to the consistency between the actor's wishes and beliefs, or to the truth or falsity of their beliefs. In the former case, the question is whether or not they knowingly act in ways that are inconsistent with their wishes and their beliefs concerning how these might be satisfied. For example, if someone knows that they are suffering from diabetes, knows what this means, and continues to eat sweets to satisfy their craving for sugar, this action is inconsistent with what they know to be in their best interests and so is irrational. But if the diabetic does not know about the disease, and it has not been diagnosed, they may continue to believe that the problem is not eating enough sweets. A person acting thus will be consistent in their own terms, yet you would still presumably wish to maintain that the action is irrational. This is because whatever the perception of the diabetic, you know that eating more sweets will inevitably be harmful, and be inconsistent with their other wishes – like staying alive. Indeed, contemporary medical knowledge indicates that certain actions are always bad for the unsuspecting diabetic. These two varieties of irrational action – those which to the actor's knowledge will not produce an outcome consistent with their wishes, and those which will not do so because of the actor's ignorance – are both all too common. Consequently, the empirical law 'All actors are rational' is simply false.

Of course, the comeback might be that however actors choose to act, they will still be doing so for reasons – they still have aims which they are trying to achieve on the basis of their beliefs, whatever comments we might make about their reasoning. So even if one may wish to criticize a person who says 'The idea of lung cancer makes me so nervous that I'll have another cigarette to calm myself', the reason for their action seems clear enough. Does this make it feasible to claim that all actions and agents are rational in that their actions must always have intelligible aims and beliefs? In fact, such a claim does not yield a law-like generalization but rather a definition of what an action is and therefore provides no means for effecting any reconciliation between causal and intentional explanation. 'All actors are rational' becomes consistent with all possible actions, and like 'All bachelors are unmarried' cannot be regarded as a falsifiable, empirical law of nature, whose truth enables the explanation and prediction of new events. Hence an action is not irrational in the sense that it lacks *any* reason. Rather it is the adequacy of the reason that is at issue – one which has nothing to do with the capacity of either good or bad reasons to prompt related actions. What makes a reason good or bad – the criteria by which they are normatively evaluated – is a complicated issue we shall explore in later chapters.

The last nail in the coffin for any reconciliation between intentional and deductive-nomological explanation concerns the evaluation of actions as good or bad *attempts*. Explanations in terms of reasons account for what you might be trying to do even if you fail. This means that although they make predictions – that you will succeed – such explanations are not falsified if those predictions do not come true and you do fail. Let us set this out in a little more detail, so that the disanalogy between reasons and causes is apparent. If you explain an event nomologically – in terms of the natural laws and initial conditions sufficient to make it happen – then you describe a real state of affairs, the cause, which actually has to happen if it is to make its effect occur. Clearly no event can be the 'effect' of a 'cause' which itself has not taken place. However, a reason, a purpose, a motive, an intention, a wish, a choice, or any of the other notions employed in intentional explanations, all look forward to the future. Whereas a cause lies in the more or less immediate past and actually has to happen for its effect to occur, an intent concerns what is meant to come about as a result of the action that it explains. The question which should be asked when an action is to be explained is, 'What do they do that for?' So the action is understood in terms of the desired outcome on which the agent necessarily places a value and which, of course, may not turn out as hoped.

Consequently, the normative character of reasons and rationality joins with this aspect of intentional explanation in the prospect of failure. You can attempt to do anything you like, provided that you are able in principle to describe – to yourself and others – what you want and how you think you can get it. If you are successful then you explain this by providing descriptions of this kind. If you are understood, so is your action – unless you are lying. Yet your reasons equally explain what you do when you try to act in specific ways. There are all sorts of ways of failing in what you do. Your understanding of your circumstances, of the value of your objective, of the proper way to go about getting it, and of much more, can all fall short of the appropriate standards of adequacy. The simplest case, though, is where you can only discover whether circumstances allow you to do what you wish by actually trying to do it. For example, suppose you try to clear a six-foot-high jump. You have already cleared five feet eleven and a half but you fail at six feet. The reasons for your actions will be the same in both cases – to see how high you can jump. Knowing these reasons allows us to predict what you will do, but our explanation is not falsified if you fail. It is not falsified even if, expecting failure, you suddenly decide not to act on reasons we nonetheless know you to have, for up until that moment your action is still identified with reference to them. A supposed law of nature only retains its status as such so long as it is never broken, but reasons seem quite unlike this.

If the prospects do not look too promising for the explanation of human action by means of natural laws, does this mean that there is *no* way in which reasons can properly be regarded as the causes of actions? After all, it was claimed in example B that the worker seeks shelter because of the rain, because of the desire to stay dry, and because of the belief that the shelter at hand will do the trick. Can it not simply be assumed that the particular reason for an action constitutes its cause and that consequently the explanation of human action in terms of purposes and beliefs remains causal despite the fact that it may not be nomological? What else could be meant by 'Jones did Y because of reason R' than that the possession of reason R was the cause of Jones's performing action Y? For reasons and causes to be analogous with causes and effects in nature, the possession of the reason and the action it explained would have to be separate events, the possession of the reason always occurring before the action. Do you not mean something similar when you talk of your present reasons dictating what you will do next? Surely, the argument continues, you would not do anything unless you had what has been called a 'pro-attitude' towards it. What could such an attitude be other than the acceptance of a particular set of reasons which would then determine your subsequent action? Even in the absence of correlations between reasons and actions which may be said nomologically to determine what the actor does, ordinary experience seems still to suggest that reasons are causal in some sense. What other explanation could be given for feelings of compulsion to act in particular ways? Such feelings are often linked to specific reasons and may precede actions which have never been performed before and never will be again. Thus, 'Since I suddenly decided to test my bravery by doing something dangerous, and diving off the cliff seemed the obvious thing, I had no choice but to do so.' In this case, the reason certainly seems to have caused what occurred.

The claim we must consider in stricter terms, then, is something like this. 'For the range of actions of which a given person is normally capable, all but one of the conditions are met which make up the set sufficient for the occurrence of that action, so that all that is required for the set of sufficient conditions to be complete is that the final condition – possession of a reason for that action – be present. The action will then take place.' Put more colloquially, this is to say that you are capable of very many actions and that the only further condition that has to be met to cause the action to take place is that you have sufficient reason to do it. This model may be understood by analogy, say, with a computerized cash dispenser at the bank. All but one of the conditions that would be causally sufficient for it to give you some cash are already met before you approach the machine. By what you do – inserting your card and tapping out your number – you present the machine with a request for cash and the information it needs to check that you have money in an account in that bank. The machine is so constructed that these logically sufficient conditions for giving you money being met – the appropriate digits in relation to the machine's programme – complete the set of *causally sufficient* conditions for you to receive the cash from the dispenser.

Thinking in similar ways about the causal status of reasons would mean that it would no longer depend on any past association of reasons and actions. The 'cash dispenser model' thus accounts for how a totally unprecedented action can be caused by reasons that a person has never had before. This sort of model is much less restrictive than the supposition that human action might be explicable in terms of nomological regularities. Here, all that is needed is the general belief that a mechanism exists which can convert the *logical sufficiency* of reasons, which defines the memory of actions, into *causal sufficiency* for their occurrences. Of course, the cash dispenser seems to have a limited ability to do this. It can only dispense cash, even though it can do so on the basis of a set of digits it has never been given before. With human rational capacities, the ability to convert logically sufficient reasons into causally sufficient conditions for action seems more or less unlimited. Whatever you want to do, from among the range of actions of which you are capable, can be caused by no more than your having a reason for so doing – or so it seems. Do you feel like having a cup of coffee? Your having a pro-attitude to a cup of coffee, given all your other circumstances, will complete the set of conditions sufficient to cause you to go and make or buy a cup. But if you do not, then another pro-attitude to something else – a beer, a cup of tea or whatever – must have tipped the scales in the inner argument you conduct when you decide what to do. Try it – it *feels* as though it is correct.

When an account of a causal regularity is given within a deductive-nomological explanation, the aim is to provide an exhaustive specification of the conditions causally sufficient to produce the effect to be explained. By contrast, when people talk about the cause of an event in a more colloquial way, then the specification they give of the cause is far more partial and deals basically with a piece of information which is *missing*. This is what gives the 'cash dispenser model' of reasons and actions its plausibility. Similarly, think of the many different factors which might be entertained – things, properties, events – when the cause of an event is requested. A child asks, 'What caused the window to break when my ball hit it?' 'Its brittleness,' you answer, since this is the missing bit of information about the set of sufficient conditions for the event from the child's perspective. An adult asks, 'What caused the window to break?' 'Jimmy's football,' you answer, realizing the adult does not need to be told that glass is brittle, but does not know what brought about the breakage. In another context the detective might ask after a fire which is suspected arson, 'What caused this window to break?' Here she/he would want to discover whether it was heat, falling masonry, blast, vibration, structural distortion, or impact from without (the possible site of entry of the arsonist). A materials scientist can, of course, give an exhaustive account of the general conditions under which glass will break. But when you ask for the cause of a particular event, what you usually want is the history of the circumstances which led to its occurrence. What is included in such a narrative explanation will depend on what you do not already know.

On the face of it, to the extent that narratives can explain specific events in nature, they can similarly be developed to account for particular actions in society. In both cases, a previously unknown event is described which, in conjunction with the occurrence of other known conditions, is considered to be sufficient to produce the event/action in question. If this unknown event is a reason, then why on earth should it not be regarded as a cause? There is a sense in which it should, although this statement needs careful qualification. To see why, consider the following explanation: 'Jones's indiscretion caused the discovery of his plot to rob the bank.' This seems a reasonable sort of account – if Jones had been more circumspect then he would not have been found out. Therefore, can it be regarded as a case of a reason causing an action? No. Jones's mistake is not in itself a reason at all, assuming of course that he is not being deliberately indiscreet. Neither does his indiscretion cause the discovery of the plot in the same physicalistic way that his accidentally setting off explosives might cause both him and the bank's safe to be blown to bits. Suppose that a successful detective has been hired to determine whether or not a bank robbery is going to take place. She will have good reasons – aims and beliefs – to discover a plot if one exists. Yet her reasons do not in themselves cause the discovery. It requires Jones's indiscretion as a necessary condition. But surely, given his mistake, are not her reasons sufficient to explain the discovery of the plot and therefore identifiable as its cause? Not yet. She still has to make the correct inference from the indiscretions to the plot itself and there are considerations which might make her unable or unwilling to do so. Three are important for our purposes.

First, it may be that the logical connection between a reason and the action that it justifies is rather less easy to see than that between believing John to be a bachelor and asserting that he has no wife. A person may easily fail to make the necessary logical inference from, say, the instruction for the use of some machine, to what actually has to be done in order to get it to work properly. Nonetheless the instructions provide a very good set of reasons for performing a particular set of actions and explain the actions of a person who successfully follows them. Second, there is the possibility that someone might perfectly well understand how to follow the instructions, have done so successfully beforehand, but make a mistake while doing so on this occasion. In this case, they would fail to accomplish their expected goal, despite continuing to have the reasons that explained their previous success. And third, there is a problem in the history of philosophy that stretches back to ancient times – that of 'weakness of will'. A person may possess all the reasons for an action, understand perfectly what actions they entail, make no inadvertent error, yet still not do what you expect. Why not? When you ask, the person replies, 'I know, I know, but I just couldn't be bothered.' This problem appears most paradoxical when you knowingly do wrong. If you know that an action is wrong, then you know that there are reasons which are logically sufficient for you to refrain from that action, but you still do it.

Of course, none of the preceding should be taken to suggest that it is impossible to be wrong about a person's reasons for action. There is a host of ways in which this is entirely possible and, no doubt, your ordinary experience of misunderstanding the actions of others is testimony to this effect. As this book progresses, we shall outline more and more ways in which such mistakes can occur, even on the part of the actor's own understanding of why they do the things they do. For the moment, all that we are suggesting is that, unlike the case of beliefs about causes, a failure to predict what someone does is not tantamount to incorrectly understanding their reasons. Unsuccessful predictions may just as well be because of something else about the agent which has not been understood, over and above her or his reasons. What all this adds up to is the advisability of viewing the causation of action as a complex package of factors of which reasons – as events rather than justifications – are only one part. And since such causation is totally dependent on both the agent's ability and willingness to infer and to act on inferences based on such a package, perhaps it is best simply to think of her/him as the cause of what they do rather than overemphasizing the causal importance of any one of the package's logical contents.

As we shall show, an explanatory emphasis on the agent of an action is important because it relates both to the use of reason in the conduct of human affairs and also to the notion of moral responsibility. We have already suggested that refraining from an action is as much an action as that from which you refrain. If you have any doubts, ask someone on a diet, or trying to give up smoking! Thus not doing what you have a logically sufficient reason to do is doing what you do not have a logically sufficient reason to do. It is precisely because of what a reason is in relation to a human that its logical sufficiency must be distinguished from any sort of causal sufficiency. Causes in themselves suffice to produce their effects. Reasons are not sufficient for actions to occur unless someone infers that an action worth performing follows from a reason or reasons logically sufficient for its occurrence! This is why such inferences are narrative in character. They dictate what *should* be done – how one should choose to act in order rationally to abide by one's professed aims and beliefs. Thus a logically sufficient reason is one which makes rational choice a meaningful human possibility. But just because reasons provide such choices, the logical sufficiency of any given reason must fall short of the inescapable determinism of causal sufficiency. The choices may well not be taken up. In short, 'ought' implies 'can'. No one can be obliged to do, or blamed for not doing, what cannot be done.

So to conclude and summarize, physical states of affairs may be presumed to cause other physical states of affairs, but only actors can be presumed to cause actions, albeit in conjunction with their conscious or unconscious aims and beliefs. Their reasons may specifically concern their physical/physiological environment ('I take my medicine in order to get better'). But, as soon as some aspect of this environment is postulated as the sufficient condition for actions ('I took the medicine because I was hypnotized' or 'I'm a criminal because of my genetic structure'), it no longer remains an action. It becomes just another example of behaviour, no different from the operations of those parts of your body of which you are unaware. To act and to have your action identified as yours, you have to be able to choose. To explain what you believe your action to be, it is *your* reasons that must be called upon. Yet, again, you may get it wrong. Your description/explanation of what you do may not be the best. Indeed, it may be terrible. How can this occur and when it does where can one look for more successful explanations?

Annotated bibliography

Despite the enormous wealth of literature on the issue of human action, works which ease the reader into the field are scarce. It is better, perhaps, to begin with some blatantly partisan classics which set out opposing stances. The view that human activity is susceptible to the same pattern of explanation as that employed by natural science found early expression in Mill 1974, book V, especially chapters 1-2. An excerpt is included in Brown *et al.* 1981, section 6. A position similar to Mill's, but in a more global and less restrictive form, is set out in Hempel 1965, chapter 12, and in Nagel 1961, chapters 13-15.

Determinism as regards human activity has taken a variety of forms – psychological, biological and sociological. Skinner 1953 sets out a sharply formulated version of psychological determinism, the social consequences of which are explored in Skinner 1972. Following the publication of Wilson 1975, there has been a resurgence of interest in biological determinism in the form of 'sociobiology'. The essays by Trigg and Benton in Brown 1984 give a brief introduction to the opposed positions in this debate. For a philosophical analysis of the tenets of sociobiology, see Trigg 1982 and for criticisms see Rose *et al.* 1984 and Birke and Silvertown 1984. Finally, Midgley 1978 is concerned with the general issues raised by the biological dimension of humanity. The influence of social institutions has also been interpreted in a deterministic fashion. The essays in Merton 1968 and Smelser 1968 struggle with the problems involved, which are critically discussed in Bernstein 1979, part I. A more recent, highly sophisticated interpretation of social determinism is to be found in Hirst and Woolley 1982.

The opposite view, that human activity requires an explanatory approach fundamentally distinct from that employed in natural science, had long been held by German philosophers when it was introduced into sociology at the beginning of this century in Weber 1964, chapter 1 and

Weber 1950, chapter 3. This contrast was expounded in a more forceful and extreme form in Schutz 1972, especially chapters 1 and 3. Arguments to a similar effect, but within the analytic philosophical tradition, were advanced in the 1950s and 1960s, in Winch 1970, Anscombe 1969, R. Taylor 1966 and C. Taylor 1964, among others. C. Taylor has written extensively on the topic of intentionality and its implications for the social sciences. For further references see C.Taylor 1985. Bernstein 1972 provides a good account of the convergence of arguments of philosophers and social thinkers from diverse traditions which focus on this specific problem. Ryan 1970a introduces this debate as it stood in the philosophy of social science before the influence of Davidson's arguments and developments in artificial intelligence made themselves felt – see below. Finally, Hampshire 1965, Louch 1966, and Norman 1971 explore the relations between the explanation of human action and issues in moral philosophy.

There are a number of anthologies which gather together useful essays. Those in Giddens 1974 and in Dallmayr and McCarthy 1977 largely argue for the unique character of the explanation of human activity, while deterministic and intentional approaches are contrasted in the essays collected in Brown *et al.* 1981, sections 6-7, Braybrooke 1965, Emmet and MacIntyre 1970, and Borger and Cioffi 1975. White 1968 is an anthology of contributions to the discussion of action as such in analytic philosophy.

While we have attempted to write an introductory account of the problems involved in explaining human activity, we have argued for definite conclusions which are by no means uncontroversial. The questions raised are discussed from rather different points of view in a number of general books on the philosophy of social science: Giddens 1976, chapters 1-2, Hindess 1977, chapters 1 and 2, Keat and Urry 1982, chapter 7, Pratt 1978, chapters 1-5, Papineau 1978, chapter 4, Trigg 1985, chapter 3. Finally, Hollis 1977 explores the philosophical issues arising from the explanation of human activity in social science within a broader historical and philosophical perspective.

Two recent developments have had a profound impact on discussions of human action since the debates of the 1960s. One of these has been the rapid strides made by work in artificial intelligence, with the attendant apparent premise that the causes of human activity can be modelled on computational processes. Boden 1977 gives a comprehensive introduction to these issues. Sloman 1978 is unhesitatingly optimistic as regards the potential of computers to illuminate human activity. Searle 1984, by contrast, argues against the view that a machine could think. Crucial to this debate is that feature of intentional explanations which we dubbed the last nail in the coffin for any reconciliation between intentional and deductive-nomological explanation, namely that reasons cited as explanations are about results as yet in the future, which an agent attempts to bring into being. This is one aspect of a supposedly logical feature of the mind known as 'intentionality', and is discussed in Boden 1978, chapters 2, 4 and 8, in Dennett 1969 and 1979, especially part I, and in Searle 1983. Torrance 1984 is a collection of recent contributions to the mind/machine debate, while the contributions to Brown 1974 illustrate the links between this debate and more general issues concerning human action.

The second development has been the influence of the philosopher Donald Davidson, whose article 'Actions, reasons and causes' in Davidson 1984a cast considerable doubt on an argument which had been central to much of the analytical philosophy of action of the 1960s. This was the claim that reasons could not be causes because a logical connection exists between a reason and an action, whereas no such logical connection could obtain between a cause and its effect. Davidson showed that a logical connection between two events did not debar a causal connection, yet he argued, in Davidson 1984a, chapters 11-14, that no nomological relation exists between mental events and actions which would allow the reduction of intentional explanations to natural laws. The articles by McGinn and Pettit in Bolton 1979 are good introductions to the style of philosophy of action influenced by Davidson's arguments, and Macdonald and Pettit 1981 is a systematic application of this approach to the philosophy of social science. Russell 1984, chapters 1-4, provides an up-to-date introduction to many of the debates above in relation to problems in psychology.

Both the computational and the Davidsonian approaches imply that a reason can explain an action as a cause which combines both logically and causally sufficient conditions for that action, without needing to fall under any causal generalization of the type involved in the deductive-nomological pattern of explanation. For reasons we briefly sketched, this places in a central position the problem of 'weakness of will'. This is a very ancient philosophical puzzle, often called 'akrasia' – the name given to it by the Greek philosophers who first considered it. Davidson's approach to this problem can be found in Davidson 1984a, chapter 2. Another relevant discussion is Dennett 1979, chapter 16. A general introduction to the problem of weakness of will can be found in the essay collected in Mortimore 1971. Pears 1984 is a recent study of this and related topics.

Finally, although economics as a discipline is not discussed in this chapter, it would be wrong to omit some reference to the debates that have preoccupied economists concerned with issues very much like those raised in this chapter. Dyke 1981, chapter 8, provides an excellent introduction to the issue of determinism in economics and, in chapter 1, a treatment of the rationality of action which has clear links with the issues raised in our discussion. Friedman's essay in Hahn and Hollis 1979 is a famous statement of the view that theories in economics are of a similar character to those in natural science, while Robbins's essay in that collection presents economics as the science of rational choice – a divergence of view which is the keynote for most of the remaining essays in the collection.

4
THE SOCIAL CHARACTER OF ACTIONS AND PERSONS

In the last chapter we began by distinguishing between human behaviour and action. Behaviour consisted of observable physical movements. Action was composed of these same movements overlain with interpretations of their 'mental' origin – individual intentions, reasons, purposes and the like. But things were not so simple. Not only may one pattern of movement be a component of many distinct actions, there are also many physical ways to accomplish the same action. Moreover, the notion that actions were determined by individual mental *causes* seemed increasingly difficult to sustain. In this chapter we shall further explore this problematic relationship between actor and action by examining in more detail the concept of a *reason* for action. We shall demonstrate that there is an important sense in which individual action is *essentially social* and that there is something fundamentally misconceived about the romantic notion of the individual person totally in control of her/his destiny. These conclusions will be seen to have important implications for many popular ideas concerning privacy, autonomy and freedom, ideas which falsely minimize the centrality of community in individual personal life.

The social character of action

It certainly goes against common sense to claim that even actions of the most private and intimate character are basically social. For example, suppose you are taking a bath. What on earth is social about that? You are not interacting with anyone. Indeed, other human beings may not be a part of your consciousness at all. It is you who decides which soap to use, how hot to make the water, how long to soak and so on. Where does society enter the picture? If the problem is to understand your action, why will it not suffice simply to ask you, the agent, to explain it and to leave it at that? To provide answers to these questions, we must examine three further aspects of the nature of individual action. First, individuals must *learn* to act from others. Second, people learn to act through learning to follow *rules* which are essentially social in character. And third, information about *social institutions* must be incorporated into any explanation of individual action. Through a more detailed analysis of these various factors, we will reveal the sense in which there is no such thing as a purely individual action.

Beginning with learning, you are not born with the ability to act. Others have to teach you. Of course, you are born with the capacity to behave in certain ways – to suck or to sleep, for example. But it should be clear by now that action and behaviour are quite different. The social dimension of learning to act is made even more important by the close association between action and language. You use language to do things and not simply to say things. The use of language, in turn, involves a host of non-linguistic skills which have themselves to be learned through careful practice and monitoring. No matter how well you can mouth the language of car mechanics, surgery or marathon running, without further instruction in how to apply this language in practice, you will still be unable to repair your car, to remove an appendix or to win a race. So your being taught what to say in specific circumstances is intimately connected with your learning how to execute activities in ways which conform to accepted social practice.

The assessment of both types of skill is essentially social in two ways. Initially, you will require teachers who will help you both to perform new actions and to evaluate your performance. But your teachers will not be your only assessor or be forever by your side. Thus if you wish to execute these activities successfully in the future, you will also have to satisfy those who are socially recognized as capable of performing/evaluating the activity in question. Indeed, your actions will constantly be assessed by all of those with whom you interact. To take a simple example, in any kind of formal apprenticeship you will have to act according to the specification both of your masters and, eventually, of those to whom you wish to offer your skills. In short, in order to act successfully in specific ways, you have to learn to join in those activities with others. Further, in the process of learning to participate in the social practices which characterize their own particular culture, actors not only have to learn from others how to identify and assess their own activity. They must also learn to become the assessors of the activities of others, and the skills required for this do not necessarily entail the ability to carry out the actions themselves. Thus, people receive the training to recognize and evaluate a host of social activities which they do not themselves perform. For example, even though you may not be a good cook or able to drive a car, this does not keep you from recognizing and avoiding bad cooking or driving when you come across them. But this capacity for evaluation raises in an even more acute form the problem of interpretation which was discussed in chapter 1 – and not just for philosophers but for people going about their everyday lives.

How do you identify and assess specific activities? Obviously the significance of an action is not necessarily going to be consistent with the purposes and beliefs with which you want to identify it. Different interpretations of a particular set of observations will always be possible no matter how committed you are to your own. For example, if you are already absolutely convinced that you have witnessed a theft then further attention to these observations alone can neither confirm not refute your explanation. In this case, it is not the observations but the meaning which you impute to them that can be called into question (e.g. 'I disagree. I don't think that's what she was doing at all.'). The possibility of making recognizable mistakes about others is a corollary of the fact that you yourself have to *learn* the social significance of your own actions. If your assessment of your own actions were entirely your own decision – a private rather than a public matter – then it would be impossible for you to be mistaken about yourself. But this is clearly not the case. For example, you may intend to bake a fantastic soufflé based on your favourite recipe. If the success of the dish were entirely decided by you, your dish would – of logical necessity – always succeed. A comment from someone else like 'That's not a soufflé – that's a mess!' would simply make no sense.

The importance of making mistakes in social life brings us to the second reason outlined earlier for the social character of individual action – the role of *rules* in learning to act. Even when you view your actions as successful, you must have a reasonably clear idea of what it would have been like for you to have failed. Otherwise, how would it be possible for you to identify your success as a 'success'. Although you choose the specific strategy for achieving your aims, the same cannot be said of the means by which your act is judged a success or a failure. Your success depends on the extent to which your action conforms to existing standards mutually perceived and sustained by others in the form of rules which dictate what is and what is not appropriate in specific circumstances. If your action conforms to these rules then you will receive social approval and learn in the future to identify that mode of activity as successful. If not, your failure will be socially communicated to you in ways that conform to yet other rules. If you wish to make your actions more successful in the future, they will have to be altered in the light of such feedback. In short, you do not become a good judge or a good chef merely through wanting to be or thinking that you already are. You must learn the appropriate language and skills from others. You must practise and improve in relation to the relevant practices of others. You must learn the rules before you learn to bend or break them.

But what do we mean by rules in this context? Rules are socially accepted conventions or norms which give meaning and expression to different types of social activity. They dictate what to do in specific situations and how to do it. Games provide the simplest examples of what rules are and how they are employed. For example, in order to play chess in a recognizable way, you have to adopt a set of aims (e.g. checkmate your opponent) and a set of beliefs (e.g. that this can appropriately be done through a combination of acceptable moves which you believe to be most effective). More complicated social rules function in essentially the same way. In order to purchase food in a college canteen you must obviously think it reasonable to formulate the aim of so doing.

You must also be aware of the publicly accepted strategy for going about it (e.g. not sampling the food before you pay for it and paying with money rather than with, say, your least favourite essay). Of course, rules of this kind have to be individually interpreted, otherwise there would be no reason to regard chess as a competitive game or to be offended by the brash manner of some people in canteen queues. But the rules themselves are essentially social in character. This is why learning to act in particular ways involves learning to assess individual interpretations of rules in terms of their consistency with the rules themselves.

Thus in order recognizably to follow rules, individuals must be capable in principle of breaking them – of making mistakes. Remember 'ought' and 'ought not' must both imply 'can'. Again, were the success or failure of their actions *entirely* up to the individual, mistakes and therefore rule-following would be impossible. But this means that individuals cannot be regarded as the best judges of what they are doing and how well they are doing it. How often do you think that only you are fully conscious of what is 'on your mind' when you act – especially when you feel that your actions have been misunderstood? Yet such thoughts are profoundly problematic. Again, if you have to *learn* to act, then you can learn wrongly. This is why, for instance, a rule book is so important in games where sincere and passionate disputes about the rules are likely to occur. To take another example, children can be quite convinced that they are doing one thing (e.g. helping to cook) and doing it well (e.g. a 'mixture' is produced) without them really doing either. Their intentions do not necessarily have any bearing on whether or not they are doing what they proclaim – whatever the intensity of their commitments.

But are we suggesting that individual aims and beliefs have nothing to do with the identification and assessment of the actions concerned? Surely this would contradict all that we have argued in the last chapter about the distinction between action and behaviour. Such a counter-argument seems strongest when the sorts of actions under consideration are ostensibly *moral*. In these situations responsibility is apparently attributed on the basis of individual beliefs. So, for example, when a person is praised or blamed for what they say or do, what they believe themselves to be doing seems crucial. Suppose a thief in a hotel lobby steals a briefcase which, unknown to him, contains a bomb, and hides it in a wood where it explodes harmlessly. He deserves no praise because he did not intend the heroism which that action would have required had he known there was a bomb in the bag. This is a clear-cut case because the thief's belief about what the bag contained was quite fortuitously mistaken and has a purely accidental connection with what the bag actually contained. His action would be regarded as theft, regardless of its good consequences, when moral responsibility came to be apportioned in a court of law.

This example seems to show that the beliefs of the agent concerning what is done or said are definitive of what the agent 'really' does. But we have seen that this does not apply in many non-moral instances of learned activity (e.g. children learning to cook) and it is often not true even in a court of law. If agents' beliefs about their actions are sufficiently unreasonable in that they inexplicably violate widely accepted social rules, then those beliefs will be seen to be irrelevant in the identification and assessment of the action in question. Suppose a man accused of threatening behaviour says that he chased his neighbour down the road brandishing an axe and shouting threats 'for a joke'. This will not refute the accusation of assault, even if he sincerely thought that it was a joke. Similarly, an employer who fails to safeguard dangerous machinery because 'I thought my employees would have enough sense not to put their hands inside while it was going round' will be considered negligent, even if it never occurred to him that any employee would be so silly. Negligence is often identified socially on the basis of rules; they define what it means to be negligent in particular contexts. Nonetheless, those found guilty nearly always protest their innocence.

Thus, the question of what agents really do or say is not settled by appeals only to what they believe to be the case about their action. This is not to say that such beliefs are irrelevant. The views of individuals concerning the significance of their own actions do have some bearing on what they are socially identified as doing even in a court of law. Doing or saying something knowingly in the full knowledge of its meaning is different from doing or saying it intentionally but in ignorance of its social significance. For example, someone who committed a crime knowing that it would involve violence would presumably be regarded as more culpable than someone who committed the crime sincerely believing that no one would be hurt. Similarly, someone who knowingly engaged in child neglect would presumably be convicted of a worse crime than someone who carelessly or unintentionally did so. Yet in both cases, the actors would be convicted, irrespective of their own perception of their activity. So your ignorance of the law cannot prove you innocent of a crime though it might be a mitigation of your offence. Thus, even in the case of moral action, the crucial determinant for identifying what is done, whether or not it is good or bad, and what reward or punishment should follow, is not the identification and evaluation of the particular actor in question. Rather, the crucial factor is the consistency of the actor's interpretation of the rules with the social practices which give them their significance. It is such practices and not individual aims and beliefs which will always be the final arbiter.

Part of the reason it is so widely accepted that individuals know better than anyone else what it is that they are doing is the ease with which people forget the social processes by which they learned to follow rules in different ways. For example, there are rules for playing chess which you have to learn from someone who already knows them. We have shown how that other person is just as important to your realizing your potential as a chess player as is your personal capacity to act as an agent. As you learn to play, the other person(s) will monitor your activity and inform you when you are following the rules and whether you are doing well or badly. On the basis of these responses, you will incorporate a sense of the 'rules of chess' into your consciousness and acquire the capacity to monitor yourself. Therefore, even when you 'play yourself' at chess, you are not completely self-sufficient. Your capacity to play this and other games reflects your teaching. Your assessment of your ability and the merit of your specific actions presupposes a range of assumptions about what others would say about it were they there. Remember, it is perfectly possible and meaningful to say while playing yourself at chess, 'My, that was a good move I just made' – only to be reminded by an expert how bad it really was! Were action simply the product of individual agency, this would be meaningless for, as we have seen, mistakes would be impossible. And what goes for chess goes for all other forms of action.

Generally, therefore, you have to learn to act from others and to evaluate your actions with reference to their reactions. Your ability to do both of these things will reflect your understanding of those rules in terms of which your own purposes and beliefs are formulated and acted upon. When this ability has reached a particular socially defined point, you achieve the capacity for self-monitoring, but still with reference to relevant rules which are not your creation and which you share with other actors engaged in similar activities. Recall the relationship between learning a rule and learning a skill in this connection. It is only after a long apprenticeship that a carpenter knows how to assess the merit of his or her work in socially acceptable terms. The same holds for the most public activities (e.g. making an effective political speech) and also the most private (e.g. making love).

The third and final argument against the simple equation of human action with the reasons and agency of the individual stems from the fact that explanations of actions explicitly refer to social institutions. In this context, 'social institutions' can be taken to mean those rules and related patterns of action by which a culture is socially organized. Rules dictating what it means to buy and sell, to be in a family, to be treated for an illness, to go to school, to work in a particular trade or profession are all 'institutional' in this sense. Although commonly thought of in physical terms (e.g. 'That's a nicer school than mine') institutions cannot be identified merely with buildings of particular types. A building designed as a hospital can be used for many different types of activity, while a hospital can be created in almost any type of building. It is not the building that is important but the rules followed within it which convey institutional status. Similarly, while the rules which characterize social institutions may sometimes be written down (e.g. in law books), they cannot usually be identified with specific texts. Indeed institutional rules may be informal and discernible only through careful observation of what people do – which may often be different from what the formal rules stipulate. In other words, if rules are to acquire institutional status, they must be associated with specific social practices believed to form integral components of the general organization of a society.

Institutional rules of this kind play an important part in our ordinary explanations of what may seem to be private and individual actions. Consider the following description of two very private actions: 'She purchased a box of chocolates with a cheque and took it to her lover in hospital.' The actions described here are explained in terms of a set of purposes and beliefs which have been learned and are applied in a social context. True, the agent causes her action in the sense that she is accountable for it. However, she clearly does not have sole responsibility for the way in which others interpret it. She wrote the cheque, purchased the chocolates, went to the hospital ... but in order for the act to be successful, all of these things had to be done and responded to in specific ways. These ways are stipulated by the institutions referred to in the description/explanation of her action. For example, her purchase is intelligible only in terms of the existence of the institutions of monetary exchange. Her cheque is only intelligible within the context of banking institutions, and will only be acceptable if written accordingly. In any given society, what it means to offer gifts, to have a lover, or to be in hospital are not decided simply on the basis of what the agent says or does. Thus all of the preceding actions possess at least the potential of being publicly identified and evaluated as being of a specific institutional type. It is your capacity for such identification and evaluation which accounts for your ability to explain both your own actions and those of others as often as you do.

Much contemporary social science is devoted to the description and classification of such institutions and to the assessment of how they either support or conflict with other social practices. Studies of specific institutions like the education system, the family, religion, the media or the economy attempt to discover the sorts of rules which are character-istically followed in these particular contexts. Other social scientists see their task as examining the extent to which different sets of rules and associated practices might be called a 'social system' – a coherent environment of institutions in terms of which actors produce and distribute the kinds of goods and services which they collectively perceive themselves as needing and wanting. Thus they assume that accurate information about particular institutions is already available and the problem is whether or not these institutions reinforce or contradict their respective aims. It might be asked, for instance, whether, whatever their formal aims, schools also help to reinforce the social values characteristic of the family or the state. For some, the question of the overall economic and social stability of British capitalism is even more interesting. Still others attempt to analyze the relationships between the different institu-tional components of the entire social and economic system of the western world! But whatever the scale of the operation, it is rules which are being investigated and the private aims and beliefs of individuals can never in themselves provide the answers to the questions posed in this kind of research.

To summarize, we have discussed a range of examples which indicate that in so far as human action is intelligible it is essentially social. Intentional explanations enable actions to be understood in terms of reasons – purposes and beliefs about how to accomplish them – that belong to a *type* of action of which the particular action to be explained is a *token*. The symmetry between explanation and justification found in intentional explanations arises because such explanations make actions intelligible by revealing the rationale that an action of that type must possess regardless of who performs it. To identify a particular person's action as a token is to impute a commitment to the rationale for actions of that type, whether or not it was consciously entertained.

The repertoire of actions you perform is therefore like the vocabulary of the language you speak. It is the collective possession of the social group within which those actions are performed and that language is spoken. So, just as the conscious formulation of what you want to say depends upon the prior social existence of language rules in terms of which words have their meanings, so the conscious formulation of an intention to perform an action depends upon the prior social existence of rules in terms of which actions have their justifications. You can only form an intention to do something that already makes sense to you as something that might be done. Thus it is fundamentally mistaken to view yourself as acting with total self-sufficiency – by yourself and for yourself – without reference to anyone else. Social life is an essential characteristic of individual humans, unlike the situation of an individual tree which just happens to be in a forest. Grown from seed in isolation, a tree is still a tree; but humanity is the gift of society to the individual.

The social character of persons

Yet the conclusions of the previous section do have implications that seem to conflict with the most cherished ideas of what a person is. What is it that makes someone a person? If you want to be sure that this is the same Fred Bloggs you met yesterday, then criteria of bodily identity, continuity of physical processes and behaviour may well suffice. But this tells you very little about what makes Fred a person – why you should act towards him in the way in which it is appropriate to act towards people, as opposed to animals or things. To identify a person by purely physical criteria is analogous to considering human activity as mere behaviour – physical movement alone. Of course, if you use strictly physical criteria in your identification of Fred, you will not find yourself with the wrong man. However, possessing a physical identity is something he shares with his dog – you can identify the same dog by this means too. This does not explain what is accomplished by identifying Fred as the man who should, for example, keep the promise he made to you yesterday. If Fred had since had an accident and lost his memory of the relevant events, then you would not hold him to his promise. It is Fred himself – his beliefs, reasons and purposes – and not his physical continuity who has the obligation to you. Arguments like this make it very tempting to believe in *crude mentalism* – the view that having an individual mind is the very essence of being a person.

We have already introduced one of the key arguments from which crude mentalism derives its authority – the belief that the mind is the seat of agency and responsibility. It states that you can no more doubt that you have a particular intention when you perform an action than you can doubt that you are entertaining a specific experience or idea at the moment you are having it. It is this intention which links you to your related action. So if you knock over a vase you are not to blame provided that you did not *mean* to do it. For the action to have been 'knocking over the vase' and to have been your action rather than someone else's, it would need to have been done with that intention 'in mind'. While others (e.g. a jury) may guess at your motivation, the crude mentalist argues that at the end of the day, you alone really know your reasons for acting as you do. You understand others by entertaining hypotheses about their mental states which bear an analogous relationship to your knowledge of your own mental states under similar circumstances. This empathic capacity to put yourself in the place of others is sometimes referred to by social scientists and philosophers as the faculty of *'verstehen'*. The idea here is that you know the reasons that *you* would need to have to act in such and such a way and for want of any better assumption, you presume that others are just like you in that they too would need to have just those reasons in mind to do the same thing. Such hypotheses about inner mental life can only be corroborated by 'circumstantial' evidence provided, for instance, by avowals of intention on the part of the person you seek to understand. But these are not self-validating – the agent could lie. According to crude mentalism you cannot, therefore, know the minds of others with the same authority that you know your own mind. It also sadly follows that others can never really understand what it is like to be you.

The primacy that crude mentalism accords to individuals' knowledge of their own states of mind implies that each person thinks quite independently. For this reason, whether or not two people agree with one another depends upon whether or not they choose to think alike. But precisely the same assumption that implies that agreement between people consists in their identical thoughts also implies the inability of anyone else to know what is in your mind in the way that you do – to know whether you and they really do think alike. Indeed, it prevents you also from knowing this because analogy with your own case is all you have to support your belief that others think at all. The assumption that you know your own mind in a way that others do not seems to be a bulwark of human individuality. Yet were your individuality protected by a barrier which is impenetrable in principle, then it would be more like total isolation.

This kind of paradox arises because crude mentalism argues that what you mean by, for example, the word 'pain' must derive solely from your own acquaintance with pain. Surely, no one can feel another's pain to know what that other person means by the word. Must not each person therefore understand the use others make of the word 'pain' by analogy with their own cases since they have no direct acquaintance with what other people are talking about when they say that they are in pain? Now it is true that you can tell that a person, or an animal for that matter, is capable of feeling a pain under certain conditions of stimulus by analogically inferring this from the sorts of noises and movements you observe (e.g. screaming and writhing). But this is not to say that 'Aargh!' has the same meaning as the word 'pain' when uttered by the person who screamed. When you say 'my pain' or 'your pain', it has the same sense – a sense you learnt that you can express in the English language by the word 'pain'. If we were both to receive an electric shock and shout 'Aargh!' at the same time, we would not be agreeing with one another. But when we then said to one another 'That hurt!' we would be agreeing. You learn how to use words like 'pain' and 'hurt' from the way others use these words, and not simply by suffering your own pains. The meaning of 'pain' is public even when it is used to refer to a pain whose occurrence is private.

Your ability to do this exemplifies a feature of the entire vocabulary of self-awareness which has to be learnt from other people with whose minds you are not directly acquainted. To say this is not to deny that when you use these terms, you refer to your own inner states of mind, sensations, desires and so forth. 'Pain', 'choice', 'belief', 'intention', 'despair', 'understanding', 'memory', and many more such terms, certainly do refer to states of mind which you must necessarily feel or have for yourself. Yet your grasp of the sense of such terms when they apply to you cannot be any stronger than the grasp that others have of them, and 'others' will include those from whom you learnt to use those expressions of yourself. They used the term 'pain' of you in the very sense you subsequently learnt to use it of yourself. The same goes for all those terms you use to describe your mental states. There can be no reason to doubt that all the terms used to describe inner mental states apply to others in exactly the same sense in which they apply to you. Of course, people may exaggerate or conceal their thoughts, feelings or desires. But your capacity to impute such states of mind to others – including the desire to deceive – rests on their capacity to do likewise in your case.

Thus the meaningfulness of the vocabulary of introspective self-awareness has a necessarily collective character. The mind viewed broadly as individual self-consciousness turns out to be a product of social reflection and negotiation. For you must learn from others the language you employ to describe your innermost thoughts and feelings. They teach you not only the rules of individual action as we showed in the preceding section; they also teach you how to describe and explain yourself to yourself. Human individuality is not mere peculiarity or uniqueness. Modern findings in immunology have shown that the chemical signature of the proteins of the bodies of humans and of very many other species defines each individual as absolutely unique (except in the case of identical twins). But this has nothing to do with the specifically human uniqueness which is attributed to each conscious rational being. This type of individuality which makes a person the recipient of rights, the possessor of duties, the holder of beliefs and the seeker after knowledge, is not a uniqueness that persons possess whether or not they know it, like the specificity of their chromosomes. Rather it is the outcome of a process, beginning in earliest childhood, that grows with socialization and the gathering awareness of ourselves and others.

Yet the crude mentalists might still try to retort that however much they must be learned from others, the meanings of words and rules must ultimately be reducible to the mental states of separate individuals. When you make a judgment, say on whether a line is straight or the sky is blue, it is by looking to see whether what is before you corresponds with the idea which you express by 'straight' or 'blue'. Entertaining the idea of the colour blue, you know what the word 'blue' means. The idea must come first because you have to know what you mean to say before you can start to find the words to express it. So all of our arguments concerning the social character of such meaning are neither here nor there. While there might well be *public* dispute or doubt about the collective understanding of words or rules, there can be no such doubts concerning your *private* understanding of the ideas – the thoughts – that you seek to express. It is in this way that we reach the centrepiece of the doctrines of crude mentalism: 'I must know what I am thinking because I am thinking it.' This assertion, or something like it, seems to offer an unassailable certainty as regards the grasp of inner states of mind – thoughts, ideas, sensations – which are presented as the real substance of what language and thought outwardly express, however much such states are socially mediated. They are the inner private language of thought, the essence of personhood.

So, finally, we must consider Ludwig Wittgenstein's celebrated argument that there can be no such 'private language'. There can be no doubt that in one sense your personal identity does consist in your awareness of *yourself* – which in turn can be reduced to a range of mental and physical states (e.g. your memories and the behaviour of your brain). Whether or not there is more to you than these states – than your sense of being connected to and continuous with your past, present and future – is the subject of fierce contemporary philosophical debate. Happily, the point of our argument thus far is not to deny that inner states of mind exist, nor to deny that a person has direct acquaintance with them. Rather, it is to point out the limitations of such acquaintances as a form of explanatory understanding. When your tooth hurts you are acquainted with the pain. There is no room for doubt because there is no way to feel pain 'incorrectly'. But that just means that there is no 'correct' way to feel it either. This is a realm where doubt is impossible, not because certainty abolishes doubt, but because here the distinction between doubt and certainty, right and wrong, correct and incorrect, simply cannot be made. The trouble then with 'I must know what I am thinking because I am thinking it' is not that it is false, but that it is just too good to be true. If it were true then you could never be wrong about anything! To understand the implications of this for the essentially social character of your ideas and therefore your consciousness, it is necessary to look further at what is involved in judging ideas to be correct and in following a rule.

How do you judge that a state of mind is the *same* this time as when you had it before? Presumably, some sort of *criterion* is required for such a judgment. If the crude mentalist accepts this, then, as another idea, it must be internal and private too. It cannot be some sort of *aide memoire*, like a diary or a knot in your handkerchief. For it is precisely your inner private certainty that is viewed as the basis for your judging that what you see before you *is* a knot in your handkerchief or an entry in your diary. The only criterion for making the required judgment would presumably be memory itself. But it is not necessary to doubt the reliability of memory in order to see that it will not do. You might recognize a friend who has shaved off his beard and remember him as having been different. It is just because there are criteria for his identity other than your memory of him that such recognition is possible. These are criteria which are outward and public, not inner and private. Your friend greets you, and despite looking different, he says and does all you would expect. Your idea, sensation or state of mind, by contrast, has no existence outside your mind. It is entirely inward. You use your memory alone to recognize it, so it makes no sense to say to yourself, 'Let me recall this idea and see if it is the same as I remember it.' If *that* is what you remember, it cannot be other than the same as what you remember. To consult your memory *again* is like buying several copies of the morning paper to assure yourself that what it says is true. You might wish to claim that a memory is correct if it corresponds with the past. But only corroboration in the present can support the accuracy of memory because the past is past and gone. Such assessment, therefore, clearly involves more than reference to your own internal states. It involves others – Brian, who obviously does not rely on your memory of him for his identity, along with the people who might have introduced you to him or who remind you of his name if you forget.

Similarly, and in relation to language, if the individual mind has the autonomous capacity to originate and confer meaning on actions and utterances, then every word 'means just what I choose it to mean' as Humpty Dumpty put it to Alice. As Carroll intended, this is an outright absurdity. For if words did not already mean what they do mean, then they could not be used to express what you mean to say. For a private and personal state of mind to be communicable, there must already exist a public medium for its expression which others recognize. Try to *make* a sound mean something. Pronounce 'INGY', and make it mean something that no English word or expression can be used to say. Now get somebody to understand what you mean. Remember that this is a meaning that you originated and conferred on 'INGY', so that you will not be able to answer 'Yes' to any query which proposes a translation of what you mean into English. Do you think that you will succeed in making your private and personal state of mind which means 'INGY' communicable to others? Failing that, it is unclear how such a state of mind can be thought of as 'correct' or even as intelligible at all – even to you. Consequently, no sense can be made of what it would mean for people to agree about rules – or anything else – simply with reference to their private mental states. Of course, this is not to deny that you have particular states of mind when you follow rules. It is to deny that the content of the rule can in any way be reduced to them. This means that judgments about the correctness of what you think as well as do are essentially social.

But if it is not their presence in individual minds that gives rules their explanatory force in making sense of human action, what on earth does? We have shown that the existence of a social rule is in turn predicated on the existence of a group of persons who *agree* upon the social constraints which have to be conformed to if a related action is even to be attempted in any identifiable way. It is normative agreement of this kind which accounts for the explanatory significance of rules. Such agreements cannot reside in any mental or physical characteristics that a single person or object might possess. In a sense, you obviously agree with yourself about the content of your consciousness and the physical dimensions of your body (in the same way that, say, two congruent triangles can be said to be the same). Yet if normative agreement amounted to no more than such mental or physical congruence then its violation – a mistake – would become unintelligible for all the preceding reasons. This yet further underlines the extent to which rules are inherently collective and social in character and not merely contingently so. They must concern the sort of agreement that you can have with others and not with yourself, agreements which may be kept, broken, entered into and renounced. The ability to follow rules and to refer to them in understanding the actions of others does not depend on individual judgments made within the questionable privacy of your own mind. It rather entails the agreement in judgments between persons about how to proceed in specific circumstances. Therefore, since to become a person it is necessary to understand and act on the basis of such agreements – to interpret and follow associated rules – the social character of personhood is guaranteed.

In general, then, the whole vocabulary of self-awareness consists of terms and expressions that you learn to apply in your own case from their use by others in talking of themselves and of you. If the particular knowledge you have of yourself – your knowledge, for instance, that you regret an action – is dependent upon your conceptual understanding of regret itself, then the conceptual understanding embodied in the vocabulary of self-awareness is seen to be no less social than other non-personal modes of understanding. In this sense, the mind has a collective existence – a shared ideal of individuality towards which particular persons aspire, in order to define themselves for themselves and for others. It is not a notion which a person understands simply and solely by acquaintance with his or her own case. It arises instead as a social construct of reflection. The dawning realization that you are a person with the capacity for rational choice is, at one and the same time, the beginning of your understanding in general of what a person is, and of what other people are like. Understanding yourself and understanding others are not two separate conceptual tasks, but one and the same. For this understanding arises by the imputation back upon yourself of the rules you first impute to the actions and utterances of others in order to understand them. In this respect our understanding of ourselves is *reflexive* in a stronger sense than is sometimes supposed. 'Reflection' here does not mean mere introspective pondering and is, of course, absolutely distinct from a nervous 'reflex'. You discover yourself 'reflected' in others. Without the mirror that the actions and utterances of others supply, it is inconceivable that you could ever grasp what manner of thing you yourself might be or become. However, this 'mirror', unlike silvered glass, does not passively return your image to you. Rather, it is what others do and say, taken as a result of their recognition of what you are and might become, that reveals to you how you are perceived. This is an active process to which you too contribute.

Thus the philosophically abstract conception of the self-sufficiency of the individual mind, free and independent of others, serves to conceal its origins as a social product of rule-governed reflection. 'I think therefore I am' totally obscures the social process whereby the use of the term 'I' is acquired. The person as a knowing subject and a moral agent, enjoying freedom, owing duties and owed rights, does not magically appear with a determined pull at his or her own mental bootstraps. A young child is a person, yet takes eighteen or twenty-one hard years to learn how to be a knowing subject and a moral agent before the rest of us will grant her or him the full rights and duties of a rationally autonomous individual. Equally, Descartes's own analysis of the individual mind itself emerged only after a long period of philosophical examination. Moreover, it is clear from many empirical studies of child development that there are complex conditions which a child's social circumstances must fulfil if this development is to proceed as it should. Yet in placing so much emphasis on the social character of others and personhood, have we not risked throwing out the baby with the bathwater? For it might appear that we have dismantled the notion of the individual human being as a free and autonomous agent, to replace it by a picture of the person as a puppet. It will be the purpose of the arguments in the next chapter to show that the conception of a person as a rule-follower does not have such disastrous consequences for human freedom.

Annotated bibliography

In this chapter we have argued for a particular thesis concerning action strongly influenced by the considerations found in Wittgenstein 1973, by the interpretation of these arguments in Winch 1970 and by the further commentary in Pitkin 1972, especially chapters 6, 7 and 11. A similar thesis is discussed in Rubinstein 1981, chapters 6-8. The contemporary discussion to which our arguments owe most is in Giddens 1976, chapters 2 and 3, and Giddens 1979, chapters 2-4. The line we have attempted to follow falls midway between two broad camps. One sees all action originating from and explained by the consciousness of individuals. The other conceives of action as being determined by, and explained in terms of, social structures which exist independently of individual consciousness. Arguably, the sharpness of the division between individualist and collectivist camps is in part an imposition on some of the classic texts concerned with social action – see Giddens 1971 in respect of Weber and Durkheim. Weber 1964, chapter 1, Weber 1950, chapter 3, and Durkheim 1982, chapters 1, 2 and 5, contain their key discussions. Weber has been widely taken as the founder of the individualist camp and Durkheim's discussion of 'social facts' as the foundation for the collectivist view. The division became more marked in the subsequent discussion respectively of Schutz 1972, especially chapters 1 and 3, and of Parsons 1968, summarized in chapter 18. Mead 1964, section 3, long ago presented a view very much like that for which we have argued, albeit from a very different philosophical starting point. Goff 1980, chapter 3, provides an illuminating commentary on Mead related to the concerns of this chapter, as does Joas 1985. The elaboration of a theory with very much the same general features, but from yet another philosophical starting point, is to be found in Harré 1979 and 1983.

This being said, none of these classic texts can be recommended as introductory reading. A text written to introduce sociology as a discipline, such as Bilton *et al.* 1981, section 1, would be a better place to begin.

More recently a literature has grown up in a more conceptual and philosophical vein, sparked off to a large extent by the claims in Popper 1961, chapters 3 and 4, for what he termed 'methodological individualism'. Contributions to this debate can be found in the essays by Watkins, Lukes and Mandelbaum in Ryan 1973, and in the essays collected in O'Neill 1973.

For further discussion of the social character of action, from a variety of viewpoints, see Keat and Urry 1982, chapter 8, Macdonald and Pettit 1981, chapter 3, Hirst and Woolley 1982, chapter 2, Papineau 1978, chapters 1 and 4, and Trigg 1985, chapter 3.

The second section of this chapter is a brief introduction to the philosophy of mind, with a strongly Wittgensteinian flavour – particularly towards the end, where we give a brief account of the celebrated 'private language argument' in Wittgenstein 1973, paras 200-72. Shaffer 1968 and McGinn 1982 are two introductions to this field of philosophy which reveal how problematic is crude mentalism, irrespective of any commitment to a particular resolution of the issues raised. Kenny 1973, chapters 8 and 10, gives a good introduction to Wittgenstein's contribution to the philosophy of mind, while Hacker 1972, chapters 7-9, gives a more sustained discussion. Taking crude mentalism as our target we follow Ryle 1963, which ranks with Wittgenstein 1973 as a classic modern contribution to the philosophy of mind.

We have attempted to give a simple account of why the 'private language argument', and its relation to following a rule, strikes us as important to an understanding of what it is for humans to be *social* beings. The significance of these arguments, however, has been an issue of considerable and difficult debate amongst philosophers. You will see that there are differences both between our account and those in the references we have given, and between those other accounts themselves. Holtzman and Leich 1981 contains articles indicative of the continuing dispute. Kripke 1982 and McGinn 1984 are two substantial contemporary contributions to the debate.

Finally, on the more general issue of 'persons', Parfitt 1984, parts 3 and 4, illustrates the scope and importance of the questions we have begun to raise and links very closely with the issues raised in Hollis 1977. The discussion of the self in Mead 1964, section 3, is instructive to compare with the diversity of views found in Mischel 1977 and in Hofstadter and Dennett 1981. As we indicated at the start of the discussion of persons, the centrality of the question of individual personal identity for moral philosophy forms a very powerful barrier to construals of the self as in any way a social construct.

5

FREEDOM, SELF-UNDERSTANDING AND IDEOLOGY

If, as we argued in chapter 3, human actions are to be explained in terms of their reasons, then the capacity to choose is an essential feature of human agency. Yet it might seem very hard to reconcile such a claim for the freedom of human agency with our conclusions in chapter 4 about the social character of action and the status of the individual as a rule-follower. If you are to be said to act, then you must be free to make choices. But it would seem that if you are to be said to act then you have no choice but to follow rules which you individually do not make or choose. This is the first of two puzzles that confront anyone trying to make sense of human freedom. The first section of this chapter shows why there is no contradiction between following a rule and exercising freedom of choice – that in fact these are but two ways of describing the same thing. The second puzzle concerns the ability that people possess to act against their own interests. Assuming that there is a fundamental sense in which all humans are free, why do so few of them attempt to free themselves from tyranny, hardship and exploitation? How can freedom of action and continued suffering be reconciled? To begin to answer this question, we first distinguish the capacity to choose from the opportunity to do so. We then introduce the concept of *ideology* in order to show that many rules serve the interests of some people better than those of others, and that the impact of the distribution of power in society on the understanding of social life can serve to disguise this fact.

Freedom, rules and creativity

If you view systems of social rules as so comprehensive and restrictive that they remove all possibility of choice, reducing those who fall under them to little more than machines, this may be because you are failing to distinguish between *political freedom* and *freedom of agency*. Confusion of this kind is exemplified by the following statement: 'It's all very well for philosophers to talk as though we had free will but we all know that in reality, society often gives us no choice.' This apparent contradiction arises from a failure to recognize the fact that if humans did not at least potentially have the capacity to choose between alternative courses of action – to exercise their freedom of agency – then there could be no complaint about their being denied the opportunity to choose. Thus any criticism of society which argues that individuals are denied freedom of choice must assume that, if given the opportunity, they would be *able* to make such choices. Otherwise, it would make no sense to suggest that they would take advantage of political freedom if it were offered to them. You cannot reasonably criticize a form of political organization which you regard as totalitarian unless you believe that, given the opportunity, its members would choose a different system. Similarly, it would seem to be absurd to sing the praises of democracy while at the same time assuming that political actions (e.g. voting) are entirely determined by factors other than the chosen purposes and beliefs of the citizens. The concepts of political freedom and freedom of agency are necessarily distinct, though the intelligibility of the former depends on a belief in the latter.

It is fairly easy to remedy the confusion of the social critic who fails to see that you can avail yourself of the opportunity to choose only if you possess the capacity to do so. Our more serious concern must be with the critic who despairs of both forms of freedom through not being able to distinguish between the constraints of rules and those of laws of nature. When someone holds a gun to your head to coerce you and says 'You have no choice', this is not literally true. It is just that the alternative to choosing to obey – death – is something you can be expected not to choose! The proverbial 'offer you cannot refuse' is in fact an offer you can refuse only at a price no one would rationally choose to pay. It is for this reason that the actions of those under duress are still theirs. The extent and severity of the coercion into, say, wrongdoing, is something you weigh when considering how far someone is to blame for a crime. 'I was only obeying orders' was the plea of mitigation made by German war criminals. The question which had to be considered at Nuremberg was how much coercion was employed to enforce their obedience. Did the fact that it was not as much as was used to procure the obedience of their victims ensure their culpability? How much is too much? Whatever the answer to this question, no amount of coercion puts a person on the same footing as a machine whose repertoire of behaviours simply does not contain items which would count as disobedience. Coercion and duress consist of sanctions – punishment – for making the choices your oppressor does not wish you to make. They therefore exist to enforce adherence to rules. It makes no sense to coerce people except where what counts as following and breaking the rule are both equally within the capacity of those who have to obey. Coercion is a means of dissuading people from making choices they might otherwise make.

But no matter how coercive a system of rules might be, the constraints which they impose must be distinct from the constraints exerted by laws of nature. Where such laws determine the course of events, there can be no sense in imposing a rule, either to command or to prohibit it. A rule commanding you not to 'obey' the law of gravity – like King Canute's attempt to command the obedience of the waves – is vacuous. One would have been equally unimpressed had Canute commanded the tide to rise and been gratified when it did just that! If a law of nature so dictates, then what will be will be, regardless of whether it has been commanded or prohibited, or whether anyone even has knowledge of its existence. The constraints of natural laws thus require no enforcement and entail no coercion or duress. By contrast, the exercise of coercion which denies liberty is only possible in the context of rules which may be disobeyed, thus calling down sanctions upon the disobedient.

Coercion obviously requires rules. However, our critic may still argue that the same cannot be said of freedom. We would respond by asking, 'Would you have more or less liberty if no one enforced *any* rules?' Consider, for example, laws which protect you and your property from arbitrary attack. The forbearance of others is essential in order for you to enjoy whatever liberties you possess. Not only is a social framework of rules necessary for this purpose, it is also necessary in a more fundamental sense for the exercise of freedom of agency itself. Stranded on his desert island, Robinson Crusoe is freed from all the coercive agencies of social life – but not, thereby, from the need to follow rules. In order to reflect on his plight and adopt rational strategies to deal with it, Crusoe has to retain and apply a repertoire of rules acquired from society. In so far as he is free, it is not because he has no rules to follow. Indeed, it should be remembered how many of the liberties of which Crusoe was deprived are ones which can only be enjoyed in a social context. A prisoner in solitary confinement perhaps enjoys less liberty than a castaway, but the sort of punishment adopted when criminals are deprived of their liberty is less severe than casting them away on a desert island. Liberty, then, is not a state enjoyed at its maximum outside society. Rather it is enjoyed largely within a social context and requires the regulation of social life in order to be maximized. Most important of all, liberty requires that persons enjoying it should understand those rules by virtue of which the actions they choose to perform take on their sense *as* actions. That is to say, the arguments of the last chapter concerning the social character of action must equally imply the social character of liberty.

So the capacity to choose is necessarily bound up with following rules, but does this mean that the only 'freedom' people enjoy is to *break* them? Much of social life is very regular and predictable. Does it follow that because they generally follow social rules most people actually exercise very little liberty? To begin to answer this question, we must examine more carefully the ways in which rules socially constrain human activity. Most rules are not so simple that they allow only the choice between following and breaking them. Consider the way in which you play a game like chess. In order to play chess, rather than draughts, bridge or monopoly, you must follow the rules. They constrain your activity to the extent that they dictate your general aims and specify the strategies appropriate for their achievement. Yet the rules do not dictate either your particular interpretation of them or the way in which you put this interpretation into practice. Your interpretation may be deemed correct if not masterful or it may be regarded as slightly if not completely misconceived (i.e. 'That was a brilliant checkmate' vs. 'That's not quite the right way to move a knight' vs. 'You don't jump men in chess as you do in draughts'). As for the *application* of your interpretation of the rules, here your individual agency becomes obvious. Experienced chess players do not dispute the meaning of the rules of play. They compete with each other against the background of these rules and in ways which provide maximum opportunity for individual self-expression. Chess is a struggle between two individuals freely deciding again and again 'what to do next' but in ways rigorously constrained by the rules of chess. In the context, individual self-expression and social constraint are therefore seen to be perfectly compatible.

Think of your own favourite examples of individual creativity. Take literature, for instance. Here, authors are constrained by a host of rules, beginning with those that govern the intelligible use of language and ending with more specific conventions concerning the 'genre' within which the work itself is to be located. Thus, there is no question that to write a popular and/or critically successful novel, many conventions have to be strictly adhered to. Yet equally there is no question that it is the acceptance of these conventions which itself constitutes the opportunity for an infinitude of individual self-expression which would otherwise be denied. So social rules or social instructions do not constrain people's action through determining precisely what they will do, any more than the language people speak determines what they say. The institutional embodiments of rules (e.g. 'the social system', 'the ruling class', 'the state', 'the church', etc.) do not themselves wield power, or do things at all, any more than a language speaks. However, the knowledge that a person belongs to a given society, church or ruling class does help to explain what they do, just as our knowledge that a person speaks a particular language helps to account for the meaning of what they say. Again, far from impeding individual choice, it should now be clear that the constraint of social rules actually makes it possible. To do anything recognizably creative means to follow and therefore to be – to a greater or lesser extent – constrained by such rules. If it is argued that animals are not so constrained and therefore are more free than humans, the response must be a question: 'But what price such "freedom"?' To be 'free' of rules is to be in the grip of natural laws or of chaotic and arbitrary randomness.

So people have the capacity to choose, whether or not they possess the liberty to do so, and it is precisely the possession of such agency which justifies our concern about human freedom. You do not, for example, worry about whether or not machines are doing what they 'want to'. You may break a machine, switch it off or on, but not deprive it of its liberty.

It is also the possession of individual agency that enables the attribution of moral responsibility, including that of blame for, say, illegally depriving someone of their political liberty. For you to be responsible for your action, you must have been able to do otherwise under just the same conditions as those in which you chose to act as you did. The ascription of blame or praise requires that the conditions under which a person makes a choice could not in themselves be causally sufficient for that choice.

So, suppose that you have a phobia about spiders and found yourself incapable of staying in a room where you think there is one. Then your obligation, say, to cook the dinner in a kitchen with a spider in it is one that you cannot actually perform. If, on the other hand, you found yourself unable to enter the kitchen to steal the housekeeping money, this would be an act of wrongdoing that you could not actually perform. Neither blame nor praise would attach to your reluctance to enter the kitchen in either of these instances. They illustrate, by what they lack, a necessary condition which must obtain before it can be said that a person has an obligation and can be praised for fulfilling it or blamed for not doing so. In order for it to be true to say of you that you ought to do something (cook the dinner), it must be the case that you can do it, as we have repeatedly emphasized. Equally, in order for it to be true that you ought not to do something (steal the housekeeping money), it must be the case that you can do it. If a law of cause and effect governing your phobia prevents you from entering the kitchen, it is not the case that you *can* do what you ought or ought not. For it is only if you are not constrained by a causal law from doing either what you ought or what you ought not that moral responsibility, praise or blame can attach to what you do. It does so because the action you actually perform – not being determined by a causal law – is the action you freely choose to perform.

In general, then, free actions fall into two categories. First, there are the numerous simple, everyday decisions about food, work, rest, etc. which conform to established social norms. Although the scope of such choices will vary with social environment, people will survive in their different ways through acting and not just being acted upon. In these cases, the rules of the social environment within which such activities occur will not be challenged – no matter how rigidly they are enforced. Rather, against the background of the rules as understood, agents formulate individual aims and assess beliefs about their attainment. Even in the most extreme authoritarian situations (e.g. concentration camps) survival has often depended not on flouting the rules but on working creatively within them. Actions which are obviously deviant constitute the second category of freedom even in oppressive social circumstances. Here rules which might or might not be instruments of oppression are flouted, although not necessarily openly. In such situations, the spectrum of deviant activity is extremely wide, ranging from open rebellion at one end through to secret acts of sabotage on the other. Certainly, any admiration expressed for political 'dissidents' reflects a recognition of the fact that it is possible to choose between different courses of action, even in the most difficult circumstances. Conversely, any blame directed towards those who carry out the orders of tyrants similarly presupposes that they too had a choice in the matter. In both cases, the belief that individuals *can* choose to act in different ways rests on the belief that they *do* select from a pre-existing environment of purposes and beliefs in order to make their behaviour understandable to themselves and others.

Consequently, even within highly regimented cultures, people still choose how to interpret rules which they accept as 'natural' for the circumstances in which they find themselves. If they rebel, their act of rebellion must also be understood with reference to the rejection of such rules. There is no difference *in principle* between the way in which you explain the actions of the oppressed or rebellious and those of someone in a supposedly 'free' society. In both cases, you refer to the rules followed by the actors and to their individual interpretations of these rules. When agents say something like 'In our society, we are not free to do what we like', what they usually mean is that they have no say about the institutional rules of their social environment and that they have to interpret them carefully in order to avoid conflict. Since they are not robots, they have to be regarded as capable of entering into such conflict and so it must be assumed that they have *chosen* not to become so engaged. Of course, this decision may or may not be in their best interests and, as we show in the next section, they may well make unintentional mistakes in trying to make such an assessment. However, their ability to discuss whether or not they have made mistakes – indeed their very capacity to make them – presupposes the existence of freedom of agency of a sort which philosophically is no different for politically free and politically unfree activity. But this being said, a new and important problem is now raised. Why does this freedom of agency which we have been stressing not lead to anarchy? Why is so much of social life so regular and predictable? To begin to answer this question we must examine more carefully the ways in which rules socially constrain human activity.

We spent some time in chapter 3 arguing that causally sufficient conditions for actions cannot be specified in terms of the reasons for those actions – however 'reasons' might be construed. In the natural sciences events which are individually unpredictable are generally accommodated within the deductive-nomological pattern of explanation by the use of statistical laws. However, there is a particular limitation upon explanations of this type. If you make a small hole in a container of gas, where the inner pressure is twice that outside the container, then it will escape until the pressure is the same, inside and out. Since the volume of the container remains constant while the pressure is halved, the kinetic theory of gases implies that there will be half as many gas particles left in the container as there were when we began to release the gas. Which half escapes? You do not know, cannot know, and do not need to know. The point of the statistical model is to explain the phenomenon of the equalization of pressure between the inside and outside of the container in terms of the motions of the mass of molecules that it contains. From the standpoint of such a theory, all the molecules of a pure gas are identical in their properties and it is immaterial which individual particles do and which do not pass through the hole.

The unpredictability of human action subject to choice is not like that of gas particles subject to statistical laws. In response to a particular opportunity – say, to buy a secondhand car advertised in a newspaper – it is true that you do not know in advance which individuals will choose to do so or even how many. Yet you would have no hesitation in explaining the actions of those who do offer to buy in terms of the reasons the advert supplies. Advertising managers may have well confirmed statistical generalizations about the effectiveness of their products, but these do not explain the responses to them. One does not need to know why particular gas particles that escape do so – those that escape can be identical to those that remain and particles of that sort always behave in that way in that proportion. By contrast, the small proportion of people who respond to an advert or, say, refrain from stealing when no one could discover them, or conceive an invention, are *different* from those who do not. This is so even though the conditions under which they acted may in all relevant aspects be the same as those experienced by a far larger proportion who did not act thus. To understand the difference between these two groups, it is necessary to understand their respective reasons for performing or not performing the actions in question, remembering that in both cases rules will be followed in the process.

The diehard determinist may accept that statistical laws are inadequate for the explanation of patterns of apparent choice and argue that somehow there just must be fully determining causal laws which govern individual actions in the same way as the individual trajectories of the gas particles. This is not the place to pursue that issue. All that we can say for now is that there could be no rules of any sort if all actions as well as all physical events were determined in this way. If rules can exist, then the notion of choice made within their framework brings a measure of intelligibility to events which are individually unpredictable from a deductive-nomological standpoint. This is particularly important when one considers situations where there is no regularity in the frequency with which people perform an action. Even here you can perfectly well understand the reasons for individual choices. Equally, there are rules which are so widely obeyed that a vanishingly small number of cases arise where they are broken – driving on the left for instance. Yet this regularity in no way persuades you that a statistical law, like that governing gas molecules, is in operation. Unlike a law of nature, whose mere existence explains the events that fall under it, it is the intentional justification of the rule 'Drive on the left' that explains the regularity you observe. You do not understand why people drive this way, unless you understand their reasons.

So the incorporation of choice into the explanation of human action – so that a person is considered capable of doing otherwise even under the very same conditions – is very far from implying that human activity is potentially chaotic because it is free of the constraints of natural laws. To

the extent that you understand the reasons for an action and to the extent
that these reasons are acted upon, you can predict what actors will do in
relevant circumstances, although as we showed in chapter 3, you cannot
necessarily conclude that they will be successful. The existence of rules
and of individual reasons for following them ensures that it is rational for
you to choose how to relate to others on the basis of your expectations
concerning what they will do next in a variety of situations. If you did not
already have this capacity – despite the individuality and uniqueness of
each human – then you would quickly go mad. You would just as quickly
go mad if you tried to base your expectations on either universal or
statistical generalizations about their past actions. Think of the trouble
which lovers get into in this way!

   Yet it still might be argued by the determinist that while this is fine and
good at the level of the individual actor, what happens when one moves
from the individual to society? Surely, the *system* of social institutions
which we identify with society possesses such regular and reoccurring
characteristics that it must be acceptable simply to refer to these in
accounting for the *patterns* which collective actions form. Consider
economic activity, for example. Economists do appear to utilize a
deductive-nomological model in both micro- and macro-economics.
Laws concerning production, consumption and distribution are applied
to particular market conditions and predictions are made and explanations assessed in ways which are apparently similar to those in physics
and chemistry. Economists would not of course deny that producers,
consumers and distributors are all acting for reasons. That is to say, they
are all following rules according to their individual interpretations and
are not believed to be hypnotized or drugged. Yet the explanatory use of
economic 'laws' of the market and their success in yielding correct
predictions of market behaviour do seem to suggest that there is at least a
close analogy between social rules and such laws. To the extent that this
analogy is taken seriously, might it not be argued that determinism has
crept in through the back door bringing with it the denial of the
explanatory significance of individual freedom in human affairs?

   There are two problems with this argument. The first is that, like the
other examples of coercion considered above, 'economic reality' constrains but does not abolish choice. There will always be a 'foolish'
option open to you, although on the assumption that you have an
understanding of where your economic interests lie, you can generally be
relied upon to choose the course of action which best serves them. The
business person who because of 'market forces' has to choose between sack-
ing many workers and going bankrupt can be compared with the chess
player who has to choose between checkmate and the sacrifice of the queen
– except that business is not a game. Other members of society will either
withhold co-operation or even phsyically coerce you if you break these
rules. But of course people do break them and suffer the consequences when
their assets are seized. Unlike the law of gravity, the laws of the
market, as well as laws in the legal sense, have to be enforced. Their
regular and reoccurring pattern is a result of their enforcement and

learned acceptance – not of their causal necessity. The market is a human institution governed though not determined by normative rules. It is not a natural phenomenon which would proceed independently of the conscious participation of those affected by it.

Yet to the extent that they are not challenged, rules feel as if they have a life of their own. They dictate what is right and wrong – what must be done and how it should be attempted. They convey their sense of determination precisely because they are accepted. Think again about those rules which you do not accept. Here, your feeling is not one of determination of 'rightness' or 'naturalness' but of oppression. This is because, in most cases, the rules you reject are clearly identifiable with the social practices of some group whose aims and beliefs you dispute. Similarly, think of those examples in history (e.g. the French or Russian Revolutions) where long-standing institutional rules were overthrown because of dramatic alterations in social practices. These examples indicate that, far from themselves determining social practices, rules are in fact merely their linguistic expression. That is to say, it is the practices themselves which give credence to specific formulations of such rules – which determine what sorts of aims are acceptable and what sorts of beliefs are correct. Therefore when rules are oppressive, it is not the rules as such which are socially constraining but those *people* who accept and follow them. Even the rules of chess could change, provided enough people could be persuaded to change them.

To see this more clearly, consider the example of what are probably the most rigid and precise rules of all – those of mathematics. Surely, one might argue, the correctness of mathematical calculations is determined by their conformity with the essential truths of mathematics, which exist externally to any particular mathematical practice. What sense could it make, for example, to claim that the rules of addition would change if enough people decided to add in other ways? Yet this is precisely what we are suggesting. Assume, for example, that you were trying to explain to someone the meaning of the mathematical expression 'add 2' and that they indicated that they understood you by writing out the following sequence: 2, 4, 6, 8, 10 . . . etc. Suppose, however, that when they got to 100, they then continued: 104, 108, 112, etc. No doubt you would then inform them that they were mistaken. But think about exactly why. You might say, 'Because the rule said add 2.' But their *interpretation* of the rule might well have been add 2 until 100 and then add 2 *more* thereafter. If you replied, 'But that's not the *correct* interpretation,' then we would still be no closer to understanding exactly what *made* it incorrect and, by implication, your own interpretation the correct one. In fact, all that you have to go on in such cases is the shared mathematical practice of the culture of which you are a part. The interpretation in question is incorrect not because it violates an essential mathematical truth existing in some quantitative heaven but because it is inconsistent with accepted practice.

This is an important insight. It illustrates once again how rules are normative but not in themselves causal and can be broken without ceasing to be rules – as long as they are not broken too often. So when people talk of rules – including, as we show later, the rules of language – they are primarily talking not about immutable physical realities but about people and their social relationships. Everyone participates in making cultural rules what they are. Hence one cannot divorce oneself entirely even from those social practices which one claims not to like but continues to participate in (e.g. 'It's nothing to do with me, guv . . . '). More positively, however, it follows from the preceding analysis that most rules – although, as we show later, perhaps not all – may in principle be changed, provided enough people *choose* to alter their social practices. This is a point of fundamental philosophical and moral importance.

In our discussion of freedom, we have drawn many analogies between social life, language and games. But those analogies should not be pushed too far. Language obviously lacks many of the most important features of social life, expressed at its most basic in the saying 'Sticks and stones may break my bones, but names will never hurt me'. Games are such that you can opt out of them at will. But you cannot do the same with social life – if you want to eat! Furthermore where games usually serve purposes which are easily recognizable, the same cannot be said of the institutional rules of social life. The role which they play in the life of their members and in society at large is vastly more complicated than it may at first appear. Even in the case of the Soviet communist party, an institution which has the most explicit conception of its role in transforming Soviet society, it quickly became apparent that the rules governing its operation had many consequences other than those it explicitly avowed – many of which were in fact antithetical to the intentions of its founders. While you usually know just what you are doing when you participate in a game, the purposes served by social action are not generally so transparent.

This question of conscious participation brings us to the second problem with the parallel between institutions governed by rules and causal mechanisms governed by natural laws. The notion of 'conscious participation' in social activity would seem to presuppose that those who participate understand what they are doing. The explanation of actions in terms of conscious reasons which are clear to the agent – for example, the case of answering adverts or driving on the left – certainly seems to make this presupposition. By contrast, explanations of social phenomena in terms of natural laws governing causally necessary processes assume that the events thus explained will occur regardless of whether or not people know what is happening. On the one side, the explanation proceeds in terms of explicit reasons which can be assumed to be part of the self-understanding of the participants. On the other side, the operation of causal laws proceeds quite independently of any such understanding. The weather is a good example of the latter. People may adopt all sorts of strategies to mitigate the effects of the weather and seek to predict it as accurately as they can. But the wind will blow and the rain will fall regardless of whether anyone understands why. The temptation is to view, say, the economy in much the same way because, just like people being caught in a storm, individuals seem to find themselves caught up willy-nilly by forces beyond their control. Yet the character of any economy seems determined by nothing more than the aggregate of all the individual economic actions of the people who participate in it; and these actions are consciously chosen. How can these two perspectives be reconciled?

In order for it to be said of people that the actions they perform are theirs, they must be making choices. We have repeatedly shown that to do so they must follow rules, consciously or not. But this need not mean that they fully understand the rules they follow or that they are actually doing what they think they are doing. Let us take a simple and well understood example – a run on a bank. The rumour goes round that a certain bank is in difficulties, and depositors all rush to withdraw their funds. Because the bank lends as well as borrows, not all the money deposited is sitting in the vaults for the depositors to withdraw on demand. All the depositors, however, think that they are safeguarding their money and demand that the bank pays them on the spot. Unable to realize its assets in time, the bank cannot meet these demands and none of the depositors is repaid in full. What the depositors individually think is the significance of their action – safeguarding their money – is not what they are collectively doing which is to bring about the collapse of the bank. In this sense, the collective significance of their actions is *opaque* to them, though not necessarily to others.

Though simplistic in social terms, this example nonetheless illustrates four important points. First, the actions of the depositors are clearly theirs and follow from their understanding of the situation in which they found themselves. Had they not understood the rumour about the bank's impending failure in the way they did, they would not have acted accordingly. Second, it was an objective feature of the situation, and not some subjective interpretation, which gave their actions their real as opposed to their intended significance. This highlights the difference between the intended and unintended consequences of their actions. The latter can rebound on the former in ways which depend upon the aggregate effects of individual actions, effects which individuals them-selves may well have no awareness of. Third, the opacity of individual actions in their collective form may be fairly readily penetrated, so that an alternative course of collective action might suggest itself – for example, a meeting of all the creditors to make an assessment of how best to secure the future of the bank and with it of their savings. Fourth, the superior self-understanding which would have enabled the depositors to act with greater rational autonomy and responsibility was of a sort that could only be possessed *collectively*. The predicament of the depositors is essentially a social one. That this social character must at least potentially be reflected by any improvement in human self-awareness can be seen by referring back to the argument that the conceptual task of understanding yourself is no different from the task of understanding others. It is for this reason that literature which emerges from the most intimate self-examination is also intelligible and illuminating for others, rather than senseless scribble with no application to anyone but the author.

We have analysed freedom into two components, freedom of the will and political liberty – the *capacity* and *opportunity* to make choices. We have argued that the capacity to make choices and the ability to follow rules are necessarily linked to one another. Unless they can be interpreted as choices between meaningful alternatives in relation to the following or breaking of some rule, events that are not determined by natural laws are random, arbitrary and unintelligible, except in terms of aggregate statistical frequencies. This is what makes so much of social life predictable, even though the basis of the predictability is not the same as it is for the physical world. Rules themselves are necessarily social in character and so too must be the exercise of the capacity to make choices. Enjoyment of the opportunity to make choices – liberty – and its antithesis – coercion – are even more clearly social in character, as we argued above. So it is not surprising that we should claim that it must also be the case that people always acquire and develop the capacity and opportunity to choose either with the help or opposition of others. Thus it is in just this way – by means ranging from direct forceful coercion, through legitimate authority, to the indirect channels of contract and consent – that some people exercise power over others. Anthony Giddens has called this necessary involvement of agency on both sides of a relationship which limits the liberty of one of the parties to it 'the dialectic of control'. Whether you wield power or have it wielded over you, you equally need to be a rule-following agent. Institutions as such do not exercise power independently of their containing some people to whom power is given and others who are willing to obey. Individual freedom and societal constraint remain, therefore, two sides of the same ontological coin – human action.

Although the capacity and opportunity to make choices may analytically be separated, they do not occur in isolation. To explore the intricacies of their relationship further, it is useful to introduce a phrase which is more explicit and less ambiguous than the simple word 'freedom' – *human rational autonomy*. A person possesses rational autonomy when he or she has the capacity and opportunity to make choices in the full knowledge of their significance. Of course, no one possesses this in full, but children possess it hardly at all at the start of their conscious lives and its growth is a characteristic feature of the child's development into an adult – or it should be. Denial by oppressive authority of the opportunity to act responsibly both removes the right of adults to expand their understanding of themselves and stultifies the development of responsibility in the child. This is why rational autonomy is so valued. Children are not allowed to exercise complete freedom because it is supposed that they do not appreciate the significances of the choices involved. Some activities – injecting heroin, for instance – are forbidden by governments because, among other things, addiction has the effect of distorting the addict's appreciation of the significance of choices to be made: it impairs rational autonomy. Personal autonomy is a social accomplishment, which may or may not be achieved to the fullest degree. The term 'freedom' focuses attention only on its necessary conditions – namely that you can exercise rational autonomy only if you are not coerced to do what you do. But freedom from coercion is not enough – you also have to understand the significance of your actions. The necessity for self-awareness and self-understanding in the achievement of rational autonomy links these points with themes from the previous chapter where we concluded that people acquire their identities as persons as a consequence of their own social development. This means that the extent to which an individual develops the capacity to achieve autonomy and responsibility will be influenced by the social circumstances in which he or she grows to maturity.

While these considerations point to an important area for empirical inquiry in social science (e.g. in the fields of deviance and social deprivation), they do not imply that conceptions of rational autonomy are wholly relative to the empirical characteristics of different social systems. By criticizing crude mentalism and arguing for a social-developmental component to the notion of rational autonomy, we have attacked the way in which rational autonomy is widely articulated today. The notion of the heroic, self-sufficient, free individual gains its plausibility by overemphasizing one aspect of rational autonomy to the exclusion of those we have sought to reinstate. The rules of the vocabulary you employ to describe and explain yourself to yourself and others must, like those of chess or mathematics, be socially acquired. But at the same time, once you have mastered them they do allow you to reason about yourself and your actions, by yourself. Indeed, this is precisely what makes the achievement of self-awareness at the same time the achievement of autonomy. The defect of the view of the mind as wholly self-sufficient is that, mesmerized by its own autonomy, the speculative intellect fails to inquire *from* what and *from* whom the possibility of creative choice derives. However, by the same token, those who stress the social origin of self-understanding risk robbing the concept of all its explanatory relevance in accounting for human action if they fail to acknowledge the capacity of people to reason *independently* and so to be the authors of their actions and utterances. Without some measure of independent reasoning, the concepts of action and utterance at an individual level disappear. Institutions or societies do not act, nor do languages speak.

In general, then, we have shown that there is no incompatibility between human freedom and the social rules on which all free action is predicated. On this view, individual autonomy becomes linked as much to education – to understanding the individual and collective consequences of choosing to follow (or to break) rules in particular ways – as to having the actual opportunity for such choices. Defining autonomy in this way underlines the possibility of its being limited by both ignorance and coercion. Indeed, we shall now show that contrary to popular belief ignorance can be as great an obstacle to the exercise of liberty as outright coercion. One thing is clear. Were social actions transparent in the social significance of their associated rules, there would be no mysteries for social scientists to unravel: footballers do not need to have their game explained to them when they come off the pitch in the same way that planners need to understand the societies which they attempt to plan.

Ideology and human understanding

We have argued that it is not contradictory to believe both that individuals can choose what they do and that choice is always socially constrained. We have also shown that individual people are not necessarily the best judges of what they are doing or of how successfully they are doing it. These ideas will now be taken a stage further to enable us to solve a problem which has probably already bothered some readers. Time and again we have insisted that when people can be said to act, it is because they can be said to choose. Many of the examples which we have given to support this contention have shown how actors try to achieve what they perceive to be in their interests through choosing to interpret rules in particular ways. Thus, we have used games as a consistent source of illustrations because there is no question that competitors are acting in just this way.

But one might well question such examples, arguing that they place too much importance on freedom of agency through focusing on situations where actors are in a position to do what they want – albeit in accordance with rules. What about those situations where people are clearly not acting in their own interests? 'It's all fine and good,' you might continue, 'to argue that people can change social rules by helping to change the social practices which give them their significance. So why don't they, then, for example in exploitative situations where acts of successful resistance are clearly possible?' If we answered this question merely by saying, 'Because they do not choose to do so,' this would rightly be regarded as vacuous. To defend our approach to explaining human action we must show how actors who choose not to act in their own interests do so without realizing the full significance of their refusal – do so thinking that they are doing one thing when they are in fact doing another. To understand how such mistakes are possible for groups as well as individuals, it is now necessary to examine the *ideological* character of much human activity.

To begin, consider a little more closely what one might mean by 'interests'. There is much confusion surrounding this concept, much of which arises from not differentiating perceived interests from real interests or (assuming that it is in your interest to try to acquire what you need) perceived needs from real needs. In ordinary language, perceived needs are identified as wants: 'I want a new car, a new stereo, a steak for dinner, a holiday in Tahiti, a victory in all my forthcoming chess matches, and so on.' What are identified as 'real' needs (e.g. minimum standards of health, nutrition, education, housing, recreation, etc.) may or may not overlap with what people declare they want. Doubtless many people believe that they need at least one of the above examples of wants but would be hard pressed to justify this belief. Medically uninformed diabetics might want sugar but need insulin. Children may want a variety of things that they do not need and so forth. Of course, this is not to say that actors never want what they also need. Needs are obviously at the root of many wants. For example, the desire for particular kinds of food is often – in part at least – an expression of the need for a basic level of nutrition. But, this being said, the distinction between wants and needs is a fundamental one which everyone makes in a variety of contexts. Think of the last time you said to someone about an object of their desire, 'But do you really need it?' Also consider the political debates which surround pronouncements such as, 'They may want a pay rise but they don't need it.'

This distinction between wants and needs has profound and often highly problematic implications for the understanding of human action which we explore further both at the end of this chapter and in chapter 8. For the present, we will simply assume that there is such a distinction, that all ordinary people use it, and that it concerns the types of things which they try to achieve or avoid in their everyday lives. We can then go on to show why the fact that actors do not always act in their own interests – i.e. do not attempt to satisfy what it may be argued are their real needs – does not invalidate the explanatory model of human action which has been elaborated.

It should now be clear that in order to do anything (i.e. recognizably to follow identifiable rules) you have to be taught both the appropriate language and the relevant set of skills. Two important consequences follow from this. First, the particular social environment in which you learn largely determines what you perceive as needs and wants and what you see as the relationship between them. The fact that you have to be taught how to act is – ironically – just another way of saying that you have to be taught what to want and whether or not you really need what you want. For example, you will not want a car unless you have some of the understanding and skill associated with driving one. Yet even if you have those skills, it is doubtful that you will buy one unless you also believe that you need it – for work, play, fulfilment or whatever. Second, still operating on the assumption that we can unproblematically believe that some needs are real irrespective of what actors have been taught (e.g. that an excess of certain foods is bad for you whatever you may want), it now becomes possible to explain how people can learn freely to act against their real needs. Since freedom of agency is always exercised in the context of consciously perceived aims and beliefs which do not *necessarily* represent the real interests of the agent, actors may easily try to satisfy wants which they do not need. Indeed, they may be taught or encouraged to do just that.

Think again about all of those dramatic mistakes which you have freely made in your life. When you think 'If I had only known then what I know now', you are not assuming that the mistakes in question were not *yours*. Indeed, you may well have thought that you were being quite clever at the time and, against your own background of accepted rules, your creative formulation of aims and beliefs may well have been quite spectacular. For many people their first long-term relationship often provides ample illustration of this phenomenon. The relevant rules are learned in an adolescent subculture and the patterns of courtship activity that then occur can be individually creative to the point of genius. Yet later you can recognize them as folly and even as violating your current principles of love, compassion and human dignity. But in so far as you participated in what now seem foolish or even degrading spectacles, it was not because of your lack of freedom. It was rather a function of what you had been taught was normal. So if actors are taught to have purposes and beliefs which are not in accordance with their real needs, they will continue *freely* to act against their interests – at least until they have found the means of formulating their interests in alternative and more accurate ways.

This possibility not only shows how individuals can be taught freely to act against their best interests, it also makes it easier to understand how some social groups can control what other groups do without the use of physical force or any other form of overt oppression. Such power is derived from the capacity to shape the consciousness of others. For example, there may have been a time when your parents and teachers instructed you to believe that you should act in ways which you now realize were against your own interests. Indeed, the wants which they teach you to see as your real needs may well be positively damaging. Feminist writers, for instance, have documented the disastrous influence of much parental and social teaching on the formulation of sexual identity. Thus girls are often taught that they are not as innately intelligent or generally capable as boys and should therefore have different expectations about their creative potential. It is important to emphasize however that, having been socialized in this way, women are not being denied their freedom of *agency*. They can still interpret creatively the rules associated with, say, being a housewife, a poorly paid industrial or health worker, or a primary school teacher, as is evidenced by the success they often individually achieve in these activities.

Through their control over channels of argument and persuasion, a wide range of powerful interest groups shape our attitudes about needs. Those with such power do not have to be insincere or disingenuous, although they sometimes are. The 'motoring lobby', for example, are – to a man – passionately in love with cars. Because their sincere persuasion serves their own interests so well they become ever more powerful – shaping our environment into an *objective* force that shapes our needs. Just think of how the image of the motor car has reached almost mythic proportions in popular literature, films and songs. If they were to be transported to our society, innocent Aztecs would be astounded at the carnage the populace willingly inflicts upon itself at the altar of a myth of freedom and potency which is far more obviously bogus than the Sun-God!

Those who exercise power through controlling understanding are not necessarily conscious of whatever they are helping to perpetuate. They may well believe that their teaching is in the best interests of all

concerned and will often identify their own wants and needs with those
which they impart to others. Equally, we do not intend to paint an overly
passive picture of the learner – refusal to go along with orthodox
teaching is always a possibility. Yet the degree to which this is possible
will – in part at least – depend on the existence of alternative rules which
the deviant actor can learn and interpret. Without such an alternative
culture or subculture it will be difficult for an actor to develop the
appropriate consciousness for the implementation of deviant actions.
Against the background of the need to learn to act, this is just another
way of saying that to challenge authority successfully, you must have
alternative guidelines as to what will constitute a meaningful and
successful challenge – a recognition which, incidentally, puts paid to all
crudely individualistic forms of anarchism as adequate theories of social
and political change. Again, rules and action – even of the most
revolutionary kind – go hand in hand.

It might be objected that it is both dangerously arrogant and highly
implausible to maintain that people are largely ignorant of the real
interests their actions serve. A liberal individualist might concede, 'I may
not be the best judge of my own best interests but I would still prefer that
I should judge rather than have my future decided by someone claiming
to know what is best for me.' However, any investigation that reveals
that people are *not* correctly judging their best interest will hopefully
persuade them to act differently. Far from removing personal control of
their own lives, such understanding will make possible a measure of
control that they had previously lacked. Moreover, the reality is likely to
be that most individuals are heavily constrained by the actions of
strangers primarily concerned with what they perceive to be *their*
interests, for example, the profit of the enterprise for which they work.
Until now we have given only scattered examples of how individuals may
misrepresent the way their society works. A more systematic breakdown
of the possible varieties of such error is as follows: misunderstanding
natural laws; misunderstanding social rules; mistaking natural laws for
social rules; and mistaking social rules for natural laws.

Like unsuspecting diabetics who do not realize that they should not eat
sugar, people may be unaware of the natural laws governing hygiene, soil
management, nutrition and the like, which similarly affect their well-
being. This means that they are ignorant of the laws of cause and effect
which determine whether the outcome of their actions will benefit them,
regardless of their intentions. Thus they may try to satisfy their basic
needs in impossible ways or they may mistake wants for needs in the
ways already described. On the other hand, the example of the run on the
bank illustrates a lack of appreciation on the part of the depositors of the
character of the social rules in which they participate. Thinking to
advance their own interests, they rush into actions which bring about
their ruin. Unlike the chess example, however, their downfall requires no
opponent to take advantage of their not having seen the implications of
their actions. Rather it is just that the significance which each withdrawal
would have had if done in isolation is not the same as each has

when all the depositors withdraw their money from the bank at once.

Not only may people be ignorant of the natural laws governing their actions and of the rules they follow when they perform them, they may also mistake one for the other. So there is a type of error, still not uncommon in modern society, which is disparagingly called 'superstition'. This is where events which are actually governed by natural laws are believed to fall under the same sorts of rules that constrain human conduct. For example, a good harvest might be regarded as a reward for the appropriate religious observances – as tokens of reverence towards a divine or spiritual agency which chooses whether or not the sun shines or the rain falls. Such beliefs may have a substantial part to play in the regulation of social life in some traditional communities. In western society it plays a minor role, but even today there are people who claim that the new disease AIDS is some sort of divine retribution for what is regarded as 'immoral' conduct. And just as the operation of natural laws can be mistaken for the actions of a supernatural agent, so the converse error is possible. This is all too common and arises when the consequences of following social rules are mistaken for the consequences of the operation of natural laws. Thus, some believe that the sexual division of labour in society is determined by 'Nature', despite the fact that boys and girls spend years learning their future roles. This error is often termed 'reification' – the attribution of a spurious thing-like or natural character to what is in fact the product of human activity.

The 'value' of gold is a fine example of reification and also shows why Marx chose to call this error 'fetishism'. Though gold is undoubtedly attractive and has some uses (e.g. for dentists), it also has an aura of intrinsic value, as though its possession were a more dependable form of wealth than any other. The emotive term 'fetishism' seems peculiarly appropriate when one recalls that governments uselessly hoard huge quantities of the stuff as a monetary talisman with the magic property of giving their paper money its value. Obviously, a monetary system could be devised if the element gold were not found in the earth's crust. Its value is no more than an artefact of human monetary superstition, which was by no means abolished when currencies were taken off the 'gold standard'. It is merely the scarcity of gold which enables it to perform its economic function. If the medieval alchemists had actually found a way to make as much gold as they wanted from other metals, then it would have become as 'intrinsically valueless' as paper money, which can be produced in any quantity. It is the idea that value is a natural attribute, so that goods may be exchanged in proportion to how much of it they possess, which convinces people that they cannot do what in fact they can. In principle, people could decide that goods should be supplied in proportion to their *usefulness* – how much they contribute to satisfying needs – rather than in proportion to market demand.

Superstition clearly involves humans either imagining that they can change what is actually unalterable or thinking that their devout participation is necessary to produce what would happen anyway. Such beliefs stand in the way of the discovery of natural laws and condemn those who share them to pointless efforts and groundless fears. By contrast, whenever the methods of the natural sciences are applied where they do not belong, the phenomenon of reification constantly threatens. It works to render the possibility of choice invisible. People who are capable of exercising their rational autonomy are convinced otherwise by doctrines which misrepresent social rules as natural laws. For if they mistakenly believe that something in their lives is the consequence of a law of nature and so unalterable, then it will never strike them that there is any alternative to choose. Moreover, even if some people do attempt to criticize such beliefs and to alter their consciousness and circumstances accordingly, they may well be derided by others for making futile efforts to 'change nature'. So, for example, when oppressed groups claim the right of equal standing in society, 'facts of nature' are paraded by their opponents to demonstrate that their aspirations are ridiculous. The weight of beliefs and expectations that stem from assuming that inherently social arrangements are rational in this sense creates the very circumstances which then appear to confirm them. For example, if a woman accepts that her 'natural place is in the home' then she will not attempt to work outside it, will regard other women who have the same views as normal and those who do not as abnormal. The more women she meets in situations similar to her own, the more she will (falsely) believe that her lifestyle is inevitable.

Ideology and politics

A further characteristic of ideological understanding has been implicit in our discussion thus far. As we have already pointed out, everyone has experienced situations where they have been deceived into formulating false beliefs and into regarding a particular state of affairs as natural or normal. But not all misunderstandings of this kind are necessarily ideological. To use a cliché, we all make mistakes − but the resulting errors need not tell us about anything other than our gullibility as actors. For a set of mistaken beliefs to be ideological, it has actually to keep one group in a position of power over another. It is for this reason that the identification of modes of consciousness as ideological can be a complicated affair, since it involves much more than just the recognition of distortion and misleading beliefs. It is also necessary to have a theory about the social situation within which such beliefs occur. At the very least, such theories consist of hypotheses about the different groups which make up the situation, their real and perceived interests, how power is distributed between them and, most important of all, how these various factors combine to form the mode of material production that ensures the survival of the group as a whole. This should be clear if you think back to previous examples, since their meaning was to a considerable extent dependent on prior theoretical assumptions about the social groups concerned (e.g. women and the social role of domestic labour). It is in this sense that identifying a particular type of understanding as ideological is − at least in part − an exercise in *political* analysis.

As a more detailed illustration of what is meant by an analysis of this kind, consider the institution of slavery. It is hardly tendentious to claim that this is a clear case where one group exploited another, but the institution was not maintained simply by brute force. Read *Uncle Tom's Cabin* – not a fashionable book these days – and you will see how much power an ideology can exert. The perpetuation of a slave society requires that everyone – masters and slaves alike – believe that slaves are inherently inferior beings. Even now we use the word 'slavish' in a derogatory sense. Slaves were not just taught this as an intellectual idea. Because of their economic relationship with their masters, everything about their material circumstances contributed to an experience of themselves as dirty, stupid, ugly, cowardly and brutal. Their environment had already brutalized them, destroyed their pride, deformed their bodies, kept them ignorant and deprived them of the means of civilized existence. All their experience confirmed the general, ideological belief about them – they hardly needed to be told as well. Thus slaves often became convinced that they could never obtain and indeed did not deserve those benefits denied them. Understandbly, they mistook the reality of their particular situation as the only possibility open to them. For their part, when the masters experienced the self-demeaning actions of their slaves, they became even more convinced that their position of dominance was right and natural.

This is not to claim that slaves were incapable of ever understanding the falsity of the ideology which legitimated their position. After all, why else would the instruments of forceful coercion have been necessary, if not to guard against just this possibility? But even the use of force in society requires similar legitimation. To see this, you only have to look at the way the labels 'terrorist' as opposed to 'freedom fighter' and 'forces of law and order' as opposed to 'authoritarian state' are applied by people with different perspectives in such places as Poland, South Africa, Afghanistan, El Salvador or Northern Ireland. It also illustrates a further feature that ideologies must possess to perform the task of justifying political power. They must make a claim to *universal validity*. The actions of a 'freedom fighter', for example, are presumed to have the justification that the actions of a 'terrorist' lack. The actions of the 'forces of law and order' are taken on behalf of society against a minority which threatens it, while those of 'authoritarian state' are seen as the actions of a government without popular support. In general, if an ideology succeeds in misrepresenting social and economic life in the interests of the exercise of power by one group over others, it will do so because it presents the exercise of that power, or the consequences of its exercise, as being right or natural, without qualification. What will be obscured by such claims to universality will be the sectional interests served by the organization of social and economic life that the ideology legitimates.

As the example of slavery shows, ideological modes of understanding can of course affect the consciousness of both exploited and exploiter, albeit in different ways. Both groups share the incorrect beliefs involved. Again, it is not as if the exploiters were analogous, say, to a used car salesman who knew all along that the customer did not need or could not afford his wares. Since both groups are socialized into the same environment of rules, it is hardly surprising that exploiters will often be amazed by accusations of trickery and injustice. In other words, despite the contradictory interests of the two groups, the consciousness of the members of both is often quite similar. Of course, this is not to say that exploiters and exploited are never aware of the falsity of their under-standing. This is clearly possible provided that they have somehow been introduced to alternative conceptual perspectives. In situations of relative social stability, where the process of reification is strongest, the ideology of the day will usually prove resilient and existing social relations will be perpetuated by the free activity of oppressed and oppressor.

To recognize false consciousness from *within* the set of social relations which nourishes it, it is necessary to become critical – to develop the perspective of an outside assessor. This means trying to determine whether or not what people say about their mode of social organization – including yourself if you happen to be a member – makes the sense which they claim it does. But as our previous discussions of such assessment indicate (e.g. in the case of trials by jury), this is no easy task. At the very least, it will involve suspending your own convictions about the situation in question in order to 'see' even the possibility of other options. Yet since we are assuming that the assessment is taking place from within the social relations under scrutiny, there are no clear external standards by which to judge the ideological status of specific aims and beliefs. In short, because of the problem of reification, the appearance of the social relations will always tend to confirm the already accepted views about it. Yet it is these views themselves which are under critical review. To carry out the review, it is therefore necessary to formulate alternative explana-tions of the social relations in question, explanations which attempt to go behind their appearance and to determine what is really going on.

As an illustration of this, consider the development of modern feminism. So much of western society is characterized by sexist beliefs and practices that in the early stages the 'revolutionary' claims of feminists were said to be refuted by what other women said about themselves and their daily lives. But what was necessary was to look behind these appearances to determine whether or not sexist beliefs were consistent with the very activities which they purported to explain. When this search for inconsistency got under way, it revealed a host of contradictions between what was said about the natural abilities and suitable occupations of women and what they had really achieved both in the past and also the present. As regards the past, the crucial role which women have played in the development of the modern economy was uncovered, along with many important writers, artists, critics and just wonderful human beings who had been hidden from history. Concerning the present, many theories which women themselves had used to justify their situation were shown to be false (e.g. the belief that infants will be emotionally damaged if they are looked after by people other than their mothers, the belief that domestic labour is somehow of less importance than other forms of work). In both these respects, women helped each other to try to strip appearance from reality through providing the courage necessary to question assumptions about themselves which they had previously taken for granted.

So ideological perceptions of the social world are false to the extent that they can be shown to contradict what is viewed as acceptable evidence to the contrary. This is not to declare the unreality of actions which are made intelligible through false beliefs. Ideological illusions, if illusions they are, are real in the grip they have on the collective imagination – in the irrational order they impart to the organization and character of what is produced (e.g. pyramids, cathedrals, motorways, etc.). In one sense, provided that people are honest, then obviously they do what they think they are doing. Otherwise, the distinction between behaviour and action – between what you do as opposed to what is done to you – would collapse. Yet in another sense, we have shown that people may not be doing what they think they are doing at all. They may be mistaken about the rules which they are following or about the overall significance of the aims and beliefs which they hold, as a slave, a worker or a child might be. In this sense, people's perceptions of the reality of their activity – of what exactly it is they are doing – will alter in accordance with how they account for it. This is because of the close relationship between the way an action is explained and identified. For example, if your understanding of the wage contract is that it is a fair bargain between employer and employee, this is obviously how you will perceive it. However, if at some future point you reject this understanding of it you will describe the action quite differently. It will mean, and in a sense it will *be*, something else.

Perceptions of the physical world are not refuted in the same way by the falsifications of accepted explanations of them. For example, the discovery of a better theory of light did not entail the falsity of the existing empirical descriptions of the behaviour of light. Rather, it was precisely the truth of these descriptions that made their adequate explanation by an underlying causal mechanism an important achievement (e.g. the wave theory of light). Theories about such mechanisms, combined with hypotheses about their interaction with the sensory organs, purport to show that the phenomena to be explained *must* have the empirical character which they do. But an analysis of the real character of, say, the wage relation against the background of everyday assumptions about justice, equality and private property, shows exactly the opposite. For example, once it is realized that modern production is basically social and that low-paid labour is just as essential for the creation of a final product as more highly paid labour, then wage differentials become much more difficult to defend. Similarly, if private property is believed to be justified because it has been earned through labour, then in what sense are owners of firms who do nothing for their profits entitled to them? In such circumstances, the ideological and hence false appearance of justice may fall like scales from the eyes.

Consequently, when an ideological representation of some social practice is revealed as incoherent, it contradicts what is generally believed to be a more accurate identification and analysis of the activity in question. To the extent that you recognize its incoherence, the representation will no longer be usable in that you will be incapable of continuing to perceive the social practice in the way that you did. Think, for example, of a time in your life when you suddenly realized that your previous understanding of a person close to you was so inaccurate that you could never regard them in the same way again. In such situations, your perception changes with your understanding in the same way that any simple acceptance of the dictum 'a fair day's work for a fair day's pay' is eroded by a detailed analysis of the contradiction of the wage relation. Looked at a little differently, you cannot continue to pray in any meaningful way if you cease to believe in God. Yet the social significance of prayer does not vanish but remains something real in the sense that it is an activity in which others do believe and which you might well wish to understand both as a significant social phenomenon and as a partial explanation of whatever social influence the church continues to possess.

It should now be clear how people can act freely – though often unknowingly – against their own interests. It should be equally clear how, at least in principle, people can use their freedom to *discover* that they were acting in just such a way. Without freedom of agency neither exploitation nor liberation could occur. But it is important not to claim too much here, since it is one thing to develop a coherent theory of what ideology is but quite another to be able to apply the concept correctly. This is especially true when the merit or otherwise of a particular mode of understanding is a matter of heated debate. In analysing both the concept of false consciousness and that of exploitation, we have so far chosen examples where we suspected that everyone would agree. For instance, there can be few who do not believe that slavery in the United States was based on false premises about the abilities and needs of blacks and that slavery as an institution worked against their real interests and in the interests of slave-owners. Yet, good as this example is from one perspective, it is misleading from another, producing the slight feeling of unease which a few readers may have had with our other examples. For when it comes to questions relating to women or ethnic groups and their 'natural' abilities and needs in the here and now, there still remains disagreement and debate. Thus while obviously endorsing our own view about the ideological status of claims concerning female inferiority, we would be foolish to deny that disputes of this kind can pose problems in the attribution of ideological status to particular beliefs – problems which will raise the theme of our next two chapters.

To show what we mean in more detail, we now return to our earlier analysis of what it means to decide that you are acting against your real interests and furthering those of another. In order to make such a decision it is obviously necessary to identify what your respective interests are. This can be done if there is agreement about which interests are real and which merely perceived – that is, which aims constitute needs and which are only wants. But what do you do when there does not appear to be such agreement – when the starting points in a dispute about ideology are radically different? For example, it is all too possible for someone with sexist beliefs to claim that the real needs of women are related primarily to various forms of domesticity. And given our discussion in chapter 1 of Kuhn's concept of a paradigm, you know that once such theoretical first principles are accepted then empirical data can be interpreted accordingly. This means that as long as commitment to those principles continues, there seems to be no simple way of refuting them empirically. So when presented with evidence that many women flourish outside the home, our sexist might respond that what he claimed was that evidence also exists that some women are very unhappy at work. You might counter with the argument that his denial of your evidence was dogmatic and that to the extent that his evidence was correct, it was because women had to compete with men on unfair terms (e.g. having to work and look after a family). But then he would probably accuse *you* of dogmatism and search for other strategies for dismissing your position. As we also showed in chapter 1, such strategies will always be available. Thus the protagonists in this illustration seem to be caught in an argumentative circle which would lead each to draw different lines between false and correct consciousness and between what is and is not exploitative.

'But surely,' it might be argued, 'there should at least be consistency between what is believed and what is practised.' Presumably the sexist, for instance, cannot have it both ways. He cannot claim in one situation that women are suited only for domestic labour and also continue to rely on them to work skilfully and reliably in his business. And, of course, this is true provided that he wants it both ways. However, what happens if he does not? Just because there is a conflict between practice and principle does not mean that the principles involved are false when viewed normatively. What should be done in the face of contradictory practice seems always open to debate. There are always other possibilities than giving up the normative beliefs to which one is committed. For example, the sexist could decide to remain consistent through ceasing to employ female workers. Or he might agree that there is a conflict between his principle and his practice but still deny that this meant his principles were wrong (e.g. through arguing that if women choose to work when it is not in their real interests then that is up to them). So if by 'ideological' we mean 'shown to be normatively wrong in practice', then it appears only to be unambiguously applicable when there are already agreed beliefs about real and perceived interests. In short, social practices have to be interpreted as to their normative consequences. The fact that the beliefs which are employed to determine those consequences are the same as those which will be used to describe the practice in question (e.g. sexist consequences follow from sexist descriptions of women at work) only serves to underline the argumentative circle in which we seem to be ensnared.

'What's wrong with this?' it might be asked. After all, was it not argued at the beginning of the chapter that the identity and assessment of human action is determined by rules which themselves gain their meaning from collective assent and constraint? This apparently means that provided enough people use language in the same ways then they can do anything they like socially. For example, if 'theft' or some accurate translation of it is not a part of the conceptual environment of a culture then theft will not exist for its members. Why should the same not apply to the identification and assessment of human interests? One would then argue that at different times and in different societies, beliefs about needs, wants, rights and justice are formulated in different ways and that these should be respected. At first glance, there is an obvious point to such claims. The history of colonialism, for example, is littered with illustrations of the havoc that can be caused through forcing alien cultures to act in new ways which are sincerely believed to be in their interests but which turn out to be destructive. Such illustrations seem to lend weight to the view that different cultural groups should be left alone to do what they think best. However, we have also argued in this chapter that people are not necessarily the best judges of what they are doing and whether or not they are doing it well. This seems to suggest that it is also possible to make rational judgments about other people's actions – whatever they themselves might think. Certainly, such decisions were an integral part of the progressive history of social welfare legislation. For example, civil rights legislation was opposed at one time by the vast majority of the white people of the US as being against the interests of all concerned and a violation of white legal rights. Without some notion of what types of political consciousness are correct, then the only justification of such legislation is the power of those who formulate and implement it. For there is no fact-of-the-matter to which to appeal. So totally rejecting the view that cultural beliefs are always debatable seems to lead to one type of dogmatism (i.e. only one view of the social world can be right), while totally accepting it leads to another (i.e. a plurality of equally justifiable views entails that might makes right).

We began our discussion of ideology with the seemingly straight-forward idea of a false set of beliefs which worked in the interests of one group and against the interests of another. In this sense, the concept of ideology is an essentially *critical* one. It does not merely entail different modes of consciousness descriptively correlated with different social groupings, but purports to be able to show that some beliefs are correct and some incorrect, some aims moral and others immoral, some rules progressive and some reactionary, and so forth. Yet if needs and wants, rights and duties, justice and injustice are all believed simply to be culturally specific, the critical force of the concept of ideology is lost. All that is left is the view that some social groups do things differently from others. You will agree with those who most approximate to your own perceived interests and disagree with those who do not and what is socially progressive becomes simply a matter of whose side you are on. The rational assessment of different modes of consciousness becomes impossible – such modes are, as Kuhn would say, 'incommensurable'. From the relative certitude of the inequalities of slavery, we seem to have ended with the means of defending it and all other forms of oppression. We appear to have returned to the abyss of *relativism* which we introduced in the first chapter. Consequently, the question which we now have to confront is the extent to which human activity is subject to radically different interpretations, the extent to which language can be flexibly used to make sense of social practice and the extent to which such practice can be conceptually moulded in any way a culture likes. Unless there are constraints on such language use – unless social practice cannot just mean what we wish it to mean – anything becomes justifiable and there can be no coherent concept of ideology in the critical sense. To search for such constraints and to attempt to lay the foundation for the rational appraisal of human activity, it is now necessary to examine the nature of human language and its uses in much more detail.

Annotated bibliography

Our discussion of human freedom has a fairly narrow purpose – to argue for the compatibility of free will with social rule-following – and for the necessity of both for the notion of political liberty. Hence we have not addressed many of the problems which are generally discussed by philosophers in this connection. It should not be thought, for example, that the conception we have used of free will in relation to laws of nature is uncontentious. The philosophical literature in this field is immense. For a good introduction see Collinson 1973 and 1976 and Trusted 1984. Berofsky 1966 and Honderich 1973 are two collections of essays which give some idea of the breadth of disagreement, as does Hook 1958, which contains useful contrasting articles by Hempel and Schutz.

The relationship between the notions of free will and of human agency is explored in Royal Institute of Philosophy 1968, chapters 1-6, Hampshire 1965, chapters 2 and 3, the title essay of Strawson 1974, and Kenny 1975. These works defend a strongly voluntaristic conception of agency. Something more like the view we favour – co-existence but mutual irrelevance of causal and rule-following explanations – is argued in 'Causality and determination' in Anscombe 1983 and in Pitkin 1972, chapter 11. These arguments are distinct both from the 'two languages' thesis propounded, for instance, in Strawson 1974, and from the thesis of 'compatibilism' originating with Hume, versions of which are set out in the essay 'Freedom and necessity' in Ayer 1980a, and with great subtlety in Davidson 1984a, chapter 4. More recently, Dennett 1979, part IV explores the co-existence of 'intentional' and 'mechanistic' frameworks of description in relation to free will. Dennett 1984 is a more general discussion of the problem of free will.

Discussions of free will related to specific questions in social science can be found in Giddens 1976, chapter 2, Papineau 1978, chapter 5, and in the excellent but demanding Giddens 1979, chapter 2. The review of conceptions of action in different philosophical traditions in Bernstein 1972 is related to the problem of free will in his discussion in part II of

Kierkegaard and Sartre. The philosophical underpinnings of Sartre's existentialism are closely allied to those of Schutz's contributions to the theory of social action.

Contemporary views on political liberty cannot escape the influence of Mill. His classic statement 'On Liberty' is to be found in Mill 1972. Even if you have never touched a philosophy book you will find much that is familiar in Mill, such is his influence on the self-image of modern democratic capitalist societies. Ryan 1974 gives an introduction to Mill's work and Ryan 1970b provides a commentary on Mill's ideas. Another more recent classic is the essay 'Two concepts of liberty' in Berlin 1969 in which a view akin to Mill's is defended. Ryan 1979 is a collection of essays stemming from Berlin's arguments. The pieces by Cohen and Taylor contain important criticisms which relate liberty to the social context in which it is exercised. Popper 1961 argues the collectivist theories of society are inimical to political liberty. The relation between Popper's philosophy of science and Mill's tenets of political liberty is briefly discussed in Magee 1985, chapters 6 and 7, and at greater length in Ryan's essay in Currie and Musgrave 1985. A similar, but more extreme version of this thesis has been argued in Hayek 1982, defending the virtues of a free market economy. Condemnation of the power of the state to infringe liberty leads Wolff 1970 to defend anarchism, and Nozick 1974 to a position not unlike that of Hayek. Rowland-Pennock and Chapman 1978 contains a variety of essays on the issue of anarchism. Plant *et al.* 1980 is an excellent introduction to issues in political philosophy as they impinge on the conception of human agency, the findings of social science and the justification of social policy. Lukes 1973 discusses the issues of liberty and the individual in the context of an examination of the notion of individualism in social thought. We have barely mentioned the concept of *power*, which is of great importance in a number of fields in social science. Lukes 1974 contains a useful survey of different notions of power which have been employed by social scientists, and in chapter 14 of Giddens 1982 and chapter 1 of Giddens 1984 are further useful discussions, in which he coins the phrase 'dialectic of control'.

The approach we have taken to the notion of ideology is obviously Marxist in inspiration and strongly influenced by the account in Larrain 1979 and 1983. The essay 'Ideology and ideological state apparatuses' in Althusser 1971, and Marcuse 1964, are very different examples of the view that it is definitive of ideologies that they contain a component of falsehood. Held 1980 is a good introduction to the tradition of 'critical theory' – of which Marcuse is a representative – which takes the critique of ideological error as its main *raison d'être*. A different conception of ideology can also be found both outside and within the Marxist tradition. On this latter view, while ideological beliefs are connected as a system with the political interests of a particular social class or group, it is not definitive of ideology as such that it should contain a component of error. The opposition between these two approaches is discussed in Larrain 1979, especially chapter 6. Mannheim 1936 and Lukács 1971 are celebrated examples respectively of non-Marxist and Marxist adherents of the view that a component of error is not essential to ideology. More recently, McCarney 1980 defends the claim that Marx did not consider 'ideological' to imply 'erroneous'.

A good discussion of 'reification' is to be found in Keat and Urry 1982, chapter 8. We have reserved the term 'reification' itself for the specific error of mistakenly taking the outcome of human action – e.g. the value of gold, or the definition of the social role of women – to be the result of the operation of *laws of nature*. It is common, however, for it to be used in a less specific way to characterize *all* the forms of what we have termed 'ideological error'. So simply taking for granted that the understanding you ordinarily possess of social reality enables you to interpret the facts of social life 'as they really are' is often called 'reification'. Such a viewpoint, which treats the facts of social life as simply 'given', entails the adoption of an uncritical empiricism in social science, on which we remarked at the end of chapter 1. Such naive empiricism, which does not entertain the possibility that the extant self-understanding possessed by members of society might in any way be problematic, leads to the development of what is often called 'reified social theory'. Theoretical explanations are formulated to account for 'data' – supposedly given facts – while no account is taken of the possibility that the 'data' might be an *artefact* of people holding the very belief for which the 'data' are then taken to be 'evidence' – e.g. our example of the self-confirming character of the belief in the worthlessness of slaves. This type of shortcoming in social scientific theory is criticized from a non-Marxist, individualist standpoint in Berger and Luckmann 1967, and in articles in Filmer *et al.* 1972. For a more broadly based anthology concerned with this issue, with a useful introduction, see Giddens 1974.

The view, common among both Marxists and their opponents, that the contributions of Marx to social science should either be accepted or rejected *en bloc*, arguably rests on the second of the views discussed above, namely that it is not error but merely a systematic connection with particular political interests which is definitive of ideology. Such a conception opens the door to relativism by implying that what counts as 'error' is relative to the interests of those who subscribe to a particular ideology. These issues are discussed in Giddens 1979, chapter 5, in the context of his making a case for selectively critical acceptance of Marxian insights into social theory. The debts our presentation owes to this discussion are clear. Thompson 1984 is the most recent comprehensive survey of the debates concerning ideology and includes an interesting analysis of Giddens's views.

Leonard 1984 contains an extended treatment of the notion of ideology in relation to individuals rather than to social classes as a whole. In a similar vein, Lichtman 1982 makes a valuable contribution to the linking of Marx's approach with Freud's theory of the unconscious. A number of works by feminist writers employ the notion of ideology as 'false understanding' in relation to individuals – Eichenbaum and Orbach 1983 with respect to the formation of the consciousness of

women, and Ehrenreich 1983 with respect to men. Evans 1982, especially section 7, contains further essays on this topic.

6
RATIONALITY, LANGUAGE AND RELATIVISM

In the preceding chapters we have examined a number of ways in which beliefs about the natural and social world are underdetermined by experience. That is to say, we have shown that conflicting interpretations of physical behaviour or of social action can be 'confirmed' by the same experiences. Hence the problem of interpretation to which we have so often alluded. This problem raises serious issues concerning rationality and power, as our preceding discussion of ideology reveals. For if experience cannot arbitrate between fundamentally conflicting accounts of what is going on and if the accounts themselves do not internally contradict each other, then there is no empirical or logical way of resolving related disputes. In short, rational debate seems pointless in such circumstances and arguments must be won or lost on the basis of power alone. Conceptual change then seems to be nothing more than 'a triumph of the will' of the innovator. If there is some way out of this relativistic impasse of 'might makes right', then it seems imperative to look for it. We shall therefore attempt this in the next two chapters. Some fundamental concepts in the philosophy of language will be introduced and we shall show how they can be employed to demonstrate the possibility of rational debate between radically different views of the world. Without such a theory, different systems of interpretation become so all-encompassing that they are conceptual prisons with neither escape nor entry.

The crude correspondence theory of truth

On the face of it, relativism possesses little commonsense appeal. This is because most people conceive of establishing the truth or falsity of beliefs quite simply – through determining whether or not they *correspond* with the facts. So, for example, a simple belief expressed in a statement like 'The grass in my garden is green' is true if, and only if, a reliable observer looks and sees that the facts are as described. Were the grass seen to be, say, brown, then the statement along with the belief it expresses would be declared false and would not be accepted as corresponding to the facts in question. In this way, descriptions are thought to be analogous to pictures which accurately or inaccurately represent all of the separate facts or relations between them which make up reality. When language is employed 'indicatively' to make descriptive claims, it can be compared with reality for accuracy in much the same way that a representational painting or model might be. If what is expressed in the statement mirrors external reality then its content is true; if not, then it is false. Hence the physical and social worlds are believed to be broken down into all of the separate facts which make them up. Empirical states of affairs accepted as being 'the case' are taken to be the 'truth conditions' of indicative statements. Hence 'The grass in my garden is green' is true, if and only if (when I look) the grass in my garden is green. '*Ostensive reference*' or *pointing* at relevant facts becomes the key method by which rival truth claims – statements which describe reality differently – are arbitrated.

So far, all of this must seem straightforward enough. No doubt, when you are unsure about the truth or falsity of a statement, you make a decision through checking the facts. Yet what of more complicated beliefs expressed by more complex statements like scientific or social theories? This complexity may take two forms. It might concern the internal logical structure of the theory or its level of descriptive generality. In both cases, many philosophers have argued that the truth or falsity of theoretical assertions remains a question of their correspondence with reality as revealed by experience.

With logically complex statements which make claims about the relationships between facts, assessment can be attempted through what is known as truth-functional analysis. This reveals how simple indicative statements are connected to form more complicated ones by links called 'logical operators'. Conjunctions ('and'), disjunction ('or') or implication ('if . . . then') are examples. So a statement like 'The grass in my garden is green and it has rained in the last week' is true if and only if its two component statements are true. Were they linked by 'or' the resulting statement would be true if and only if one or both of its components were true. If two statements are linked by implication, as in 'If the grass in my garden is green then it has rained in the last week', then the resulting statement will be true except when the premise is true and the consequent is false. As can be readily seen, this same method of analysis could be applied to statements which were even more complex. The general rule here is to assess beliefs through *reducing* them to their most basic descriptive components – those statements whose truth or falsity can be determined with reference to simple truth conditions, facts of experience which are not further reducible to simpler facts. When all of these truth values are added up, so to speak, in accordance with logical principles like the above, then the truth value of the general theoretical statement can be determined. Applying this idea to language as a whole, the resulting image is of linguistic building blocks representing many different and independently describable facts, the whole collection of which constitutes reality. It is not surprising that the resulting theory has sometimes been referred to as 'logical atomism'. We shall call it the crude correspondence theory of truth. Note the close similarity between this and the theory of crude empiricism which argues that all knowledge originates in and must be verified by experience.

The crude correspondence theory seems to be able to account for the way in which everyday statements about the world are evaluated for their truth or falsity. However, when it is employed to evaluate scientific theories two problems emerge. The first concerns theoretical entities which have no immediate empirical referent (e.g. 'force', 'election', 'alienation', 'superego'). If they do not correspond to the facts of experience, how can their existence be justified? The second problem concerns the level of generality of scientific theories. In chapter 1 we showed that you cannot point to any aspect of your experience to prove or justify a statement like 'All lawns are green' in the same way that you can prove one like 'It is now 3 p.m. on July 4th and my lawn is green'. The first statement refers to too much, to more states of affairs than you are in a position to observe. This means that you cannot empirically justify the truth of the general statement in the same way that you can the truth of the particular. It will be remembered that for this reason there is an asymmetry between verification and falsification. You may be able to falsify universal statements – in the above case just one lawn will do the trick. But you cannot prove them. What, therefore, can universal statements be said to correspond to?

Even though both of these points about theoretical entities and the generality of theories are correct, it can be argued that they do not necessarily threaten the crude correspondence theory of truth. It just needs to be made more sophisticated through arguing that the *confirmability* – though admittedly not the proof – of the existence of theoretical entities must still refer to a specific set of experiences which are thought to *bear* on the question of their existence (e.g. in the case of electrons, those in an experimental cloud chamber constructed in ways which the theory under test dictates). Similarly, the confirmability though not the proof of a universal theory may be understood in the same terms – with reference to those experiences which bear on its truth or falsity. Thus the worthiness of a theory and the view of the world it puts forward remain truth-conditional. It can still be said to correspond with the facts even if it is not actually *known* whether it accurately represents all of them and even if another theory comes along which can be said to correspond to more of them. Were the latter the case, the more sophisticated correspondence theory would simply argue that more and better evidence – new truth conditions – had been discovered which better confirmed the new position than the old. In short, sophisticated correspondence theorists, such as Popper, envisage a reality which is revealed not through direct observation but through the sort of critical experimentation associated with contemporary science in all its guises. The central assumption of the crude correspondence theory remains: that independent experiences are the bedrock of scientific assessment – 'independent' in the sense that the truth of descriptions of any one experience has no bearing on the truth of any other.

Empirical or 'synthetic' truths are those which are directly confirmed by independent experiences in this sense. To state them you obviously have to use language. This brings us to another type of truth which is equally important to crude correspondence theorists – logical or 'analytic' truth. To see what this means, again consider how language seems to be employed indicatively – to describe or refer to particular components of reality. In order to make a statement which refers to some experience of reality you must follow at least two sorts of rules in the language you use: 'syntactic' and 'semantic' rules. The former refer to the logical form of statements, while the latter refer to their meaning. So the syntactic rule concerning 'and' set out above in the example 'The grass in my garden is green and it has rained in the last week' holds irrespective of the meaning of the two simple statements conjoined by 'and'. We could write 'P and Q' and this would be true only if the two statements represented by 'P' and 'Q' were both true, no matter what these letters happened to stand for. Try using it in any other way (e.g. claiming that statements like 'Prince Charles is heir to the throne and he is a man' are not true) and see how far you get.

However, it is the semantic rules which are of primary interest to our argument. It is very natural to suppose that these dictate the meanings of the words employed in statements, and so the capacity of those statements to represent the facts of experience which they describe. On this view, words are analogous to paints employed to complete a linguistic representational canvas. As in the relationship between specific paints and a painting employing them, words in their own right do not make representational claims. They must be brought together as components of an indicative *assertion* like 'The grass is green in the garden today'. Yet the separate meanings of words will obviously be central to whether or not they can be employed in such assertions and whether or not anyone understands what is being stated when they are. Just as it makes no sense to use black paint to depict a blazing sun, the same can be said about trying to describe a garden with nouns and adjectives which are more suitable for, say, the kitchen. Suitability in this respect is determined by definitions which link words to specific experiences assumed to be shared by everyone in the same way and to reveal what sorts of things and attributes the word contains. Provided one is considering written languages associated with high levels of literacy, definitional or analytic truths can always be found in those modern repositories of semantic rules, dictionaries. The truth of definitions (e.g. 'all bachelors are unmarried') does not derive from experience but from the fact that they are self-contradictory to deny. This makes them and their assessment quite different in character from synthetic truths. It makes no sense to suggest that someone should look to see whether or not there are any married bachelors. It is just as absurd to consult the dictionary to determine the current state of your garden.

But the analogy between language and the artist's palette might appear to break down when it is recognized that words can be defined in a host of different ways, whereas oil paints always retain the same physical properties. As *signs*, words are in themselves quite arbitrary. Note for example the differences between the French 'Toutes les herbes sont plantes' and the English 'All grasses are plants' which mean the same. And, of course, the list goes on and on through all the different languages with words in them which are employed in some way to denote what English speakers use to denote grass, gardens and so forth. Another way of saying the same thing is that, other than the fact that no one would then be able to understand you, there is nothing in principle to keep you from systematically substituting 'blug' for 'grass', 'plimp' for 'plant' and 'zap' for 'green' and begin to talk (to yourself) about your garden in this way. For others to understand and be in a position to assess the truth or falsity of what you then stated, they would have to agree to use language in the same fashion. And, of course, it seems that people do use different languages precisely in this way to refer to what are apparently the same things and seem to make the same true or false statements despite differences in phonetics or script.

To give an account of why this might be, the crude correspondence theorist must make further use of the concept of 'meaning'. For to claim that indicative statements in different languages either correctly or incorrectly refer to the same thing clearly presupposes that they have something in common. Meaning – the sense that is possessed by the same utterances in different languages – seems to fit the bill. So, for example, a French person may point to your garden and say 'L'herbe est verte' and you will agree because you accept that this statement is synonymous with the English statement that you would make under the same circumstances – it *means* the same thing. This synonymity entails two things. First, you and the French speaker are making the same factual claim – asserting the same *synthetic propositions* with the same empirical truth conditions. And second, you are both employing semantic rules (i.e. informally, definitions found in dictionaries) which enable you to utter words and sentences with the same meaning, conceptually structuring your respective experiences in the same way, albeit in different languages. Reality is viewed as external to language and divided into individual empirical facts which when added up equal the whole. Yet now it is combinations of *ideas* – rather than words as such – which are viewed as either corresponding to it or not. Language acquires its representational status through its capacity to express these ideas (e.g. the meaning that is captured in 'The grass in my garden is green'). That people using different languages can assert the same proposition enables them to agree and disagree with each other through their consequent ability to refer to and argue about the same things.

This reformulation of the crude correspondence theory leads to the view that one must *discover* what the natural or social world is ultimately like, in the same sense that a stranger might discover that the grass in your garden is green. Operating on the assumption that the stranger already understands these concepts which are necessary to recognize the facts in question – those analytic truths associated with 'grass', 'garden', etc. – then the relevant statement can be formulated in whatever language the stranger uses, and tested to see whether it corresponds with the facts. Your ability to translate what the stranger says will depend, on this view, on the independence of the fact that the grass in your garden is green from any particular way of saying that it is so in your language or in the stranger's. Presented with the same fact, both you and the stranger will therefore have the means, in your respective languages, of reporting that fact. Two sentences in different languages which report the same fact will have the same meaning because both have the same fact as their truth condition. It is important to note the essential link made here between the identity of the fact and the identity of the meaning of the two statements which report the same fact in different languages. If this view can be sustained, then there will be no essential difference between our stranger and, say, the modern micro-biologist or anthropologist. They are seeking to discover new facts about DNA or kinship systems in the same way the stranger might try to unearth information about your garden – through the use of their senses, aided by refined experimental apparatus and methodology. In this respect, facts and the concepts which express them are viewed as having an existence which is independent of the consciousness, beliefs or language of the individual inquirer. DNA or the truth about its structure did not suddenly materialize, the correspondence theorist might argue, when Crick and Watson made their famous discovery in 1953!

Of course, whether or not the facts about reality *will* be discovered is an open question. Its answer depends on two things. The first is curiosity, ingenuity and all of those other attributes which are associated with the history of successful empirical science. The second is more usually associated with theoretical innovation and involves a different, conceptual dimension of discovery. Here original ways are found to classify experience through the formulation of new analytic truths. Returning to our strangers, they will be unable to agree about any aspect of the garden unless they have access to the vocabulary adequate to express the relevant synthetic propositions – whatever the specifics of their particular language. This again means that they must understand these analytic truths which English speakers proclaim when they define 'garden', 'green', etc. The crude correspondence theorist would argue that the same goes for science. Without discovering the *correct* definitions of 'force' or 'mass', Newton, for example, could not have discovered the synthetic truths embodied in his laws of motion. It follows that, like synthetic truths, analytic truths possess meanings which can be expressed in a variety of languages, that such expressions may be mistaken and that there are some such truths which have not yet been discovered. Thus experience is viewed as already having a natural classification into things and attributes which is the same for all *normal* perceivers, much in the way in which Linnaeus is often regarded as having discovered – rather than created – *the* natural classification scheme for all embodiments of plant and animal life.

Before we proceed to discuss the problems with this rather neat version of language and truth, note how potentially conservative it is. Those who endorse it identify western science and dictionaries of western languages with the best available approximations of synthetic and analytic truth. Armed with this identification and the maxim that nothing succeeds like success, crude correspondence theorists simply advocate more of the same as if to say, 'We've got this close. Why should we change direction now?' This is very much the essence of Popper's conception of scientific progress and of that of all other 'realists' who believe that there is one reality which can be successfully investigated by everyone – provided they use languages which are synonymous in meaning with contemporary English and adopt contemporary western beliefs. When bold discoveries are made it is 'on the shoulders of giants' (usually white, male and European or North American!) and there is thus no great discontinuity between the old and the new. In recent years, however, this optimism has been challenged in three different ways.

First, beginning in the 1930s, a revolution took place in anthropology. Rather than dismissing traditional or 'primitive' cultures as some sort of collective stupidity or madness, it became increasingly accepted that many of their 'strange' beliefs were both internally consistent from a logical point of view and empirically consistent with the experiences of the indigenous populations. Suffice it to say that these experiences were, from that time, often classified, described and explained in ways which bore little relation to western dictionaries or western science. This suggested that such dictionaries – and the scientific theories employing their concepts – might be more arbitrary than had initially been supposed. For the simple fact was they did not automatically command universal assent among people who in the ordinary pursuit of their daily lives seemed quite rational.

Second, in the early 1960s, the work of Thomas Kuhn became widely read. As we saw in chapter 1, he argued that scientific change was not gradual and cumulative but embodied dramatic conceptual revolutions. Belief systems thought at one time to be internally consistent and compatible with experience (e.g. Aristotle's) were replaced by other, radically different ones which were equally consistent and compatible (e.g. Newton's). Kuhn's view of the rationality of such a change takes us a long way from scientists simply checking to see whether or not their beliefs correspond with the facts. For if by 'facts' we simply mean experience or even experiments, Kuhn showed that two different belief systems or 'paradigms' – conceptual schemes quite incompatible with each other – could *both* be said to correspond with the facts. As a tool of referential assessment, experience no longer appeared to be the uncomplicated arbiter of truth and falsity that the theorists made it out to be.

Third, and finally, the most important challenge to their views came, not surprisingly, from two philosophers of language – W.V. Quine and Ludwig Wittgenstein. During the 1950s and 1960s Quine systematized the implicit epistemological assumptions made by relativists about language, truth and meaning. In so doing, he refuted the 'dogmas of empiricism' on which the crude correspondence theory depended: (a) that experience uniquely determines which statements in language are analytically and synthetically true, and (b) that it also uniquely determines their propositional content or meaning. Wittgenstein had earlier developed similar arguments, although in a much more suggestive and less organized way. It is therefore to Quine that we must now turn.

Empiricist dogma

Let us begin with so-called analytic truths. For Quine, statements that are held to be analytic are in fact reducible to the *conventional* designation of terms as synonymous – as substitutable for each other in different synthetic statements with no alteration in their truth value. This criterion of substitutability must apply if one word can be correctly said to have the same meaning as another. Yet 'conventional' is the operative word here since the necessity that is associated with analytic truths is only apparent, Quine argues, and based on nothing more than a history of using language in particular ways. In other words, though we may *feel* that statements like 'All bachelors are unmarried' are logically necessary, the feeling cannot be said to derive from a correspondence with the way in which experience is already naturally classified. For other internally consistent definitions can be formulated which stipulate incompatible classifications and thereby incompatible analytic truths. Therefore, there is nothing fixed, permanent, natural or normal about experience to which the content of dictionaries can be said to correspond – nothing 'out there' to reveal what words mean. For instance, the necessity of the statement 'All rulers are objects used to measure length' is not of the same kind that is associated with a law of nature. It is true by definition. However, the definition in question could in principle be quite different, although changing it would entail all sorts of revisions to other analytic and synthetic statements in English. Think about 'All rulers are vehicles used to travel from one place to another' and this should become clear. Similarly, whether or not statements should be classified as synthetic truths cannot be decided through checking to see if things 'really are like that'. So 'This ruler is one metre long' appears to be an empirical claim which everyone would have to assent to or deny in the presence of the ruler in question, provided that they employed the same dictionary. But its status as a synthetic assertion, or the truth-conditional status of the bit of experience to which it refers, has no privileged status in the ultimate nature of things. Again, things could be or might have been different. For example, leaving aside the havoc that it would cause in other aspects of language use, 'ruler' and 'one metre' *could* be regarded as meaning the same thing, and 'This ruler is one metre long' as analytically true.

Therefore, Quine argues, there is nothing about reality or the experience of it which forces language-users conceptually to divide up the world in one way rather than another. Those divisions which already exist – dictionaries and the descriptive uses to which their contents are put – obtain their sense of permanence from nothing else but habit. This does not mean, of course, that you are not entitled to say under the appropriate referential circumstances that a statement like 'This ruler is one metre long' is true. You are, if the circumstances warrant it, depending on your conceptual scheme of things and what you do in fact experience. But for someone employing a different conception of measurement, 'This ruler is one metre long' might be false under precisely the same empirical circumstances which led you to believe it was true.

Consider another example to illustrate the same point. Before Captain Cook went to Australia, the statement 'All swans are white' and 'All swans have long necks' were very much on the same level. Since all swans in Britain were white and had long necks, both statements might have been used to express either analytic or synthetic truths. However, assume for the sake of argument that it was Cook himself who discovered what he took to be black swans. Identifying the birds as *swans* was entirely his choice. He could have denied that they were swans precisely because they were black, thus continuing to use 'All swans are white' as if it were an analytic truth. But if in fact he *chose* to use the statement in a synthetic way – to accept the existence of black swans – then his decision to use language in a particular way was just as relevant to his 'discovery' of black swans as were the birds themselves. In short, it is true that there must be some accepted differentiation between the analytic and the synthetic in order for users of words like 'swan' to know how to use them. However, as the example of Cook's discovery shows, there is no reason to believe that there is anything unique, permanent or irrevocable about such decisions. As you have seen, dramatic innovations in scientific theory always entail changes in language use which make new empirical discoveries (such as black swans) both possible and intelligible. Yet if it really is the case that experience cannot arbitrate between disputes about what kinds of statements are themselves to be regarded as classificatory rather than as true or false, then how can such disputes be settled rationally?

The response of someone who continues to believe that empirical facts can be unambiguously used in such arbitration would be to refer again to the successes of modern science. Just because people *can* define words in different ways it does not follow that they *have* to or that some definitions and some associated beliefs are not more progressive than others – closer to the truth that western science has revealed. If it is not presupposed that this is so and is not accepted that there is more to the status of interpretations of experience than mere convention, then how can the remarkable success of western science be explained, along with the dramatic control over nature which it has facilitated? If a language is not rich enough in its development to make possible the utterance of a simple propositional truth like 'Snow is white' or a more complex one like 'On earth, the mass of a body equals the force acting on it multiplied by its acceleration,' then, says the crude correspondence theorist, so much the worse for it and the culture that employs it. Of course, words can be defined in different ways and in abstraction strange distinctions can be drawn between the analytic and synthetic dimensions of a language. But unless it is believed that people with radically different beliefs actually live in different worlds, it is surely necessary to believe that some true propositions can be uttered in all languages and that experience is ordered in such a way as to indicate their representational meaning and to demonstrate that they are true or false.

Without the existence of propositions and corresponding empirical facts in this sense, the crude correspondence theory becomes untenable. For if experience cannot be shown unambiguously to dictate truth and meaning in ways which are independent of differently constituted dictionaries, then language and consciousness are set adrift in a sea of cultural diversity. Quine raises the anchor through arguing that there is nothing to indicate the existence of a conceptual realm of propositional truth and through claiming that experience is compatible with widely divergent and inconsistent descriptions.

Returning to our previous section, when the French speaker states 'La neige est blanche' and the English speaker proclaims 'Snow is black', they certainly *seem* to be disputing something other than the meaning of what they actually assert. That is to say, they appear to be *disagreeing* rather than *misunderstanding* each other because it is clear what proposition they are contesting, albeit in different languages. Were they not able unambiguously to argue and disagree about propositions – about their representational claims – then rational debate between them would indeed be impossible. Of course, people *might* misunderstand each other but this, again, does not obviate the possibility that they will not. It just means that once the two speakers have pointed to the truth conditions of their respective propositions (the colour of 'la neige' or 'snow' in the appropriate circumstances) and are sure that it is indeed this thing (or event or attribute) that is the object of their disagreement, the wherewithal exists for empirically settling the dispute. Even where their terminology is seen not to be synonymous, the crude correspondence theorist still argues that experience can be used to help the disputants agree on the sense of what they both want to assert. One might say, for example, 'Ah, I now see from the way that you consistently refer to your experience that you are leaving open the possibility that those birds I call swans and define as being white might be other colours. OK, let's look and see whether or not your proposition is correct.'

The existence of propositions – shared conceptual representations which do or do not correspond with empirical facts about reality – is even more important for ensuring the possibility of rational debate between members of radically different cultures or supporters of radically different belief systems. Relativists who deny the existence of universal standards of rational appraisal are fond of pointing to the fundamentally different ways in which radically different cultures define, describe and explain experience. Here there is certainly the opportunity for misunderstanding on a large scale. Unless some way exists for disputants to realize that they are talking about the same thing, through uttering propositional content in one language that can be recognizably translated into the same propositional content of the other, then disagreement would become impossible and misunderstanding inevitable. In other words, unless it is possible for one of the disputants to say something like, for example, 'I see what you're talking about. We call that snow', then the crisis of rationality which relativism envisages would indeed be upon us. To be more specific, let us return to the debate between the western doctor and the traditional healer which we briefly introduced in chapter 1.

You will recall that the traditional healer maintained that illness was a manifestation of witchcraft which could be both detected and cured if proper magical rituals were rigorously adhered to. The western doctor interpreted illness primarily as a physiological malfunction to be under-stood using the western medical model (e.g. in the case of infection, the germ theory of disease and the technology of antibiotics). The debate was about which of these approaches constituted the more accurate explana-tion of what was really going on in a particular illness as well as the more effective approach to cure. In this dispute there is certainly a radical difference in fundamental beliefs. For critical communication to occur between the disputants, the one must attempt to understand the beliefs of the other. Only the achievement of understanding that is accurate allows the possibility of coherent disagreement. And as we showed in chapter 1, it is more difficult than might at first appear to generate a resolvable disagreement between our medical protagonists.

When presented with an example of apparent success on the part of the traditional healer, the western doctor will account for it in ways which are consistent with scientific medicine (e.g. 'The success was an accident or only apparent and really due to other naturalistic factors'). Equally, the traditional healer will explain the apparent success of the western doctor in supernaturalistic terms (e.g. 'It was really due to the casting out of the devil'). When presented with examples of the apparent failure of their opponent, both the western doctor and the traditional healer react in the same way, suggesting that failure indicates the explanatory poverty of the rival conceptual scheme. If the patient dies, for example, neither the traditional healer nor the western doctor will accept the death as evidence of their own failure. Both will blame other factors. The western doctor might suggest that prescribed medicines could have been faulty, that such medicines were not properly taken or administered, that a diagnostic mistake was made, that the disease was exacerbated by other 'complications', that the disease was an 'incurable' type . . . and so on. Similarly, when presented with failure, the traditional healer might argue that prescribed magical potions were incorrectly mixed, taken, or administered, that prescribed rituals were improperly followed, that unknown magical forces were at work which required further investiga-tions . . . and so on.

So the disputants seem to be trapped in what might be regarded as the interpretative prison of their preconceived views of the world. What they accept as relevant truth-conditional evidence for assessing statements made from within their conceptual scheme is itself based on an overall acceptance of the scheme itself. The traditional healer sees and points to what are already accepted as particular examples of witchcraft, whereas the western doctor sees and points to what are already accepted as particular examples of infections. It will be recalled from chapter 1 that Kuhn argued in similar terms about the 'incommensurability' of 'paradigms' in the natural sciences. Again, in these circumstances, disputants argue in circles and do not have enough conceptually in common to be said to disagree. Rather, trapped in their respective belief systems, they talk past and thereby misunderstand each other . . . or do they?

It should now be clear what the crude correspondence theorist must say in these circumstances. Just as the dispute between French and English speakers about the colour of snow could only be rationally decided once a translation of their respective descriptive statements was accepted as accurately expressing the proposition which the disagreement was about, the same goes for the competing healers. For them even to disagree, let alone to settle their disagreement, there seemingly must be something on which they disagree – again, propositions and the specific facts to which they refer. Thus one disputant asserts that an actual state of affairs exists (e.g. that referred to in English as 'witchcraft') and the other asserts that it does not. It must be possible for the alien to point and say in her/his language, 'Oh yes, I see that what you mean by "infection" is what we mean by [their word for] witchcraft. I was not sure what you were getting at but now it is clear that we are simply referring to the same thing – the same set of truth conditions – in different ways. Let's now do an experiment to see who is right.' In other words, in order to show that speakers of different languages are disagreeing about the same things, the crude correspondence theorist must demonstrate that there exists only *one correct translation* which captures the representational meaning of the rival claims. It would thus be about the truth conditions referred to by this single proposition (analogous to the apparent single meaning of 'Snow is white' and 'La neige est blanche') that the disputants could be said to disagree, despite their linguistic differences. What Quine dramatically does is to show that it is impossible to isolate one 'determinate' translation of this kind. In so doing, he undermines one of the central principles of correspondence theory – that experience presents itself to users of different languages in conceptually prepackaged form which enables them to refer to it in the same ways and to know that they are doing so.

The indeterminacy of translation and ontological relativity

Quine argues that no matter how complete and seemingly accurate a translation of alien linguistic behaviour might appear, it will *always* be possible in principle to devise different and conflicting translations which are equally compatible with the same empirical evidence. It would follow that there simply is no one determinate propositional content which is the same for everyone and into which experience can be naturally divided. If correct, this supports the relativist case because it then becomes impossible to be sure that people using radically different languages are agreeing, even when they think that they are. Since experience may bear many radically different interpretations, it cannot be used for the purposes of rational arbitration. Quine develops this argument through examining hypothetical examples of radical translation between such interpretations.

How, he asks, does a typical translator/anthropologist begin an inquiry? Initially, the problem seems to require a decision about whether or not specific nouns, verbs or short sentences in the new language are used to refer to things or events in ways which can be systematically correlated with the ways in which the translation refers to them. So when the alien utters a sentence and then points to an object or seems to be referring to an event that has just occurred, the translator can record that in English the sentence means such and such. Remember that in this connection those who believe in the existence of propositions would say that for a translation to be correct, the objective meaning of both the alien's statement and the translation must be the same. But how can the translator set about trying to demonstrate that this is the case? Any such attempt will involve the ways in which the aliens *use* language – for example, to single out a thing, attribute or event for attention. So to show that the propositional content of an English translation and the alien's use of language is the same – that both sets of assertions are making the same empirical claims – it will be necessary somehow to *demonstrate* that the respective languages are being used to refer to the same truth conditions. But, Quine asks, how could even this be demonstrated given the degree to which all ostensive reference is subject to different interpretation?

Presumably, the translator will begin the search for the sense of the alien language through pointing, say, at a plough and pronouncing the alien word/assertion which is considered appropriate. Suppose the alien seems to agree (e.g. through various acts of apparent affirmation like nodding vigorously) and does so regularly to the same action of the translator. Also, suppose that the alien consistently dissents in some recognizable way when the same word/assertion is ostensively used to refer to objects which are not ploughs. Surely this would be evidence enough of successful translation and thereby proof that the objective meaning for 'plough' was the same in English. Yet Quine shows that even in such an apparently straightforward situation, the translation remains indeterminate. The alien might be using the assertion in question to refer to a specific part of all ploughs like the handle, to 'plough' as an abstract noun, to 'plough' in the sense of a particular technique of ploughing, to 'plough' as an event, and so on. In trying to decide what is meant, neither the translator nor the alien can point to the propositional sense of what is being stated. For it is this that they are trying to determine through their references to what seems to be the relevant experience in question. All that they can do, therefore, is point to further objects, attributes and events in the hope that they will mediate apparent misunderstandings. But then the translator is right back to square one.

Quine argues for the *indeterminacy of translation* – that a translation hypothesis need not be uniquely correct – even if it is consistent with *all* of the translator's evidence and that this is *all* the evidence that there is or ever will be! It will always be possible to imagine other translation alternatives which are equally consistent with the evidence. Consider, for example, the following illustration which harks back to Quine's analysis of the conventional character of the analytic-synthetic distinction. Suppose that the word 'gup-gup' is translated into English as 'bachelor' because it appears to be used in the same way that it is in English – to refer to an unmarried man. Assuming that all the possible evidence is already known (e.g. the aliens have mysteriously disappeared), let us further suppose that this translation hypothesis is shown to be consistent with *every* known use of 'gup-gup' in the alien language. Even in this case, Quine argues, an alternative translation could work equally well. What if by 'gup-gup' the aliens were referring to the absence of a ritual scar made on the forehead of all men when they were married. This hypothesis would be compatible with all of the ostensive evidence as well as explaining the apparent synonymy with 'bachelor' in English. In short, nowhere in the evidence would there be any suggestion that where 'gup-gup' was used to refer, an unmarried man was not pointed at. Thus, according to Quine, since experience itself will bear any number of rival interpretations and since there is nothing other than experience to decide between one interpretation and another, no clear meaning can be attached to the idea of one interpretation which is uniquely determined by experience – which unambiguously reveals the facts.

Since it is possible to divide experience into such incompatible but nonetheless equally consistent categories, why have so many people come to believe that it possesses a natural order which is the same for every one? Presumably it is because of the commonsense conviction that, say, English and French speakers just must be talking about the same thing when they agree or disagree. If 'Snow is white' and 'Le neige est blanche' do not have the same meaning in that they are expressing the same proposition – ascribing a real attribute to stuff that is really out there – then why are they accepted as 'saying the same thing'? Surely, it is obvious that given our ability to communicate with each other in an apparently unproblematic way, real agreements occur about real states of affairs which are the same for everyone. But it follows from Quine's arguments that the existence of objective propositional meanings simply cannot be justified. For the only thing that makes apparently similar languages easy to translate is the conviction of their respective speakers that they *are* talking about the same things. However, all this entails in practice is that they are each able to *predict* what the other will say under what are accepted to be the same experiential circumstances.

Think of your own experience of trying to understand other languages. If you feel that you have understood an assertion, it is because you are convinced that you can predict how it will be used in specific situations. It is only when you can generally accomplish this task that you will believe that you understand a foreign language and can correctly translate it. Similarly, you will only believe that you have mastered your own language when you can successfully anticipate how other people will use it and will respond to your own usage. In other words, speakers feel that they are talking about the same thing because of the ways in which they have *already* implicitly agreed to carve up experience in the same ways. According to Quine, such agreements must be understood in historical and psychological terms. Historically, patterns of language use which are quite different have evolved because the conceptual schemes which they embody meet the pragmatic needs of the members of the cultures which employ them. Returning to our example of the western doctor and the traditional healer, both belief systems and associated languages enable sense to be made of illness and therapy in a way which is internally consistent and equally compatible with experience. Psychologically, Quine offers a behaviouristic account of language learning which we shall introduce shortly. The main point for now is his demonstration that experience never can nor does determine the conceptual content of what we say because *it quite literally possesses none.*

This is the most powerful reason why it must be accepted that it is we who impute content to experience through the conceptual categories – the dictionary – that our language embodies. If this means that it is impossible to prove that people are not misunderstanding each other when they appear to be disagreeing, then, Quine suggests, so be it. All that this shows is that we must alter our views about what it means to understand a language and that it is silly to ground the conception of such understanding on mysterious entities like shared propositional meanings which cannot be observed and do not exist. Thus he argues that there is no more to understanding a language and by implication no more to understanding radically different cultures than learning how to predict what people will say in specific circumstances and when they will assent to or deny what is said to them. Therefore, Quine maintains, if you wish to make sense of another past or present culture, then you have no option but to understand it in its own terms. For there are no terms to appeal to other than those determined by the linguistic rules presupposed by the belief systems of such cultures. This point also applies to your own patterns of language use. As far as empirical assessment is concerned, if other cultures pull themselves up by their own conceptual bootstraps, so to speak, then the same must apply to us and to our criteria of what is right and what is rational.

Wittgenstein developed similar views about the conceptual plasticity of human experience. He greatly influenced a number of philosophers who have explicitly explored the implications of these views for the social sciences. One of the best known, Peter Winch, argues that any attempt to impose one set of cultural rules on to another will lead to a breakdown of anthropological and sociological understanding. A proper explanatory approach in the social sciences will therefore minimally attempt to do two things. First, it will not try to understand human action nomologically in terms of laws but rather intentionally in terms of rules, for all the reasons we examined in chapters 3 and 4. Indeed, on the basis of this discussion, it should be clear that in the explanatory use of rules, Quine's

indeterminacy principle applies twice over – first to the physical behaviour of the person which may be interpreted and explained differently
in different cultures, and second to the actions associated with such
behaviour which may have different further interpretations even if there
is complete agreement about what physiologically is taking place.
Remember our discussion of the conflicting intentional accounts which
might apply to just one example of physical behaviour – someone
running along a busy pavement. Winch argues that the second necessary
condition for making successful sense of alien activity entails a sensitivity
to the internal coherence of rules within a culture. It also requires
effective methods of getting, as it were, conceptually inside such cultures
without ducking the issue and pretending either that they are closer to
western language use than is the case or that the aliens are irrational. As
far as rational appraisal is concerned, and returning to our earlier
example, we may *wish* (like Popper) to believe that the western doctor
and the traditional healer are disagreeing in a way that can and should be
settled by experience. But however hard they try, Winch argues, joint
attempts at such rational appraisal will always reduce to misunderstanding so long as the disputants pretend that there is something in common
(e.g. 'experience', 'truth conditions', 'propositional meaning', 'reality')
that they are disagreeing about. You can understand what the aliens are
up to, and vice versa, in the sense that you can predict what they will say
and do next on the basis of your apprehension of the rules which they
themselves follow in their various actions. Certainly, Quine and relativist
writers who employ similar arguments are right: what you cannot do is
to show that the aliens are wrong in their own terms, when these are the
only terms which exist for them.

Annotated bibliography

Perhaps the nearest to an espousal of the crude correspondence theory of
truth is to be found in Popper 1972a, chapter 10, although he does not go
along with the notion that a proposition is a 'picture' of a fact.
Wittgenstein was the originator of the 'picture theory of meaning' and a
good account of this view is to be found in Kenny 1973, chapter 4. Useful
introductory discussions of the complexities involved in maintaining a
correspondence theory of truth which is not 'crude' are to be found in
White 1970, chapter 6, O'Connor 1975, Haak 1978, chapter 7. Both
Hacking 1983, part I, and Newton-Smith 1981, chapter 2, discuss the
idea that truth is correspondence with the facts in relation to a more
general examination of the rationality of science, while Rorty 1980, part
II, especially chapter 6, situates this idea in a still wider context of the
history of philosophy. In these and a number of other works the term
'realism' is used in connection with a correspondence theory of truth,
with the view that theoretical entities posited by science are *real*, and
with the view that truth and meaning have an inextricable connection.
These three views may all be held together. However, they may not and
may be justified independently – a warning against assuming that

'realism' is always used to mean the same thing. For discussion of those points and in particular of the philosopher Putnam who has adopted various versions of 'realism' in his work as it has proceeded, see Hacking 1983, chapters 6 and 7.

Despite the importance of Quine's work in recent philosophy of language and logic, introductory treatments of his ideas are few. Davis 1976, chapters 5 and 6, and Harrison 1979, chapter 7, discuss Quine's arguments in the context of introducing the philosophy of language. Grayling 1982, chapters 3 and 7, does so in introducing the philosophy of logic. Quine 1970 is an introduction to a number of his key ideas, but gives little space to the doctrines to which he is opposed. For a good account of the impact of Quine's arguments on recent epistemology see Rorty 1980, chapters 4 and 5. Domenos 1983 provides a more advanced analysis of the importance of Quine's work in relation to the philosophy of language.

At least some of the impact of the essay 'Two dogmas of empiricism' in Quine 1980 will be appreciated by a reader new to the field. The implications of the discussion of radical translation in Quine 1960, chapter 2, will be clarified by Quine's responses to the essays of Hintikka and Chomsky in Davidson and Hintikka 1969. Domenos 1983 is particularly helpful with the more difficult of Quinean topics raised in the essay 'Ontological relativity' in Quine 1969 and also on the importance of Quine's work on Tarski's theory of truth. This is also lucidly introduced in the title essay of Quine 1976. This theory is also evaluated in White 1970, chapter 5, and in Grayling 1982, chapters 6 and 8. Popper 1972b, chapter 9, takes Tarski's theory to be a version of the correspondence theory of truth. In so far as it is, this is only because it retains the *metaphor* of correspondence with the facts without the substance of the crude correspondence theory – that facts are in some sense independent of language. The whole point of Tarski's theory is that 'truth' be defined for some specific formalized language in terms of correspondence of sentences in that language, not to facts outside language as such, but precisely to *descriptions of facts* in a 'meta-language' devised for the precise purpose of talking about truth in the first 'object language'.

If the truth conditions of sentences in one language are not facts in the world, but sentences in a second language used to talk about the first language, then an intuitive connection between truth and meaning becomes clear. A link seems forged, for example, if the English sentence 'The sentence "La neige est blanche" is true if and only if snow is white' is used to talk about the quoted sentence in French. This insight is elaborated in Davidson 1984b, chapter 2. The analysis of meaning offered in this essay has been highly influential. In Davidson 1984b, chapter 3, a very far from 'crude' version of a correspondence theory of truth is defended. The subsequent debate these and other essays by Davidson and his supporters have provoked concerning the nature and defensibility of their doctrine of 'realism' is complex and difficult. Grayling 1982, chapters 6, 8 and 9, provides the best available overview of these issues. The endorsement, however, in Davidson 1984b, chapter 15, of the Quinean thesis regarding the holistic character of the relation of language to the world indicates just how far Davidson's position lies from the crude correspondence theory of truth with which we began. For an interesting discussion of realism in the social sciences see Keat and Urry 1982 and Benton 1977.

7
WHAT IS WRONG WITH RELATIVISM?

There can be no doubt that various formulations of relativism which employ arguments similar to Quine's have proved popular, particularly during the last decade. The idea that different systems of belief might possess an internal autonomy which makes them immune to criticism by 'westerners' has held an obvious attraction to opponents of economic and cultural imperialism. It has also appealed to members of the anti-science or 'counter-culture' movements through reinforcing their conviction that 'alternative' modes of understanding are possible. These might be used to make coherent sense of the world in ways which would not, they argue, lead to the ecological and human disasters associated with modern science.

Whatever their intellectual and political contexts, relativistic arguments appeal to humanistic sentiment through arguing for a principle of *charity*. According to this view, 'aliens' of whatever kind are just as interested in maximizing the truth content of their beliefs as any other rational person. Arguments similar to Quine's reinforce this principle through claiming that the concept of truth cannot be employed to arbitrate between radically different systems of belief independently of the language in which they are formulated. Thus the investigation of such beliefs should focus on an accurate description of their key principles and on the means by which they provide a consistent interpretation of experience. Hence the interest among relativists in those studies in anthropology and the history of science which take this descriptive or ethnographic orientation. Such research is essentially *sociological* in the sense that it is concerned with why the social, economic and environmental characteristics of particular cultures led their members to adopt some beliefs rather than other, equally coherent, alternatives. It does not ask whether or not these beliefs are true or rational in the way in which the crude correspondence theorist of the last chapter would prefer. However, there are major problems with such 'strong' programmes in the sociology of knowledge.

136

The conceptual foundation of human understanding

The central idea of the principle of charity is a good one. If you want to understand what people are doing in any cultural context then, as we have shown, you have to understand the rules that they are following. Though remember that it is possible to follow a rule without necessarily deliberating about it or 'having it in mind'. So if your neighbour does something which you believe to be strange and irrational (e.g. throwing a rock through your window) then, exercising the principle of charity, you will assume that there is a good reason and ask why. With any luck, there will be an explanation which is acceptable in that it is consistent with beliefs which you assume that you and your neighbour share (e.g. 'I was chasing away a thief who was climbing through your window'). More problematic examples from your own culture will be those investigated by, say, criminologists or clinical psychologists. Again, if the principle of charity is exercised, it means accepting that those defined as deviant or mentally ill only *appear* to be irrational in that their beliefs and their actions make sense as internally consistent responses to what they perceive as their situation.

There can be little doubt that an approach of this kind will imply programmes of care and education which would be unthinkable if the deviants in question were dismissed as lazy, stupid or mad. Indeed, the terrible conditions in many prisons and mental hospitals are testimony to the urgent need for applying the principle of charity in social policy generally. It goes without saying that a similar urgency exists with regard to so-called 'underdeveloped' peoples and cultures. The damage that has been inflicted upon them in the name of 'progress' has revealed much more about the selfish barbarity of agents of 'western civilization' than it has about their concern for those whom they were supposedly civilizing. If there is to be any real concern for the welfare of traditional peoples, it must start with an accurate understanding of their culture and why they are so committed to it. Only then will it be possible – without domination and dogmatism – to help them to create scientific and technical choices for themselves. This, of course, implies nothing about how they will choose or about what they in turn can culturally offer the west.

Thus the principle of charity, with its apparent endorsement of relativism, seems to have much to commend it. Yet the implementation of the principle entails more than that cross-cultural understanding is possible. It follows that such understanding should be *maximized* to ensure that nuances and ambiguities which might be regarded as manifestations of irrationality are seen to be logical and coherent against the background of the other beliefs of the culture/person involved. Is this not just another way of proclaiming the necessity for *accurate radical translation*? For without it – without the assumption that the alien beliefs under investigation have been understood – there will be nothing to be charitable towards. But this poses the question of how relativists are to reconcile their need for correct translation with the philosophical barriers which they erect – partly with Quine's help – against that very possibility. If different cultures really are locked into the conceptual prisons of their systems of belief, if the meaning and truth-conditional status of their experience are based on no more than the different conceptual schemes of their members, then it is difficult to see how successful communication can occur between them. Recall our discussion of Quine (or Kuhn): would not such members simply continue to talk past each other, unable to get even the most crude translation off the ground? Remember, for Quine this point holds, irrespective of how much people might *think* that they are communicating. In short, the relativist cannot have it both ways – on the one hand believing that supporters of radically different beliefs agree on nothing that might act as common ground for rational assessment and debate, and on the other hand assuming that they agree on enough to make possible a disinterested sociological appreciation of their respective beliefs.

To grasp this contradiction more clearly, imagine that you are an anthropologist trying for the first time to make sense of a radically different culture. Assume for now that you have learned enough of the aliens' language to try to communicate with them about beliefs which you think that you have understood. In order to apply the principle of charity, you will have to ask further questions, the answers to which you assume will fill in the conceptual background to the rationality of these beliefs. The first thing to note here is that these questions cannot even be asked unless you think that you and the aliens share minimal logical principles. So, suppose for example, the alien makes an assertion which you translate as 'Children are birds with the ears of rabbits'. Since, given the principle of charity, the whole point of your investigation is *not* to assume that what you are hearing is illogical and stupid gibberish, you must assume that there are common standards of logical consistency and coherence on which your translation must build. The most important are those of *identity* (i.e. If any statement is true then it is true), *contradiction* (i.e. No statement can be both true and false) and the *excluded middle* (i.e. No statement is neither true nor false). Provided that it is assumed that the aliens also accept these rules, along with the discovery that in all other known linguistic contexts children are never equated with birds or rabbits, the principle of charity leads to the view that language is being used metaphorically. So it might be argued that what is being asserted is that children are *like* birds because of their swiftness and *like* rabbits because of their acute sense of hearing. In fact, without a 'bridgehead' of shared principles of logic, successful translation could never get off the ground. This is because until a language is learned, it will be full of apparent inconsistencies and ambiguities which can only be resolved through assuming that language users are rational in the above minimal terms. Think of your own experiences with learning languages in this respect. If a foreign speaker or teacher utters a statement that seems silly or absurd because of its illogicality, you do not blame them. You blame yourself and seek another translation which 'makes sense'. As with the anthropologist, this will at the very least entail that you believe that the speaker in question accepts the same basic logical principles that you do.

Of course, the relativist might immediately respond that they can accept such minimal agreement on logical principles without giving up their main contention. This is that the truth conditions of conflicting conceptual schemes simply do not match – that there is no set of common experiences which are neutral to such conflict and to which appeals can be made in order to resolve it. For example, the traditional healer and western doctor might well recognize the internal consistency of their respective views. Yet they will continue to be unable to resolve their dispute about the general nature of health and illness on empirical grounds, even though there will be resolvable empirical disputes among the supporters of either view. This formulation of the relativist argument now claims that there is nothing other than logical principles that radically different views of the world have in common. But the difficulty with this view is that it still does not take into account the actual process of translation that leads to enough understanding to identify other systems of belief as being radically different in the first place. Since the principle of charity says 'Always assume that a successful translation is possible which will reveal the logical coherence of alien systems of belief', what makes this revelation a real possibility?

For radical translation to be possible, aliens and translator must have more in common than a few rules of logic. There must be 'core' *concepts* and *beliefs* about which agreement is also assumed to exist. So, for example, aliens will have translatable linguistic expressions for differentiating objects, attributes and events, as well as for making causal, spatial and temporal judgments. Were this not the case, they would be unable even to think, let alone assert, that one identifiable person made an identifiable event occur, that one identifiable thing was in front of or behind another, or that the same event that occurred yesterday might not do so tomorrow. Unless translators think that aliens are capable of making these judgments in ways which are reflected in their language, they will have no idea of how to get their translations off the ground. For these modes of ordering experience will be so fundamental to translators' own conceptualization of the world that alternatives become literally unthinkable. Even an alien statement correctly translated into English as 'Yesterday, that tall man over there to your left made one small cooking pot and one big one' becomes impossible because it could not be assumed that the aliens were capable of thinking such a thing. This is not to say that translators must agree with the details of alien judgments. The fact that anthropologists who believe in western medicine can investigate and understand traditional medical beliefs demonstrates as much. Yet if alien beliefs are generally to be understood as coherent attempts to describe and explain experience – something which must presumably be done to apply the principle of charity at all – then it must be believed that at least in certain respects, both translator and alien are employing language to try to do the same sorts of things.

But the list of what alien and translator must be presumed to have in common to understand each other does not stop here. Imagine how difficult it would be to translate a language which had no synonymous words in your own for the myriad of ordinary experiences of daily life. In fact, it is not clear in what sense it would even be possible. Suppose, for example, that you were an anthropologist especially interested in the agricultural techniques of an alien culture. How could you begin to make sense of their language if they had no words which were similar to 'plough', 'sow', 'seed', 'spring', 'summer', 'autumn' and 'wheat', 'rice', or 'maize' (whichever was most appropriate)? Of course, this is not to mention all of the other words which you can think of (e.g. nouns for different plants and animals or adjectives which make it possible to differentiate plants from animals and different members of each group) which makes experience characteristically agricultural as opposed to, say, nomadic. Thus, successful translation and cross-cultural understanding presupposes that you are able to take words of the alien language and correlate them with those which you conjecture that you use in your own language to refer to the same or similar experiences. If you cannot do this, then you cannot be charitable. Since the principle of charity is a cornerstone of relativism, it paradoxically follows from it too that there is a further translational bridgehead of shared experience between aliens and translators which they interpret in the same ways and about which they are perfectly capable of communicating.

Another and influential formulation of this type of argument has been put forward by Donald Davidson. He starts from the necessity that translation must begin before the possibility of mistranslation can arise. This necessity rules out the extreme relativist scenario of two complete and absolutely incommensurable conceptual schemes. For how is the translator to know that the sounds and marks of the aliens *are* a part of a language? In order to do so, it must be possible to identify at least some of them as *expressions* and this can only be done by showing that they are equivalent in meaning to some expressions in the translator's own language. For Davidson, this evidence entails the same truth conditions for both expressions – the belief that irrespective of their semantic differences they are referring to the same experience which we have just outlined. Were it not possible to establish commensurability between languages through such translational equivalences, he argues, you would be no more entitled to ascribe the term 'language' to the sounds and marks made by aliens than you would to the songs of birds or the babble of babies.

Davidson's resulting version of the principle of charity is that you always choose these equivalence rules between the alien language and your own which minimize the ascription to the aliens of what *you* take to be true and false beliefs. You will assume, for example, that when translating an alien statement like 'The sun moves', it would be more charitable to ascribe what *you* take to be a single false belief than to believe that the expression means what you do when you say 'The sun is stationary'. If you did the latter, Davidson argues that you would be forced in other contexts of movement to ascribe a much wider range of false beliefs to aliens – that rivers, clouds and fleeing animals were also 'stationary' – and that this would be much more uncharitable! In short, he maintains that you have no choice but to recognize other languages or conceptual schemes in terms of your own and that, ironically, you also have no choice but to be charitable towards others in relation to what you believe to be the truth. The very idea of a language or conceptual scheme which is so radically different to your own that these two things are not possible becomes fundamentally unintelligible on this view. And since it is precisely the existence of such schemes that is the cardinal tenet of relativism, then, Davidson suggests, so much for relativism.

These arguments are powerful, and are the subject of much contemporary debate which we cannot do justice to here. Suffice it to say that the relativist might come back at this point and argue that we seem to be contradicting ourselves. In the previous section we apparently accepted Quine's demonstration that from a logical point of view translation of all kinds – indeed your conviction that you understand what your own neighbour is saying – is indeterminate. That is to say, just because you think that you disagree with an alien or anyone else, it can never be proven that you will not discover that you have misunderstood them instead. Any principle of charity which suggests that it be simply assumed that you disagree, leaving unquestioned the correctness of your own language and beliefs, is tantamount to condescension. Again, 'reality' or 'facts' simply do not exist in any unambiguous form capable of settling the issue of who is right and who is wrong. How can we endorse this rigorous form of ontological relativity and continue to believe that all cultures have the sorts of conceptual/linguistic agreements outlined above?

The answer to this question is straightforward enough. There is simply no option but to understand alternative languages and beliefs through relating them to your own. The trick is not to assume that this entails that rival views of the world are impossible or that your view is necessarily correct. What Quine has shown is that there exists a level of inductive uncertainty of the sort which we examined in chapter 1, which goes above and beyond the fact that universal descriptive statements like 'All swans are white' can never be proven by particular instances of white swans. He shows that in understanding anyone else, it can never be demonstrated that you and they mean the same thing by 'white swan' even if you both think that you do. However, just as one has to learn to live with inductive uncertainty of the first kind – scientists do not call a halt to their inquiries because they can never be sure that their theories are certain – the same applies to anthropologists, sociologists and psychologists who have read (and understood) their Quine. The fact that they can never be certain that their translations are correct does not entail that they can never have good reasons for believing that they are. These reasons will stem in part from their ability to anticipate the linguistic responses of the subjects of their inquiries; but they may also derive from other sources, as we now show.

The practical foundation of human understanding

Things get even worse for the relativist when we look more closely at a further necessary condition for the successful application of the principle of charity. This is the necessity to *learn the alien's language to begin with*. So far, we have just assumed that at least some linguistic competence already exists on the part of the translator, enough to enable her or him to ask questions, for example. However, given Quine's arguments for indeterminacy – especially his and Wittgenstein's emphasis on the ambiguities of ostensive reference – it is still not clear how translators ever gain entrance into alien webs of belief. For, as Quine argues, when the alien points to what, say, for the translator is a rabbit and utters, for example, 'gavagai', they might be referring to anything from the rabbit, a particular part of the rabbit, the event rather than the thing, a potential meal, and so on. Imagine trying to learn a language where it was assumed that *none* of these questions already had a correct answer – where what you and they referred to by particular expressions could not ever be assumed to be the same. This suggests that there must be something about all humans which is intelligible in and of itself, about which there is general agreement and which helps to account for the existence of those shared syntactic and semantic principles which we have already outlined.

Obviously, some activities would be impossible to identify – much less to join in with – without having some prior understanding of their rules. In this sense, such activities can be said to be *culturally specific*. Examples will range over those practices which give a culture its particular identity. Thus games, rituals, cosmologies – the spectrum of customs which are characteristically 'local' – are all culturally specific in this sense. Indeed, it is these activities which are employed with such effect by relativist writers in illustrating their relativistic arguments. Culturally specific activities may well hold little interest beyond linguistic or anthropological curiosity. But if they hold more, prompting a desire to assess the merits of, say, supernaturalistic versus naturalistic approaches to understanding and treating illness, then it follows all the more that accurate translation becomes imperative. More specifically, until one develops the linguistic competence to identify potions, charms, spells and things natural as opposed to supernatural, it will not be possible even to describe what is going on, let alone evaluate it. Therefore, how can the radical translator gain entry into the alien language without already knowing something of alien rules – a contradiction in terms for anyone who argues that you must understand an alien culture *entirely* in its own terms.

One thing is clear. Unless communication of some form is possible prior to learning the language, radical translation cannot get off the ground and charity cannot be exercised. That is to say, it will be necessary to have the confidence that a yet further translation bridgehead exists which is not language-dependent at all. Otherwise, translators would have no way of identifying themselves as humans – much less as friends – or more importantly, no way of assessing the very first translation hypothesis on which their later work must build. In short, they must presuppose that there are some alien *activities* which are the same as their own and that this explains why alien language-use translationally will correlate in some measure with their own. These practices about which a measure of agreement can be said to exist prior to translation we shall call *constitutive activities*. Both translator and alien will already have theories in their respective languages about the nature of these activities because any form of human life will require them in some way or other for physical survival. For example, whatever their cultural background, both translator and aliens will share a certain measure of understanding of the distinctively human and social ways of doing a variety of different sorts of things (e.g. eating, sleeping, engaging in agricultural production, reproducing, constructing, sheltering, healing, playing, etc.). None of these can be done in just any old way. They are constrained by the laws of nature, as they affect, for instance, human biology and health, the communication of certain types of emotion, processes of agricultural and technological production, and the possibility of representing, communicating and storing information.

This takes us, then, to the question of what is and what is not a constitutive activity. The key test of whether or not such an activity has been successfully identified will be the translator's ability to join in it – correctly perceiving what does and does not constitute success *without necessarily saying anything*. Only then will it be possible to resolve those seemingly insurmountable ambiguities of reference posed by Quine's favourite example of pointing and naming. Again, since the alien might always seem to be referring to one thing (e.g. a rabbit), only to be later discovered to refer to another (e.g. a particular rabbit part), it will only be against the background of practical agreement that an accurate decision about what is being named will be reached.

So before it is possible, say, to identify a culturally specific activity like decorating shelters it will be necessary to recognize the constitutive activity of building shelters as such. Then what counts as decorative, rather than structural, may be distinguished. Imagine the translator confronted with the construction of a new hut in a strange culture. Many things will already be known about such construction (e.g. how to hold a support while a roof member is being positioned). Without saying anything, it will be possible in principle to join in and help, thereby communicating that something is understood of what is going on and – by implication – that translators use shelters too. It is this prior intelligibility which puts the translator in a position to try to translate some of the alien language associated with constitutive building activity – for example, their words for 'roof', 'support', 'walls', for the materials and actions involved, and for the identification of the grammatical character of their utterances. The same will go for other activities, less narrowly economic, which the translator might share with the aliens: making music, cooking food and so on.

Thus in testing the translation hypothesis in this way, more is being done than pointing, naming or asserting or, as Quine would have it, recording alien 'patterns of assent and denial'. This kind of language-use entails the active *use* of language to do things – to accomplish goals which are to some degree already understood (e.g. successfully communicating about how best to support a roof or level a floor). In a translational inquiry restricted to predicting patterns of utterance under given experiential conditions, there will indeed be an infinite variety of ambiguities which will prohibit the *certain* identification of alien concepts. For example, the translation of 'roof' is indeterminate in this sense. It will always be possible that, among other things, the alien means 'roof part', 'thatch', or 'what is going to keep me dry' by the word which the translator takes to mean roof when she/he points at one. However, indeterminacy will become increasingly less probable as one comes to understand the part that alien language plays in the accomplishment of constitutive activities. In the roof example, for instance, a translation will eventually be adopted through attempting to use the suspected word for 'roof' in the context of actually or hypothetically joining in roof construction, roof repair, etc. Thus it is when something practically turns on using words that translators acquire a cutting edge concerning ostensive ambiguity. Since relevant practical activities will be constitutive in character and joining in can occur without the use of language, it will be possible from the beginning of the translation exercise to agree – to some extent at least – with the aliens about what needs to be done and about how they use language to do it. This has to be seen as a very different kind of activity from merely pointing things out and naming them.

Similarly, it may be the case that 'rabbit', 'rabbit part', 'rabbit moment', etc. are all possible equivalents for Quine's 'gavagai' where the translator is simply being shown round the alien's forest. But the same would not hold for the 'gavagai' on the dinner table. Try eating a 'rabbit moment' or a 'glimpse of rabbit' or suggesting that the alien do so! Further, it would not be advisable in such circumstances to mistake the whole rabbit for the appropriate part of the animal which local etiquette demands to be eaten first. Constitutive activities will no doubt be described in the alien language and in the language of the translator. But, unlike culturally specific activities which are subject to infinite variations, constitutive activities present a constancy which does not change with language.

For example, one cannot build or use language to build a shelter unless certain requirements are met. This is true regardless of how the world from which one shelters is understood. A 'shelter' which provides no actual shelter is no shelter at all, for anyone. If this is what the aliens are making (e.g. a structure that consistently falls down as soon as it is completed) then their activity has simply been misidentified as shelter-building. And if an alien language contains no elements which actually facilitate the construction of shelters – some societies after all do not bother – then it does not contain elements which can be translated into the English vocabulary of shelter-building. Constitutive activities do not have to be universal to mankind in order to serve the function we have allotted to them. Which activities of the translator's society overlap with those of the alien's will be a contingent matter. An immediately intelligible activity for you, dropped in a society without a word of their language, might be buying and selling – by no means an activity universally practised in human societies. On the other hand, a truly universal activity like childbirth might be – as it has been in some societies – so exclusive a female preserve that no male translator would put it to use in establishing a translation bridgehead.

As far as culturally specific activities are concerned (e.g. telling specific sorts of stories), it appears that people may do or say anything they like. Yet those activities are made materially possible only by the constitutive activities of the society involved and there is a range of natural constraints upon such activity. For example, the successful use of any language in the constitutive activity of shelter-building will depend not just upon what is sayable within the language, but also upon what environmentally and physically can be done and the type and extent of understanding of these constraints. This, in turn, will only become evident in what, for example, actors produce. So again, as with other constitutive activities, to the extent that people produce the same sorts of artefacts and engage in the same sorts of productive processes, they can be said to agree with one another. In so far as translators can share and participate successfully in these activities, they can *in fact* agree with them – rather than merely seem to. From that real agreement, disagreements – as distinct from misunderstandings – can come to be recognized and translators can move towards real competence in an alien language. It then becomes possible to explain conceptual agreements between cultures. To the extent that translators engage in and are constrained by the same practical activities, it is hardly surprising that they have evolved similar linguistic ways of describing, classifying and explaining them – for example, those categories of objects, attributes, events, causes, times and places to which we referred above.

The translator and alien may have very different beliefs about what sorts of objects there are, what sorts of causes affect them, what sorts of attributes things have, and so on. There will no doubt be cases where disagreement and misunderstanding are hard to disentangle. However, if translators have spent days helping aliens to build shelters, hunt game, and carry out other constitutive activities *before* becoming sufficiently fluent in their language to discuss their beliefs about magic, spirits, etc., then there seems to be a way out of the original dilemma of translation. The possibility of confusing misunderstanding with disagreement may extend to a debate about why, for instance, their hunt was successful. Does, say, the 'deer spirit' really give them their quarry or not? But what translators will not discover, after chasing a deer all day, killing it and eating it with aliens, is that a misunderstanding has occurred and that they were not hunting at all.

Thus far we have shown that in order for *any* radical translation to take place – much less to achieve any degree of success – there must be a measure of agreement between translator and alien both about what is being done and the way language is being used to do it. Constitutive activities provide a practical bridgehead of interpretation into an alien language through their being to some degree intelligible prior to any grasp of the alien language. Such activities also constitute the social context within which language is learned by children within their own culture. Language acquisition has so far been equated with radical translation since this is such a useful test-bed for the consideration of problems concerning meaning, indeterminacy and truth. Yet this situation is highly problematic. If ambiguities of ostensive reference create such formidable obstacles for radical translators already in possession of linguistic expertise, then infants faced with the same ambiguities and with no linguistic clues to go on would presumably be silenced for ever. This is clearly not the case and the practical formulation of infant language learning shows why.

In light of his keen awareness of referential ambiguities, it is surprising that Quine's own analysis of language learning is behaviouristic. He argues that once the infant has learned to apply a specific name (e.g. 'blue' or 'cat') correctly to an appropriate experience, it can then apply it to other 'similar' experiences through deciding whether or not the new sufficiently conforms to the old. When faced, for example, with a different shade of blue or a different type of cat from those involved in its original linguistic conditioning, somehow the infant possesses the innate capacity to 'see' appropriate similarities and dissimilarities. On the basis of this capacity, it will then inductively generalize and use 'blue' or 'cat' correctly or incorrectly as the case may be. This is implausible. On the one hand, some names (e.g. cat) will be used to refer to a wide variety of experiences. On the other hand, different names (e.g. 'turquoise', 'blue') will be employed to refer to experiences which are in fact very similar. So even if an infant were conditioned to use the word 'blue' to apply to one shade of blue, why assume that it will be able to do so for all of those other shades to which it has not been exposed? Similarly, if the infant were confronted with other names applied to shades which were quite close to the one with which it had started, would this not destroy any consistent conditioning that had already been established? Thus ostensive reference *alone* – even with consistent patterns of reinforcement – seems too ambiguous to constitute the foundation for even the simplest aspects of language learning.

Behaviourism succeeds no better in explaining the acquisition of the capacity to combine words in a grammatical way. Again, for Quine, the innate capacity for inductive generalization provides the mechanism. For instance, the infant first learns words such as 'foot', 'hurt', or 'hand'. Positive reinforcement occurs when 'foot hurts' is asserted in appropriate circumstances and the same happens when 'hand hurts' is substituted in a similar situation. So, it is argued, the infant is conditioned to combine words and to look for analogies, and its understanding of syntax can be reduced to reinforced grammatical habits which work in conjunction with its innate inductive capacities. Therefore, the child learns the specific grammar it does because its linguistic experiences are contingently what they are. Yet the infant's initial experiences of grammar are just as ambiguous as its first encounters with names. Consider, for example, the difference between naming and asserting. Why should the infant ever learn to separate or positively distinguish between 'foot' and 'hurts' as a name (i.e. 'foot hurts') for the pain in its foot? Simply on the basis of repeated utterances, its parents will be unable to discern which use is which and will inevitably reward correct and incorrect uses. Presumably it will also be just as unclear to the child what it is being rewarded for. Indeed, even if the infant does correctly combine one set of words in a way which consistently suggests that it is following a specific grammatical rule, the same ambiguity will arise when it attempts to combine others in accordance with the same rule (e.g. 'hand hurts'). As they stand, the linguistic responses of both parents and children remain indeterminate and there is no clear pattern of positive or negative reinforcement from which to learn.

There can be no doubt that ostensive reference is indeterminate, as Quine suggests. But there is equally no doubt that since language is successfully learned, indeterminacy is somehow resolved *in practice*. It is the nature of this 'practice' which must be clarified. As with the case of the radical translator, the practice does not initially consist in the activity of pointing, naming and recording the patterns of assent and denial of those who are assumed to be using names in specific ways. Rather it involves *using language to do things* which have already been learned. For example, in English the language of tools is subject to all of the referential ambiguities which we have already described. Infants do not learn which things are 'hammers' because they are consistently called as such and bear a perceptual similarity to other objects which are also referred to in the same way. Indeterminacy is too great on too many levels for this to be possible. Learning the language is in fact preceded by learning (or at least recognizing how) to hammer and understanding that the rules associated with ascribing the name in question relate not just to perception but to a network of practical activity on which the success and failure of language use will turn. Try hammering (nails, for instance) with a mallet and see how quickly it becomes clear that hammers and mallets are very similar but different sorts of things. Without the capacity successfully to participate in some activities *prior* to learning the associated language, the infant will not be in a position to test what is and what is not linguistically appropriate to those activities with anything like the degree of determinacy that characterizes linguistic understanding. It is not experience as such that is relevant to such judgments; rather it is what the child and others are doing that focuses its attention on what others might be speaking about. On its own, the experience of the child is simply too rich and continuous to provide a focus for its attention.

Rationality, conceptual change and practical activity

So we would argue that both translators and infants develop general linguistic competence through identifying and participating in constitutive activities. If translator and alien can be said rationally to appraise such activities *prior* to the development of linguistic competence, then the rationality of appraisal cannot, as relativists suggest, be predicted solely on alien language use. This certainly appears to be the case in practice. For example, there are some ways in which a shelter just cannot be built, or crops grown or sickness healed – whatever the culture and whatever the language. Crops cannot be grown through burning them, nor sickness healed through cutting off the patient's head. Prior to the acquisition of linguistic competence, a radical translator participating in constitutive activity will therefore be able recognizably to do the right thing (e.g. hold a support at just the right angle to position the roof properly) or, of course, the wrong thing. It will also be possible to show better ways of accomplishing agreed aims which aliens will accept and adopt – or to recognize the limitations of one's own methods.

This kind of debate can occur in practice because, by hypothesis, *some* constitutive activities sufficiently coincide between *each* culture. If the shelter is built (or the crops grow or the sickness is healed) to the joint satisfaction of translator and alien, then practical communication is clearly occurring. Where there are disagreements or misunderstandings in practice, then they can – potentially at least – be resolved through practice. For Quine's dilemma of radical translation to arise, some attempt must be made to communicate with language about the reasons for success or failure. Disagreement can obviously be mistaken for misunderstanding and vice versa. However, in the above example of rational communication in the practice of construction, linguistic competence between translator and alien has not yet evolved. What can it mean to suggest that when such competence is acquired, translator and alien then learn that they have really been misunderstanding each other all along, despite persistent successful resolutions of their practical problems?

Once linguistic competence is acquired – and the test of this will be the translator's ability to use alien language in the execution of further constitutive activities – it will be possible to begin to ask questions. This will enable discussion of why the aliens engage in such activities in their own particular ways. Their answers will reveal the rules which they perceive themselves to be following and the beliefs about the world which they exhibit in so doing. In this respect, even though their activity is constitutive (e.g. seed planting), its associated language is not. Again, people can say almost anything about what they do and why. Provided that nothing constitutively hinges on what is said, then questions of rational appraisal do not arise. So, suppose the translator does not agree with the supernaturalistic explanation of an illness. If aliens are healthy in ways that both translator and alien accept (i.e. neither would attempt in their own culturally specific ways to intervene), rational debate will prove futile. For in the cycles of health and illness jointly perceived as obtaining for particular cultures, there is no practical reason for, say, a traditional healer to consider western medical views. In these cases, traditional methods will seem to work and the ostensible successes of western medicine can always be explained away. And vice versa. Parity of this sort is seldom if ever found between cultures; but none has a monopoly of wisdom, or ignorance.

Yet, suppose that through more and more determinate translation, the translator does indeed understand that elaborate shelter decorations are attempts to ward off evil spirits believed to be responsible for a new illness. Suppose further that despite such decoration, the aliens are distressed by a rapid increase in the illness. Suppose finally that from the perspective of western medicine, the translator correctly diagnoses that the illness is a form of dysentery which can be successfully treated with available antibiotics. It is at this stage of their possible intervention – where something might constitutively turn on the difference between their conceptual schemes – that the translator and alien might well engage in rational debate. Using newly acquired linguistic competence, translators will be able to communicate disagreement with alien healing methods and to suggest the superiority of their own in this case. More specifically, they will be in a position to assert intelligibly that the physical administration of a certain substance will stop the illness. From the perspective of the aliens, there is nothing *in principle* to suggest that the substance will not be tried, provided enough is perceived to turn on taking the translator seriously. There is no more reason to doubt this than to doubt that western doctors would do the same under similar circumstances. If the translator's prescribed treatment is consistently successful in the face of the alien's, there is equally nothing in principle to suggest that it will not be adopted in place of the old healing practice.

In short, despite culturally specific differences which might remain between them, the translator and alien can agree, disagree and debate about what is to be *done* in particular circumstances. To the extent that their debate reaches a conclusion which is then consistently acted upon by both, they have recognizably disagreed – in the same way in principle in which neighbours might – and have resolved their disagreement in a rational manner.

Thus, there is no difference in principle between convincing aliens non-verbally that four supports are better than three in the construction of shelters and convincing them in practice *which includes language* that pills of a certain kind are more effective than decorated shelters in healing certain jointly accepted manifestations of ill-health. As far as constitutive activities are concerned, language can be regarded as just as much of a tool as, say, a lever. With its help, goals can be achieved which recognizably demand the same action irrespective of culture. Constitutive debate which employs language is thus qualitatively the same as non-verbal constitutive debate about the efficiency of tools. Without understanding the use of the lever, one person might be convinced that a particular task is impossible. Another, who does understand its use, can *show* the first the incorrectness of her/his position without necessarily saying anything. Similarly, aliens might well believe a certain task to be impossible (e.g. one concerning agricultural yield) because its successful completion is apparently incompatible with their beliefs. As in the case of the lever, it is possible for translators to show the superiority of their linguistic tools (e.g. of their theories about how to increase agricultural yield) and for aliens to recognize this superiority in the manner already described. Translators can also learn from aliens and for the same reasons. Both, of course, may decide for other reasons (e.g. religious, economic, political) not to implement their new technical expertise.

Once it is accepted that a measure of linguistic communication has been established, we have already indicated that hard cases will obviously arise where misunderstanding and disagreement still threaten to be indistinguishable. But such problems will only arise where an aim is to some extent already shared by both translator and alien. Where aims are admittedly culturally specific (e.g. those embodied in the game of cricket) translators may not understand, but they will have nothing to disagree about. Questions of disagreement arise about the accomplishment of a shared purpose (e.g. childbirth, buying and selling, curing, cultivation, hunting, building) which turns in part upon being able reliably to predict future events of certain types either with or without a measure of human intervention. In cases like this, a resolution of the issues does not take place in terms of arbitration by objectively neutral observation. Rather, it occurs relative to the provisional agreement between both parties about what it is that they are doing or attempting to do. This kind of resolution – through practice – does not bring to translation that determinacy envisaged by those who hanker after objective criteria of synonymy between languages and a once-and-for-all decision procedure for science. However, it does define the direction that must be taken for even greater precision to be brought to the interpretation of what others say and do.

Constitutive activities – the practical agreements on which we have predicated our treatment of translation, language acquisition and rational appraisal – also serve a crucial role in conceptual innovation. In some ways this is the most interesting aspect of such activities and the one which most justifies the title 'constitutive'. We have argued that continuity of communication across generations, cultural divides and conceptual changes alike has a *non-arbitrary* foundation in prior agreement in practical activity of some kind. This foundation is non-arbitrary because the world, regardless of how or whether it is understood, places constraints upon the possible forms of practical agreement people may reach with each other. The material reality of such constraints, along with their being recognizable because they will have been experienced in practice, is what allows one to speak of a sense in which people may join in the same activity independently of the terms they may use to frame their intentions. Therefore, it is only in relation to the obstinacy of the material world that it can be recognized that there is a measure of real rather than apparent agreement between human beings.

The word 'obstinacy' is appropriate because the world resists you, rather than imposing itself on your passive minds or nervous systems. And it is only in relation to that resistance that humans can agree. As we have shown, you do not agree with one another merely by virtue of saying the same things under the same circumstances, any more than books from the same printing or records from the same press 'agree'. Rather it is because the world resists their actions in the same ways that what people do can become *concerted*, rather than merely similar; and it is in relation to their acting in concert that the point of assertion, assent, denial, truth and falsity acquires its purchase. If nothing anyone did ever turned on anything that was said, then the meaning of what you said and of what you understood others to say could be anything you pleased – words would mean what you meant them to mean. This being said, material constraints associated with constitutive activities only emerge as such, and become intelligible, in the context of the historical development of human practical activity. In the case of each such constraint, its communality extends, whatever its range, over the participants in some particular human practice. The totality of such practices, past and present, constitutes an interwoven fabric, connected at the point of each constraint with the laws of nature, including, of course, those which have yet to be discovered. Throughout the whole of this fabric, few if any constitutive activities extend as unbroken or uniform threads. Put this way it becomes clear that practical agreements are evolutionary in character and can in no sense be complete or permanent; and it is this that leads us finally to the issue of conceptual innovation.

Imagine two scientists who collaborate for years until one day they disagree over the significance of some observation or theoretical criticism; assume also that this does not result from some simple error they could both acknowledge – an error of calculation, for instance. One decides that their existing theory should be retained, and a way found to accommodate the point, while the other is convinced that a radical revision is required. Does this disagreement reveal that all along, despite their collaboration, they have held quite different theories – that they have never really agreed with one another? Clearly, before their disagreement, they agreed as far as it was *possible* to agree and subsequently, however profound their dispute, they still agree on what they were and are trying to accomplish. Thus they are not like two players at a chequered board waking up to the fact that one is playing chess and the other draughts. It is unnecessary to descend to the rock bottom of hunting, shelter-building and the like to find that it is the non-arbitrary shared practice of the scientists (e.g. what they succeed in making and/or manipulating when they conduct an experiment) which mediates between the disparities of belief and/or conceptual understanding with which they carry on their disagreement. Through such practices, two theories can be related to each other as rivals, regardless of the divergencies between their conceptual foundations. For this reason, the practical agreements in constitutive activities will always be partly invisible. Their nature will not be captured completely by any statement of the purposes they are believed to serve nor by the account given of how these purposes are accomplished. The discovery of new ways to accomplish them is thus left open and may occur in fields as specialized as atomic physics or as broad as the organization of productive labour within capitalism.

With this in mind, we are now in a position to give a far broader characterization of constitutive activities than we have thus far. They constitute those areas of human practical agreement which make specific forms of cultural life materially possible and which therefore *call for* the imputation to them of rules which will maximize their success in achieving this goal. This being said, they neither *dictate* precisely the rules that shall be imputed to them, nor can they be exhaustively characterized (as culturally specific activities can) by the particular rules which are held to govern them. Consider a firm that makes tools, for example. On the one hand, tool-making is a constitutive activity if ever there was one. It transcends both cultural barriers and conceptual innovations to provide a broad continuity of intelligibility as the *same* activity regardless of the different ways in which it may be understood. On the one hand, the registration of a tool firm as a limited company with all the specifications of its existence as a legal entity – its responsibilities under English law to its employees, customers and creditors – is clearly culturally specific. The framework of specificity might change if, for instance, the firm became a publicly quoted company, or were nationalized. Historically, of course, such companies developed from the medieval system of guilds, masters, journeymen and apprentices – further examples of cultural specificity – while the activity of tool-making has itself materially altered and become more refined. Yet one can easily see the continuity of tool-making through the development from a simple smithy to a nationalized machine-tool company, through a number of intermediate changes to the specific rules by which tool-making was progressively understood.

Thus, expressions in a language take on their sense only in relation to 'the whole of the rest of the mechanism', in Wittgenstein's phrase. The parts of the mechanism which tend to escape the attention of the philosopher are the practical contexts in which language plays a part. This must mean that the entire organization of practical activity at a given time has a bearing upon the sense that expressions of this language may have. Hence, it should be expected that major changes in such organization will call for major conceptual changes. Again, this is not to claim that practical activity determines concepts in some mechanical fashion. Alterations in practice can call for the invention of techniques and rules concerning their meaning and use without specifying how human creativity will respond, if at all. All that can be said when describing a new way of understanding as a response to a problem is that it was prompted or called for by that problem, but not caused or entailed by it – it might, after all, have gone unsolved. Similarly, innovators may not foresee the material or social consequences of their creations. This does not imply that the significance and efficacy of concepts are wholly relative to the particular interests of their originators – any more than the significance or efficacy of inventions like the wheel or the differential calculus can be determined solely by asking whether or not they served the original purpose of their inventor.

So it is immensely plausible to suppose that there existed mutually reinforcing influences linking the rise of modern science and the transformation of the contemporary view of the universe to the Renaissance, the age of exploration and colonization, the Reformation, the rise of mercantile capitalism and the decline of feudalism. The science of the socially static and hierarchical medieval world envisaged the universe too as static and hierarchically ordered according to divine purpose. This view was displaced by one which sought instead to understand the impersonal framework of causal laws which governed all natural events. The former science placed humanity at the centre of the universe but subordinate to the divine purpose exemplified by birth, growth, death, the seasons and the fruitfulness of the earth. It was replaced by a science which, through its mastery of causal laws, gave to humanity the possibility of intervention in, and eventual mastery over, nature on an unprecedented scale. This transformation took place at the same time as trade and exploration grew and, with it, the growing tendency to regard the world and humans in instrumental and exploitative ways – seeing everything with a view to the personal, primarily commercial advantage that could be derived from it. The story of Robinson Crusoe, written towards the end of the initial phase of this transformation, reveals little of the influence of the new discoveries of natural science, but much of the new individualistic and exploitative outlook which increasingly drew strength from the economic transformation that it was helping to facilitate. Mastery of his environment and of others for his own benefit was Crusoe's imperative – how different from the attitude of feudal times, with its resignation to God's purpose in giving life and taking it away.

This outlook can hardly be said to diminish the rise of science to the level of 'mere ideology' – open to assessment only in the respects in which it facilitated the rise of capitalism. Yet, at the same time, it would be perverse to ignore the evident parallel between the view of nature that science engendered and the orientation towards the world as the provider of natural resources which is equally engendered by the perspectives of commerce and industry – or to suppose that this parallel is mere coincidence. It is in this sense that the organization of practical activity and the economic framework within which it is organized have a crucial bearing upon the conceptual developments within a given society. They do so not as a causal or logical determinant, but as that matrix of practical agreement which guarantees that communication within and between such developments will remain possible. 'Pure science' cannot, any more than art, religion, literature or philosophy, be portrayed as subordinated to economic and practical activities. But each does depend upon a certain form of division of labour in society from which arises the possibility that people may reasonably concern themselves with such things in the way they do. Moreover, the problems scientists seek to solve, the matters which artists depict, or the issues to which literature, religious and philosophical doctrines are directed, do not arise in a vacuum. For a form of life and a language must already exist, within which a person's preoccupations with such things must be intelligible to some degree. Otherwise, they could not *begin* to engage in the relevant practice, no matter how innovative their eventual contribution might turn out to be. Of course, the same point applies to others who are able to understand conceptual changes and to see their relevance to the solution of problems which retain their practical identity throughout. If Einstein's innovations had been *totally* original, then neither he nor his contemporaries could have understood or scientifically acted upon them.

So language acquires its purchase on reality through its involvement in practical activities and the most important activities in this respect possess a measure of intelligibility in and of themselves. In translation, in the acquisition of language, in rational appraisal and where conceptual innovation occurs, we have proposed that disagreement in beliefs can only be distinguished in principle from misunderstanding of meaning if there is more to shared language use than mere coincidence of utterance with experiential conditions. *Concerted engagement upon the same tasks* is the only token of the real agreement which ultimately makes linguistic communication and human progress possible. Agreement in practical activities has the capacity to perform the constitutive role it does for agreement in what humans say because it is the ultimate bearer of the imputation of sense that the use of language requires. This is only revealed, however, because the same practical activities can be the bearer of divergent imputations. It is in this fashion that such activities practically mediate between conflicting conceptual schemes. They call for and constrain but do not determine the sense that is made of them.

To conclude, relativists correctly take the problem of interpretation very seriously and are keenly aware of the difficulties which it poses for any form of empiricism. Indeed, they take it so seriously that it impales them on the horns of a dilemma. For they endorse the principle of charity that an accurate understanding of the activities of others is possible in their own terms, no matter how apparently strange or perverse. At the same time, they wish to reject the existence of a common core of shared concepts and practices which unites all humans and thereby all cultures. We have shown that acceptance of the principle of charity entails acceptance of such a common core, one which provides the foundation for the rational assessment of divergent conceptual systems. This should not be surprising. The concept of charity entails that there are *standards* by which people can be judged. It is precisely these standards which are evoked, for example, in appraising the horrific poverty and brutal practices of some traditional cultures which in other respects are rich in sociological complexity, historical tradition and artistic creativity. Is it charitable to dismiss such horrors as unreal because they are not necessarily conceptualized as such and to focus one's scientific attention only on an accurate description of the richness?

One thing is clear. To try do do anything about such horror entails a belief in the universality of human *need* linked to the best available technical understanding which can be brought to bear to meet it. If human understanding does, as we claim, have a *practical* foundation, this is because 'doing something to meet your needs' is universally intelligible, however much beliefs about what these 'needs' are might vary. We shall have more to say in the next chapter about the character of such needs and their relationship to the problem of the determination of real rather than apparent human interests, raised in our earlier discussion of ideology. For now, we are content to have shown that there is no reason in principle why need-oriented understanding should not be accessible to everyone, thus enabling them to develop a critical perspective on their own beliefs and practices which does not collapse into subjectivism. Of course, what they decide to do with such understanding is an open question and the human and ecological disaster associated with much modern technology suggests that the abuses of the past must in some way be corrected. In light of the distribution of power and patterns of corporate domination within the developed and underdeveloped world alike, these choices are at present little more than abstract visions. Yet if one believes in associated struggles for liberation then it must also be accepted that they are coherent visions, a long way from the prescriptive insularity of much relativist writing.

Annotated bibliography

While the foundation for relativism rests on the arguments in the philosophy of language considered in the previous chapter, the motivation for advancing specific relativistic theses has come from a variety of sources. The work of Kuhn has stimulated a great deal of discussion of science from an unabashed relativist standpoint. In their essay in Hollis and Lukes 1982, Barnes and Bloor defend what they term the 'strong programme' of relativistic sociology of science. This is defended further in Bloor's essay in Brown 1984, and expanded and applied in Barnes 1977 and Bloor 1976, while the application of Kuhn's work to social science is considered in Barnes 1981.

A second source of motivation for adopting a specifically relativistic stance has come from the convergence of problems of ethnocentricity in anthropology and the problems of giving adequate recognition to deviant rationalia for action in subjectivist interpretive sociology. This source of relativism is reviewed in Giddens 1976, chapter 1. The modern debate among philosophers was initiated by Winch's essay 'Understanding a primitive society', to be found in Wilson 1970, along with a number of other important contributions to the debate largely initiated by Winch's essay. For further anthropological background, see Horton and Finnegan 1973, and Skorupski 1976. The continuation of the debate can be followed in the essays and bibliography of Hollis and Lukes 1982, and in the essays in Brown 1984. Bernstein 1983, part II, surveys the range of current debate and in the remainder of the book seeks to situate the relativistic dilemma in the broader context of the development of philosophical ideas. In his essay in Brown 1984, Bloor links cultural relativism and relativism towards natural science with a third source of motivation for the thesis of relativism. This arises from an interpretation of Wittgenstein's later philosophy, which he has expounded at length in Bloor 1983. A similar link is also apparent if Winch's essay in Wilson 1970 is taken together with the thesis of Winch 1970.

The importance of logic in relation to 'translation bridgeheads' is stressed by Hollis and Lukes in Wilson 1970. The non-relativistic 'principle of charity', which maximizes attributions of truth to individual sentences in an alien language, is invoked in Davidson 1984b, chapter 13. The attempt by relativists to construe 'charity' in relation to consistency between sentences in the alien language rather than attribution of truth to individual sentences is one target of Gellner's criticism in his essay in Wilson 1970. The discussion in Macdonald and Pettit, chapter 1, introduces the idea that practical activity has a part to play in resolving difficulties of translation in order to strengthen the repudiation of relativism which they derive from Davidson's arguments.

On the general issue of the constraint the external world places on human language and activity, in Wilson 1970 Winch introduces the notion that the 'human condition' might somehow unite cultures. This idea has been explored from both conservative and Marxist viewpoints, and from positions in between. Levy 1981, chapter 7, gives a conservative view, as against the Marxist approach in Timpanaro 1975, while Trigg, in Brown 1984, examines the claim of sociobiology. Midgley 1978 and Hirst and Woolley 1982 consider at length the contribution that a biologically fixed human nature might make to human social life – see also the notes to chapter 3 of this book for more on biological determinism. Quine's view that the behaviouristic constraints of stimulus and response must be those which condition language acquisition, which we criticize, is developed in Quine 1960, chapters 2 and 3, and in Quine 1974, chapters 1 and 2. These approaches, and the approach which derives its relativistic impetus from an interpretation of Wittgenstein's later philosophy, are at variance with our argument, much of which is reproduced from Doyal and Harris 1983. This provides a much more detailed bibliography than we have space for here. The key idea in that essay – that the nature of the material world constrains the variety and arbitrariness of directly intelligible 'forms of life' – derives from the discussion of the 'builders' at the start of Wittgenstein 1973. More generally, the idea that practical activity has a measure of intelligibility independently of language use is tied up with the notion of a 'form of life' alluded to at various points in Wittgenstein 1973. This is one of the more cryptic of Wittgenstein's ideas. The interpretation of the phrase 'agreement in form of life' in Wittgenstein 1973, para. 241, as a covert conceptual agreement can be found in Winch 1970, chapters 2 and 5, as convention, in Bloor 1983, chapters 6 and 7, and as natural similarity in Stroud's essay in Pitcher 1966. By contrast, argument for the view which we have taken that the embodiment of rule-following in an agreement in form of life does *not* reduce to something else, but is *sui generis*, can be found in Pitkin 1972, chapter 4, and in Giddens 1979, chapter 2, where Giddens also contrasts *following* a rule with *formulating* one. While we have drawn a specific parallel between the thought of Wittgenstein and Marx, general treatments of the interrelation of their ideas can be found in Rubinstein 1981 and Easton 1983.

8
SOCIAL STRUCTURE AND ITS MORAL EVALUATION

The first two chapters of this book mainly concerned models of knowledge and explanation derived from the natural sciences. We argued that the firmness with which natural science is indisputably established does not arise because 'facts speak for themselves'. Facts are always accommodated by natural science within schemes of interpretation supplied by explanatory hypotheses. In chapter 3 we concluded that the interpretation of human activity as physical movement – 'behaviour' – simply divides up the 'facts' in a way that has no bearing on what requires explanation and that the individual 'reasons' appropriate to such explanation were not in any straightforward sense the same as the causes of physical events. However, having rejected a deterministic framework for social scientific explanation, we then found ourselves taking issue with the model to which such a perspective is most commonly opposed – the individualistic, humanist viewpoint. This approach was shown to be fundamentally flawed through its neglect of the social character of human action and the irreducible part that must be played in its understanding by notions such as 'rules' and 'institutions'. Perhaps the most important reason for emphasizing the social context in which the individual decides to act is the possibility that what people think they are doing may not be what they are really doing. Along with the limitations on the understanding of actions achievable just by discovering individual intentions, this poses the problems which we discussed in connection with the concept of ideology. It also raises an explanatory problem of a different order – that of the *unintended consequences* of human action and of the systematic character of these consequences in the operation of social systems. This chapter will analyse this operation in order to develop a theory of social structure which is consistent with the conception of human action and rationality which we have developed. It will conclude by setting out some of the ethical consequences which follow from this theory.

The intended vs. the unintended structure of society

People may explain for themselves why their actions have the consequences that they intend. The key question we must address, however, is how far such explanations could suffice to explain *what* they intend, let alone what may follow from their actions by way of unintended consequences. It is these which require social scientific theories for their explanation. This need arises from the *opacity* of social life. It has a structure, performs functions and has effects which no one explicitly intends, resulting from actions which people perform for quite different reasons. Take economic competition, for example. This appears to those who participate in it as a competition in which each individual aims to maximize the advantage derived from each economic transaction. In a market economy, the aggregate effect of all such actions will have the unintended effect of promoting the most efficient individuals and enterprises. Individuals who are successful will always be able to offer more for sale at lower prices than their competitors – attracting customers away from those who are less efficient and prospering at their expense. And it is not just conservatives wedded to the eighteenth-century ideas of Adam Smith who harbour such thoughts. Even in socialist economies which were traditionally planned by highly centralized state bureaucracies, debates now rage about the advantages of a 'mixed economy' with a healthy private sector. These have been in response to some of the unintended consequences of central planning and the abolition of private ownership – shortages in consumer goods, poor quality and general inefficiency.

Yet many argue that there will be other unintended effects of capitalist enterprise as well. One will be that in so far as human needs are met within a competitive market economy, it will not be in proportion to the scale of those needs themselves but in proportion to individuals' capacities to *buy* what they *think* they need (e.g. cigarettes). Another consequence might be adding to the destructive pollution of the environment. For example, toxic air and water emissions might well be acceptable when viewed from the perspective of the trade-off between the capital costs of cleaning them up and their relatively minimal effects. Yet their *cumulative* effect – no doubt unintended by the owners/managers of the firms concerned – can be disastrous. Those who condemn capitalism for related reasons argue that it is hardly surprising that social inequality exists on such a large scale in societies organized around the merits of competition and that this and its unintended consequences – poorer health, education and general welfare for the disadvantaged – vitiate Smith's dream of fair competition between all. It is also claimed that the lack of economic concern for the infrastructure of society – roads, sewers, schools, hospitals, etc. – which is also the unintended consequence of so much emphasis on individual business interests requires at the very least a strong public sector to do what the private sector cannot.

These sorts of debates are important and we shall return to them. For now, they should be seen as schematic examples of what a systematic understanding of some of the unintended consequences of social actions might look like. Among other things, it would open up an entirely new perspective in the range of choices available to members of a society. These would concern matters which people had not hitherto realized were the results of their own actions and so subject to their control or choice. They would also raise the prospect of a collective choice about the kind of social and economic organization under which people have to live their lives.

Making sense of the unintended consequences of human action therefore is different in kind from the type of understanding which is either causal or intentional. For example, the discovery that a healthy market sector in an otherwise socialist mode of economic organization can help to increase the efficiency of certain aspects of production and distribution has proved enormously liberating for some individuals involved and has served actively to strengthen their commitment to socialism. Yet those individuals who are attempting to make money through this permitted private enterprise do not intend these beneficial consequences. Indeed, such benefits were not even conceived as a possibility until the economic assumptions of traditional state socialism were no longer interpreted as deterministic laws of society no different in principle from laws of nature. Similarly, the often quoted view of the current Thatcher government that 'there is no alternative' to the restrictive economic policies which have so devastated traditional sectors of British industry also presupposes such a causal conception of capitalist social relations. Those who criticize these policies argue, among other things, that their most horrific unintended consequence – high levels of unemployment and associated human tragedy – is avoidable through more government intervention in the form of direct investment in promising sectors of industry. Representatives of the government respond that the unintended consequences of *these* policies would be even worse than the present state of affairs. And so the debate continues. The point here is to recognize that the debate is about choice – how humans should choose to organize their public affairs rather than seeing themselves as the passive and determined 'stuff' of nature.

In chapters 3, 4 and 5 we argued that intentions may explain *why* people act as they do, yet it is rules which explain *what* it is they do. The accuracy of the agents' own explanations depends upon the measure of understanding they themselves possess of the relevant rules which structure their actions. Social scientists content with explanations at the level of agents' intentions alone will get no further than telling people what some will already know. This may well be far from negligible. Yet the understanding people require in order effectively to follow a given set of rules can fall very far short of their intending that all the consequences of their actions should result from what they do. Thus many of the participants in a market economy are in much the same position as beginners at chess. They know how all the pieces are moved and what counts as a loss rather than a gain, but their grasp of the consequences of any given move is very slight. The regularity with which such players lose to players who have a better understanding of the game is not unlike the regularity with which most people in a market economy do not get rich. In both cases the winners win at the expense of those who lose and do so by virtue of a better grasp of what is really going on. This said, however, a minimal level of self-understanding is necessary on the part of participants – even the losers – as a necessary condition for their actions to have those consequences which most of them admittedly did not intend and failed to anticipate. For example, to go bankrupt in business entails that you know quite a lot about the rules of the market place. What it may mean is that you are a bad business person, not that you are not one at all!

In seeking to point up the objective independence of rules from subjective intentions, we have made much of examples of games. However, unlike chess, social and economic relations are not a game but rest on foundations provided by those practical activities discussed in the last chapter – those in which members of a society must engage in order to serve their interests and sustain their lives. The most important unintentional consequences in any society will be those which ensure that these activities are successfully carried out. It is in this regard that all but the simplest societies exhibit a more or less complex *division of labour* which by and large is the unintended aggregate result of the ways in which their members conduct their individual lives. It is hardly contentious to claim that social strucures exhibit such a division – not everyone has to or can do everything necessary in order to sustain themselves. Very diverse and distinctive forms of activity, which are often specific to particular cultures, are to be found in human societies. Imagine trying to explain the occupation of an insurance salesman to a nineteenth-century Zulu warrior or a medieval European monk and you will get some inkling of just how historically and culturally specific 'normality' can be! While diverse and distinctive sets of beliefs and attendant intentions may be cited to explain this variety of activities, we argued in the last chapter that the intelligibility of diverse cultures must be found elsewhere. Rather, there are constitutive activities, at least some of which are recognizable in every society, which possess a measure of intelligibility independently of the subjective intentions of those who perform them. This enables them to serve as the means by which individuals effect an entrance into the practice, language and beliefs of a culture, either as an outsider or as a child being inducted into social life for the first time. At a collective level, it is these activities which render different societies comparable to one another in respect of the functions performed by their component institutions. They involve the production of goods and services required to satisfy the *basic needs* which all humans have irrespective of culture and which must be satisfied if cultures themselves are to survive.

Societies differ, of course, in exactly how they go about these tasks and which loom largest in their division of labour. However, practices like hunting, cultivation, shelter-building, preparation of food, child care, tool-making, etc. will be identifiable as basically the same, irrespective of the beliefs of those who perform them. There are few activities of this kind which are strictly universal but that is not the issue. Far more of them form overlapping filaments of practical activity in a thread which connects all societies. It follows from this picture that such tasks may well be consciously understood by members of some other society in terms of explicit beliefs quite different from those you would use to understand similar actions which you perform. For instance, you can imagine a society in which those who cultivate grain see this as a sacred task akin to the worship of the land and who attribute more importance to religious observance than to what you might see as techniques of cultivation. By contrast, in western society farmers will be principally concerned with the *price* of what they grow. They will do things to their crops which will be unintelligible to the first group – cover them with poison to make them look better and even destroy them during a bumper harvest to keep up their price. It is in this context that practices can be viewed as identical while acceptance of the reasons behind them can vary widely between societies. What will not vary is that a division of labour will have to exist which is sufficient for food to be produced, shelters to be built, and children to be reared.

Not only is it the case that viable social structures entail viable divisions of labour; they must also possess normative frameworks which ensure that those divisions are accepted by their members as natural and normal. This will be achieved through the existence of sets of institutional rules from which the divisions themselves will follow, by and large, as unintended consequences. Such rules will in some way stipulate duties to produce and rights to consume the fruits of human labour. In legal/ political/economic terms they will implicitly or explicitly structure the institutions of property and exchange. It is in this context that the members of the society, with a greater or lesser clarity, construe their individual and collective interests and the ways in which these are served by their participation in social and economic life. The implicit or explicit value of activities, traditions, artefacts and accomplishments is established upon the foundation of such rules. They dictate in religious or secular terms a conception of the 'good' life – of the way in which happiness, the satisfaction of desires and what is ethically right may best be reconciled with one another. So in western societies someone may accept that it is rational and normal to work at a specific type of job, to expect the sort of private space and opportunities which property and possessions can provide and to calculate their own self-interest through doing the sorts of things that they believe necessary to bring these things about. Yet they probably do not perceive themselves as reinforcing the division of labour which makes their employment, property and possessions a real possibility. Indeed, they may have never heard the expression 'division of labour'. They feel that the *point* of what they do is elsewhere – in these rights and duties which they perceive to legitimate their daily lives.

Thus despite the diversity of past and present human societies, there are objective, non-arbitrary limitations on what social structures can do while enabling their members to succeed in sustaining and reproducing themselves. Since they make possible the co-operation necessary in meeting basic human needs, social structures can be compared with respect to their performance. For example, on the basis of a crude measure like life expectancy, it is clear that Britain is doing better than, say, Nigeria, and China is doing better now than it was before the revolution. Social structures must also be organized in such a way that their rules can be learnt by new members. Formally or informally, they will contain institutions of *socialization* which will facilitate this learning – everything from the family to schools to the courts. Of course, rules do not necessarily need to be self-consciously imparted, but people must have the opportunity to *join in* related activities, learning no more than what would count as correctly and incorrectly doing what others already do. So in following rules which constrain and give identity to their social and economic relations, members of a society cohere with one another within a social structure into which each of them was born and which they sustain and reproduce through their participation. The fact that sustaining this structure is not usually the intentional goal of their participation only serves to underline again the opacity of much social activity for the participants.

In placing so much emphasis on the relationship between social structure, the division of labour and constitutive activities, we may seem to have neglected the many facets of social life which do not serve immediate economic functions. While the emphasis has been deliberate in this respect – these functions must be fulfilled in order for any others to be – two further points are worth noting. First, since divisions of labour are primarily the unintended consequences of people's actions, they are totally dependent on the intentions which inform such actions. These are enormously complex and diverse and must be investigated in relation to the spider's web of cultural rules in terms of which individual intentions are formulated. For example, in a wide variety of cultures, actors conceptualize their obligation to work in relation to their religion. In such cultural environments, therefore, religion is just as necessary for the material functions of social structure to be achieved as are the rules governing material production *per se*. In short, it is a stylistic device to separate the productive and reproductive functions of social structure from the culturally specific intentions through which it is understood and experienced by its members. The latter are no less real than the former. Second, it is also true to say that societies, like their members, do not live by bread alone. In focusing one's investigations on the real diversity of meaning in different cultures rather than on unintended consequences of related actions, one is not engaged in second-best social science. Part of the mystery of human life consists not just in the amazing ways in which people unintentionally organize themselves to produce and reproduce, but in the creativity and colour of the beliefs with which they express their artistry in doing so. To investigate this alone – the province of certain forms of anthropology – is of the highest scientific and humanistic value.

The duality of social structure

The preceding sketch of social structure and function is sufficiently definite for a problem to emerge which was touched upon in chapters 4 and 5. Is there not something wrong with a view which says that it is society itself which determines the significance of every action and utterance? We argued in chapter 5 that such a conception does not compromise the rational autonomy of the individual to make choices amongst intentions. Freedom and the capacity to deliberate and be critical are not absolutely unconditional states of the individual. You are the author of your utterances and actions and Shakespeare the author of *Hamlet* because of and not despite the context of rules within which this authorship is exercised. Total autonomy would be utterly arbitrary – unintelligible to others and meaningless to you. Without the rules of language you would be unable to speak, yet it is *you* who speaks, not language. Similarly, without the rules of your society, you would be unable to act. Yet it is you who acts, not society. Thus the importance of the individual has somehow to be reconciled with this *holistic* picture of society which says that the social whole or totality is not explicable in terms of, nor reducible to the character of, the individuals who comprise it.

This form of holism does not attribute some mysterious causal power or social mind to the totality of social relations, any more than it attributes what people say to the language that they speak. This totality does not itself 'do' or 'say' anything in its own right – only people can do this. Yet it is not people in aggregate who constitute such a totality. Just adding them up, so to speak, will tell you nothing about a social structure other than how many people are in it. To understand the totality of their relations with each other, you must grasp the grammatical and social rules they are following and the consequences that language use and activity in one part of the totality will have on other parts. For example, consider a revolution like the one in Nicaragua in 1979. The crucial events preceding the revolt were only made possible by the particular mode of interaction of its instigators. However, the consequences of these actions then began to be felt nationally and internationally in ways which were, at best, only partly realized by those involved. International-ly, the vociferousness of official American hostility to the revolution in relation, say, to broad questions of US international political and economic interests has certainly surprised and shocked many Sandinistas who did not plan for it. Naturally, many were equally unprepared for the development of a strong feminist consciousness among many women participating in the revolution who had often been educated by them. This example illustrates the extent to which social totalities overlap and certainly raises the spectre of a totality of relations which is global in scale.

The 'internal' relations between the actions constituting social tota-lities can be contrasted with the 'external' relations between the parts of a physical totality which can be explained in terms of the properties of its parts. For example, a stone which is part of a building would be the *same stone*, even if the relations it has to the other stones that comprise the building had never existed or if the building collapsed tomorrow. By contrast, a word which is part of a language in virtue of the relations it has to the other words in the language and to what that language is used to talk about would not be a word at all if those relations had never been or ceased to be – it would just be a senseless sound or mark. The same can be said about individual human actions and their relationships to other actions in a specific social environment. Without such relations they would be no more than senseless examples of physiological behaviour. This being said, internal relations are again no less real or objective than external ones. For example, it is just as possible to make a mistake as a chess-player or revolutionary as it is in stone masonry and perhaps with even more dramatic results!

Two apparently contradictory claims therefore remain concerning the relation of the individual to the social totality. On the one hand we have argued that social structures are real and exist prior to the lives and actions of individuals. On the other hand, we argued that nothing is the effect of a social totality which is not the result of the action of some individual(s). Were the first of these two claims correct, it might seem that individual agents could be no more than cyphers, acting out parts which had already been dictated for them by forces outside their control. This *top-down* representation of the relation between the individual and social structure yields a conception of human nature which can be called 'over-socialized'. Here, the stress is upon the dominance of the social totality over the formation of the individual. It is predominantly the *synchronic* relations between the two that are emphasized – the stability of the structure of relations organizing social life at a particular moment or brief period. Such a representation can be contrasted with the picture that seems to follow from the second claim above. For if nothing is the effect of a social structure that is not the result of the action of some individual(s), this would seem to attribute to individuals the capacity to construct such structures through the actions they perform. This *bottom-up* representation of the individual's relation to society yields a conception of human nature which can be called 'undersocialized'. Here the primacy of the individual over social structure is proclaimed and those relations between the two that are considered more important are predominantly *diachronic*, embracing all the detailed interactions through which over an extended period individuals participate in the creation and recreation of social life. In this sense the focus is on the detailed dynamics of social processes rather than on their structure.

It is easy to choose examples which appear convincingly to illustrate each approach. There are plenty of rules which you follow because of your upbringing, which feel like the influence on you of some external force. Try taking off all your clothes on a bus and see if you do not 'experience' a constraint! On the other hand, there are situations in which it is equally possible to feel that everything depends on what you *choose* to do. Here, your active and unconstrained decision will be the principal determinant of how matters turn out. Think of the one action in your life that you feel was *the* most important for you. These are the kinds of moments and experiences which twentieth-century existentialist writers like Jean-Paul Sartre have stressed as defining the human condition. The temptation is to choose one side of this picture as representing truth and the other as representing falsehood, rather than recognizing that each is necessary for the other. As we argued in chapter 5, freedom is thrown into relief only by its contrast with constraint, and constraint only recognized as the limit of freedom. For example, part of the beauty of a successful act of political liberation is the contrast with the tyranny which preceded it. Conversely, the horrors of tyranny present themselves as such because of the artificial and arbitrary limits which they place on human creativity.

When a social system is considered only in the form of a structural cross-section at a given historical moment, it is hard to envisage the dynamic character of the relations between such a system and those who belong to it. Conversely, from the standpoint of individuals making plans and decisions over the span of their lives, the dynamism may be apparent but not the structure in which it operates. Even institutions sometimes appear as little more than collections of individuals. For example, consider the division of labour again from two standpoints. The 'man-power planner' surveys the occupational structure calculating that it has space within it for so many doctors, lawyers, teachers, construction workers, miners, etc., and notes the extent to which recruitment to occupations is correlated with various aspects of social class. From this perspective, the division of labour appears as a fairly stable structure with an extremely strong influence on patterns of recruitment. Yet that is not how it appears from the standpoint of a young person about to begin a career. Here there are decisions to be taken, efforts to be made, and personal relations to construct, and each appears crucial to the individual's progress. Actions can appear to fit either model – acting out a role 'written for you' by social structure or taking an active and autonomous part in framing your own destiny. Moreover, it is a cliché of social observation that many self-defined acts of courageous self-expression are little more than slavish obedience to fashion and fad when seen from a more detached standpoint. Equally, it can require very considerable resources of individual resolve to fulfil a 'conventional role' under difficult circumstances – rescue workers, for example, coping with some disaster.

So the holism which we endorse entails that the complete explanation of any single action must inevitably make reference to the social totality within which the action is synchronically situated. Yet that totality also stretches backwards and forwards in time and must be considered diachronically as part of an ongoing process. It is clear how the relation of a given action to a precedent in the past has a bearing on the character of that action in the present. Conversely, setting a precedent is an action which reaches forward into the future. So too is a *blunder* – the sort of action whose nature is determined by the way its unintended consequences rebound on the perpetrator. Napoleon, for example, marched on Moscow. That he, as an individual, gave the order, is not in question. Yet the significance of that action is commonly judged in terms of consequences Napoleon hardly intended. It is important also to consider what makes it possible to say that Napoleon 'did' this at all. 'Marching on Moscow' is not a thing that a person can really do. What is needed in order to understand what is meant here is some reference to a complex configuration of social relations in both time and space which will have Napoleon's order as its *unique* focus.

Consider family life as a further illustration of these points and in a context that is central to the maintenance and reproduction of social structures. While you may know that as an institution 'the family' is found more or less universally in human societies, it nonetheless takes on a particular specificity when you examine an individual family. By comparison with many other institutions, it is remarkably self-sufficient in its initiation, maintenance, reproduction and change. Agencies external to the family compel few marriages, more in some societies than others, and do not often intervene to sustain them. They also play little or no part in the reproduction of family structure in the next generation – that is the job of your family upbringing. The initiation of almost every new family is the reproduction of structures of the previous families from which husband and wife are drawn. While you might argue that the roles of 'mother', 'father', 'son', 'daughter', etc. are determined for those who fill them by society, there is still no doubt that individual families are as unique and 'individual' as individuals themselves.

In a microcosm, families illustrate the way in which society is a two-sided ontological coin with individuals on one side and social structure on the other. Anthony Giddens has recently called this the *'duality of structure'* – the way in which individuals forming and being formed by a social institution are integrally related in the action of those who belong to it. Thus the perspectives of structure and of process, and of individual and of social totality are all partial views of the complex, concrete unity of a single thing. While parents and children perform in roles which may be understood in relation to the generic institution of the family, as found in the structure of the wider society to which they belong, their particular version of those roles will be constituted by their own self-activity. This is by no means dictated for them by the existing social structure or by the past experience of the parents. It will develop with its own history and take on a form unique to that family. It may well sustain itself through all sorts of crises – unemployment, bereavement or divorce, for instance – or again, it may not. It will also change in response to the particular ways in which the children do or do not find themselves able to establish their independence, or to changes in the health or employment patterns of its members. Key events in the history of the family can be picked out and viewed equally well as landmarks in the developments of its members' lives or as significant contributions the members have made to the family's constitution. Giddens refers generally to this two-way process as one of 'structuration'.

The interdependence between the normative structure of a family and the autonomous contributions of its members make both oversocialized and undersocialized conceptions of human action appear naive and simplistic. The top-down imposition of structure would imply far less variety or change than is actually found even in so universal and regular a generic institution. For example, just think of the diversity of composition and lifestyle among the members of those families you know best. The bottom-up construction of social relations would imply far more haphazard and arbitrary variety than is actually found. No matter how colourful, stable or in tatters all of these families are, they are still families in quite obvious ways. It is evident from the work of Freud and his successors that the historical slate is not wiped clean each time a new family is formed, but neither does the process whereby the family structure is reproduced write an unalterable script for the participants.

Our stress on the role of the unreflective imputation of rules in the act of directly joining in the activities around you is meant again to draw attention to the opacity of this process for the conscious explicit self-understanding that a society possesses – self-styled 'tradition' included. It is not the inheritance of explicit, conscious ideas which mediates, in the first instance, between individuals and the social structures in which they find themselves. Later in life a person may reflect on those formative processes, but the nearest many people get to this is nostalgia, that inchoate feeling that their lives once had a different meaning for them, which notoriously resists any clear expression. For example, when you reflect on your upbringing and what your parents' lives meant to you, it is not so much your parents' intentions or ideas that you examine as their often unreflective practice of parenthood. The significance to you as a child of the ways your parents acted towards you and towards each other is an imputation only you can make and one which they can sometimes barely appreciate. 'How could you have treated me that way?' 'But I always did what I thought best for you.' And so on. . . . They may also have handed on explicit ideas to you, but probably not a sense of what it is to *be* a mother or a father. After all, most parents just get on with it! It is the content of such unreflective practice which binds individuals to social situations, which continues unbroken as generations pass and which has as its foundation those practical activities in which the members of all societies must co-operate if they are to survive.

In short, one must resist the temptation to reify social structures as though they were *things* which existed independently of the actions of human beings. Every institution or social practice was once initiated; it is sustained by virtue of nothing more than the results of human actions, past and present; it is reproduced through no other means than by new generations joining in those concerted actions; it is changed only in so far as those who belong to it or join it change what they do when they take part in it. On the other hand, none of this implies that the actions involved in initiating, sustaining, reproducing or changing an institution or a social practice could have occurred outside an already existing institutional environment composed of rules and reinforcing a division of labour. This will be so even if no one is aware of the implications of their everyday activities. Think, for example, of how the English language has changed since the fifteenth century. Few of the writers and speakers who were instrumental in such change set out deliberately 'to change the English language'. The alterations were unintentional in precisely the sense we have outlined. This being said, the actions which led to such changes occurred through the use of the language itself and would obviously not have been possible but for its existence. Other forms of social change are the same. Thus capitalism has had the most profound impact on the family, leading to the near destruction of its extended structural form. Yet, again, modern nuclear families are still families in the same sense in which their extended predecessors were. For their function is the same in relation to those constitutive activities which they still facilitate. As we argued in chapter 7, it is this more than anything which links evolving institutions, traditions and forms of life.

The methodological consequence of our analysis of the duality of structure is that ways must be found to investigate both sides of the societal coin – individual intentional action on the one hand and its cumulative unintended consequences on the other. As regards the former, the problem is establishing/imputing intentions through some form of communication with the actors concerned. Many techniques exist for doing this, ranging from structured questionnaires (where there is only limited opportunity for interviewees to respond in their own terms) to participant observation where subjects may not even know that they are being studied. Ideally, use will be made of alternative approaches within the same study to see the extent to which the results tally. Of course, there are reasons why information from interviewees may not be easy to obtain, even assuming that actors are in some articulate fashion aware of their aims and beliefs. For example, they may simply be secretive, deceitful or have formed some notions of what they think that investigators would like to hear or perceive. There will also be sampling problems. Since you will almost never be in a position to communicate with everyone who might be relevant to a specific problem, it is necessary to ensure that those with whom you do make contact are reasonably *representative*. Finally, it is important to remember that much individual activity is unreflective and therefore not so susceptible to the preceding methods. Here it will be necessary to impute intentions of which the individuals being studied may be completely unaware. Techniques do exist for dealing with this difficulty. Participant observation is a tenable strategy in this context but because of the danger of incorrect imputation in the face of so little self-awareness on the part of those being studied, it has to be used with great care and double checked as much as possible.

The other side of the societal coin is structure. Since the object of the investigation here is the cumulative unintended consequences of individual activity, a different set of methodological questions are posed. The investigative approach in this case will be both conceptual and empirical. It will necessitate an analysis of the logical relationship between individual actions and their wider socio-economic context – the *internal* relationship between those rules which are being intentionally followed and other rules of which the actor may be unaware. Elsewhere in this book we have discussed several examples of such relationships in practice, often focusing on the market because it illustrates the points so well. Perhaps the simplest example is the run on the bank to which we referred in chapter 5. Whatever the intentions of the individual actor, if too many withdraw their money at once, the bank will fold unless, say, some sort of insurance has been taken out. That it will fold sooner or later follows logically from the rules of banking (e.g. the need for a viable bank to have so much money in reserve) and the fact that these rules will be broken if too many individual actions of a certain type occur. Yet empirically, one still has to check that the predicted results do follow. If they do not, this will indicate that there is a flaw in the conceptual analysis or some other unknown factor influencing the results of the actions in question (e.g. more reserves in the bank than originally envisaged or an unknown policy of government support). The collection of a range of accurate information about such consequences will involve still other sorts of methodologies and problems depending on the type of data involved. In the case in point the required evidence would be straightforward. In other cases – say, the real impact of a new government policy to stimulate more successful technological innovation or a new educational policy to counteract sexism or racism – the required evidence will be much more complex, and include a wide range of statistical data about the nation's wealth, health, education and welfare.

Of course, all of these methodological approaches for dealing with the duality of structure are fallible. As with the natural sciences, it is never possible to demonstrate the certainty of a theory of social structure, either as regards people's intentions or the consequences of their actions. However, this does not mean that some theories are not better than others. Some accounts of the duality in question are certainly more accurate than their predecessors. We all know more than we did about what it means to be human and to live in societies, and we can see that many past beliefs about what was natural and unavoidable in society were mistaken.

It is important to note, however, that social scientists are still faced with a question that natural scientists can ignore. They need to ask whether or not societies *should* be organized in the ways they have been discovered to be. You have seen how natural laws which causally govern material things do so irrespective of human preference. But social rules are not like this and can be changed. If people neither know, nor intend, the consequences of their actions, it may be claimed that they bear no moral responsibility for the outcome. Unfortunately, social scientists cannot claim the same ignorance. If they have broken through the opacity which clouds social life for so many of their fellows, then it is not possible for them to affect the ethical neutrality which natural scientists display towards the contents of a test tube. Only three consistent attitudes are possible for them: endorsement, condemnation or tolerance.

It is therefore to the question of the moral evaluation of social structures to which we must finally turn.

The moral evaluation of social structure

Moral judgments are widely thought to be subjective or at least lacking in any rational justification. Moreover, because they are logically distinct from factual judgments – on the face of it an 'is' statement cannot be deduced from an 'ought' and vice versa – they are often held to be antithetical to scientific objectivity. In this concluding section we shall argue that the idea that a social structure performs a function must presuppose that basic human needs are met in the process. While the satisfaction of such needs does not provide a unique and complete basis for the rational justification of moral judgments about social structures, we shall argue that failure to meet them provides a pretty good basis for moral condemnation. Your immediate response to this might be somewhat suspicious. After all, did we not show in chapter 5 that what are perceived as needs for some can be regarded as wants for others? These questions seem especially applicable when what are being compared are the perceived needs of individuals in radically different cultures. So to the extent that perception of need is shaped by social structure via culture, how on earth can the satisfaction of human need be viewed as a way of rationally and morally arbitrating between such structures? Unless we can come up with some way of identifying needs which are clearly universal to all cultures – irrespective of the ways in which their members view their situation – then there seems little way around this dilemma and relativism of at least a moral kind wins out after all.

As far as the identification of basic needs is concerned, the situation is surprisingly straightforward. At the very least humans need what it takes to be human. Throughout this book, we have developed a complex picture of what this 'humanity' entails. To be a person – as opposed, say, to a rock or a snail – you have to be able successfully to act and not simply to be acted upon. Therefore, our question about the identification of universal needs reduces to the question of the necessary conditions for successful action, whatever the particularities of the individual person or culture involved. In other words, if there are conditions which must be met for humans in any culture to do anything, then at least these conditions must apply to everyone in the same way. Returning to our example in chapter 6 of the traditional healer and the western doctor, what do they *both* have to have in common to be either one or the other? Going along with much recent writing on this topic, we believe that there are two basic needs which are crucial in this respect: *health* and *autonomy*.

In order to act successfully in any culture, the actor must be physically and psychologically able to do so. Physically, this will involve adequate nutrition, water, warmth, housing and so on. Psychologically, the same can be said for security, human contact and affection. If the doctor or the traditional healer is starving or suffering from a chronic and debilitating

Social structure and its moral evaluation

disease, they will not be able to perform their usual social roles. In relation to physical health and personhood, the limiting case is obviously survival itself, but the structure of the argument is the same for psychological needs. Acute depression can be just as incapacitating as physical illness and the limiting case here would be severe and long-term catatonia. The fact that something like this equation of physical and mental health with basic human need can be found in all cultures is exhibited by the extent to which their members identify one another as having more or less of both. Of course, the exact details will differ but there is no question that whatever the culture, someone who has what in western terms is described as cholera will be viewed as having constraints placed on their ability to do the sorts of things they normally do – more constraints than would be the case if they had what in western terms was a common cold. In short, at the very least, all people in all cultures *need* what is required in order for them to avoid being ill in this sense.

As far as the relationship between personhood and autonomy is concerned, much has already been said in previous chapters. Loosely, autonomy can be defined as the capacity to act creatively through the ability to formulate aims and beliefs and to choose to put them into effect in the knowledge of at least their immediate consequences. In whatever culture, your identity as a person is intimately vested in what you – rather than someone else – are perceived to do in a variety of different circumstances. Were you not autonomous in the terms defined above, this would be impossible since there would be no way of linking you to specific actions and holding you responsible for them. As in the case of health, the conditions for the development of basic levels of autonomy are straightforward. The most important is education in the broadest sense of the word. Since you have to learn to be you, others have to teach you. This will involve the acquisition of the language specific to your culture, along with a wide range of conceptual and practical skills deemed appropriate for the vocation(s) which you are encouraged/coerced to pursue. Yet even to the extent that the need for autonomy translates into the need for education, more than linguistic and practical skills are involved in its achievement. People also have to be confident enough to use whatever skills they possess. This will require emotional strength and underlines the link between autonomy and mental health. In whatever cultural guise, the individual's family will be an important factor here – whether positive or negative. There must also be the opportunity to exercise learned skills and to receive constructive critical and emotional feedback from one's fellows in the process. Thus, the availability of productive work will also be a need for everyone.

That something like health and autonomy in the above terms are regarded widely as basic human needs is evidenced by the universality of the distinction between needs and wants. As a reminder of how it is employed, it is worth pointing out that examples like 'Diabetics may want sugar but they need insulin' or 'Hannah may want to watch TV but she needs to do her homework' are to be found in all cultures, whether or not they contain insulin or television sets. In other words, the distinction revolves around the idea that some things are bad for you and that this does not necessarily keep you from desiring them, even if in some instances you know that they are damaging. Furthermore, focusing on health and autonomy needs in the way we suggest gives a good indication of what these hazards amount to and why. The simple fact is that an enormous amount is known about the necessary individual, social and environmental inputs to produce basic levels of health and autonomy, theoretically in ways that can be applied to all cultures in a relatively unproblematic way. As regards health, for example, organizations like the United Nations, the International Labour Organization, the World Health Organization and the Organization for Economic Co-operation and Development all emphasize the relevance of indicators like levels of mortality, morbidity and disability and link them to factors like safe water, adequate diet, the availability of primary health care facilities, warm and well-ventilated housing, safe working conditions and so on. As for autonomy, much the same holds. Here the key indicators will be levels of literacy, employable skills, artistic creativity, depression and suicide. Contributory factors will be the availability of formal education, of employment, of leisure time and facilities and of a reasonable degree of consistency in the general normative environment of the individual actor.

If someone insisted on abusing their own health/autonomy, you would presumably at least argue with them about the advisability of doing so. Indeed, it is precisely these sorts of debates which rage within one when trying to give up some harmful habit like cigarette-smoking or to 'do better' in relation to some other aspect of everyday life that concerns autonomy (e.g. to become a better parent, lover, student, carpenter, philosopher or whatever). Often such arguments also involve other people, as when you attempt to help someone else to change their ways because 'it would be best for them'. One thing is clear. You would probably have little hesitation about morally condemning others if they deliberately abused someone else's basic needs – especially if the other person was unaware of the possible dangers involved. It is this sort of condemnation that is associated with, say, parents who abuse their children through allowing them to do things which are against their interests, or husbands who do not allow their wives to do things which *are* in their interests – 'interests' being defined in relation to the satisfaction of basic needs. Why not assess social systems in the same way, through examining the extent to which they encourage or hinder health and autonomy?

There are two main objections to such a proposal. The first is that facts alone do not make value judgments true. How does the fact that, say, a child needs to be fed generate the true value judgment and consequent moral obligation that it *should* be fed. The missing premise is to be derived from looking again at the character of social life. We have already argued that regardless of the overt framework of values embodied in the way people understand their own actions, their unintended consequences have a systematic relationship to the performance of fundamental social functions. In broad terms, regardless of what people think they are doing, a large proportion of their actions are really part of the organized structure of the division of labour in society on which they all depend. That is to say, whatever individuals may believe about who is entitled to what, the satisfaction of basic human needs is what social life is *for*. People may think that it serves some other purpose and purport to act as if this were the case. However, for the reasons we have already outlined, they would not even be able to think and do this were it not for the fact that enough of their own health and autonomy needs have been met. For the same reason, if you accept that other people at least have the right to agree with you and to facilitate you in what you wish to achieve, then it follows that it is right that their basic needs should be satisfied as well. In relation to the hungry child with which we started, this is precisely the missing premise which is required to move from the fact of her hunger to the moral obligation to feed her. Her capacity to participate – and certainly the demand that she should participate – in any mode of preferred social organization seems to dictate as much.

Another argument which attempts to bridge the gap between the fact of basic need and the moral entitlement of need satisfaction returns the discussion to the division of labour itself. Someone might maintain that they have no wish to see children or anyone else starve or remain uneducated. They could further accept the previous argument that even agreement on this point itself presupposes that for those who are agreeing related basic needs are being met. Yet they might still protest that this does not mean that the satisfaction of such needs is a matter of right – of strict entitlement – rather than of charity. Ultimately, they might argue, people are only entitled to what they have individually produced themselves through the fruits of their own labour. Such a message has strong commonsense appeal and appears on the face of it to be a coherent moral theory. Why should anyone else have the right to tell you what to do with what you have created, much less to take it from you to give in part or whole (e.g. in the form of taxation) to someone else? If you wish to give, that is up to you and you alone and therefore, the gap between the fact of need and the moral obligation to satisfy remains.

This argument is clear but fundamentally misconceived. It founders on the simple fact that individuals have essentially social lives and do not provide for themselves – by themselves – at all. What they consume in the satisfaction of their needs is the by-product of the labour of many others engaged in related constitutive activities. Consequently, to the extent that individuals have participated in a division of labour which has benefited everyone, it would seem reasonable to believe that they have earned the right to share in what they have produced. It would seem just as reasonable to ensure that those who are not immediately involved in such a division (e.g. children and the elderly) should also be so entitled either because of the importance to the collective of their participation in the future or in the past. It was very much with this in mind that Marx argued, 'From each according to his ability, to each according to his need.'

Thus it makes sense to evaluate social structures in relation to their capacity to facilitate basic need satisfaction. It is also reasonable to view such satisfaction as a matter of right rather than of charity. To argue the case for this proposition in a rigorous way would require more time and space than we have available. There is a vast literature on the philosophy of entitlement and such debates are at the heart of contemporary discussions about the shape and future of the welfare state. Suffice it to say for now that if you believe that anyone has the universal right to *anything* (e.g. to compete fairly in the market place, to practise the religion of their choice, to become politically subversive, to denounce political subversives, etc.) then you must believe that they have a prior right to basic need satisfaction. To ascribe rights or duties to people without guaranteeing such satisfaction is simply contradictory since there would be no possibility of their exercising the one or fulfilling the other.

It might still be protested that all of the preceding discussion has focused on a *minimal* conception of human need – just enough health and autonomy necessary to guarantee personhood. The problem still remains of deciding how much more than this minimum to satisfy. Since different cultures generate different rules and expectations in this respect, who is to decide? The liberal relativist with whom we took issue in chapter 7 would claim that to impose western expectations on other cultures would be tantamount to dogmatic elitism. What is one to make of such claims?

Beginning with health, would the relativist endorse a set of expectations concerning, say, high infant mortality simply because they were held by people within a particular social structure? For example, the infant mortality rate in many parts of the African subcontinent is 125 per 1,000 births compared with about 17 per 1,000 in Britain, and the immorality of this situation has nothing to do with the cultural expectations of the parents. Presumably, even the most diehard relativist would accept that there are situations in which expectations do not reflect needs (e.g. among the children of relativists). The reasons for such a wide discrepancy in mortality rates are well understood and if life expectancy and morbidity *can* be improved then the task is surely to do so for all people – whatever their expectations and whatever their material circumstances. The only acceptable argument against this view would be that health provision on such a scale was a physical impossibility. No one can have a right to do something which violates a law of nature and some countries with specific types of social structures are certainly much poorer than others and might be said not to have the resources. But of course this ignores the extent to which the health problems of underdeveloped countries are an unintended consequence of international division of labour. It would in principle be possible to change this division and transfer enough wealth from North to South to make the aim of health for all a viable prospect. This is hardly a wide-eyed revolutionary claim. Its general correctness has been endorsed by groups like the World Health Organization.

Similar arguments hold with respect to the human need for autonomy. It might be claimed that all we have shown is that any society requires of its members a minimal measure of rational agency in order for them to assent to and abide by the rules of their culture. Each generation must then acquire some measure of understanding of what it has committed itself to by continuing with that form of social life. But if their understanding of themselves is mistaken – if they are not doing what they think they are doing – then they do not really know what it is to which they have committed themselves. If no one *could* be any wiser then so be it. But what if there is some way of finding out? Take an extreme case of the Japanese soldier who hid himself in the jungle of the Philippines for thirty years after the end of the Second World War. Did he not *need* to know that the war was over? Suppose there had been a whole platoon of men, with women and children in tow, all committed to undying loyalty to the Emperor. The need for rational autonomy is therefore not met by a false understanding of social life. If, as we have just argued, rational autonomy embodies the capacity to distinguish what is mistaken from what may not be, then the human need for rational autonomy is no more limited than the human capacity to discover error. To put it more rhetorically, the need to optimize autonomy is as insatiable as the thirst for knowledge and as inextinguishable as the pursuit of liberty because it is both these things.

We should now be able to see our way clear to the establishment of a number of other conclusions without too much more laborious argument. If the task of theoretical explanation in social science is, as we argued, the penetration of the opacity of social life, then social science *has as its aim the growth of human rational autonomy*. Human beings *need* this knowledge just as the Japanese soldier needed to know that the war was over, just as the woman in purdah needs to know that she is full of intellectual potential which has been artificially denied her, just as the macho male needs to realize the gentleness, warmth and creativity of which he is capable but to which he has also been blinded by the contingencies of his culture. Of course the soldier, the veiled woman and the unreconstructed man all possess a degree of autonomy, since without it they could not be even what they currently are. The point is, however, that they can almost always become more than this and that it is they who should choose how their needs are to be satisfied to this end – a choice informed by the best available understanding of the human condition.

Yet good social science is only a necessary condition for human liberation from unnecessary and arbitrary constraint. The thesis of the duality of structure entails that human beings participate in the formation of social life reciprocally as it affects the formation of their own identities. This means that social structures need to be created so that people are able not only to interpret their society more correctly but also to change it for the better. But this can only mean that the primary aim of such change should be the creation of those very conditions which are necessary *further* to sustain it – healthy, educated and skilled citizenry who recognize their mutual dependency and who have the right democratically to seek the most rational solutions to their social problems. In the abstract terms which relativists set for debates on these issues, it might well be possible to conceive of a society which reproduces itself unchanged from generation to generation, in which the unintended consequences of its members' social actions yield the performance of its social functions in such a way as to give no hint to those who belong to it that their society could be changed for the better. This is not, however, the type of society to which most people in the world belong. In the face of rapid national and international change and the emergence of dominant and coercive social structures which have long since transcended natural barriers, the importance of insisting on the intelligibility and possibility of human progress in meeting basic needs has become more important than ever. One of the most important weapons against the violation of such needs is your and our outrage that it exists at all, an outrage fuelled by the extent to which social science has shown it to be the consequence of modes of social organization which can and should be changed by the political resolve of those individuals who sustain them. The possibility of such change – and the previously unrecognized choices which they can bring about – is the moral lesson to be learned from the duality of social structure.

In short, we conclude that if you set out to understand social life, you must find yourself inexorably committed not only to criticize whatever irrationalities you discover but actively to oppose them. Perhaps you will discover that there are none, that you live in the 'best of all possible worlds'. That is an empirical question. We think it highly unlikely that this will turn out to be the case. Nonetheless the arguments we have sketched in this book proceed without assuming more than that it is *possible* that a society will be discovered to be irrational and immoral. It is just that possibility – not mere idle curiosity – that drives social science forward and inescapably with it the struggle for human liberation.

Annotated bibliography

In writing of a 'theory' of social structure, at the start of this chapter, we do not intend to produce any sort of rival to the many substantive theories of society which already exist. Our concern is, rather, to pick out some of the conceptual categories which any such theory should acknowledge if it is not to encounter problems with regard to the topics of the earlier chapters. Such problems will largely arise from a failure to reconcile the task of explanation with the fact that it is human beings – members of society – who propound and accept explanations. Explanations which allow too little scope in their account for the exercise of autonomous rationality undermine the basis on which they may be rationally accepted. Explanations, on the other hand, which elevate the category of rational autonomy beyond its evident limitations in reality simply fail to address what it is about society that requires understanding.

Hence our initial focus upon the unintended consequences of actions. This is such a broad and in a sense obvious feature of social scientific explanation that there is a certain oddity in giving just a few references. At an introductory level, perhaps, this point will come across most forcefully from a collection of vignettes on sociological theorists, such as Raison 1969. Look particularly at the essays on Marx, Pareto, Veblen, Durkheim, Simmel, Weber, Mannheim and Parsons. Widely differing views have been taken of the unintended consequences of actions that theories purport to uncover. In Durkheim 1982 and 1985, in common with many later functionalist writers, the unintended consequences of actions are seen largely as benign – 'society adapting and integrating itself' without the conscious intervention of its members. The essay 'Manifest and latent functions' in Merton 1968 discusses this from a functionalist perspective very much with the notion of unintended consequences of actions in view.

In the 'Preface to a contribution to the critique of political economy' in Marx 1975, a similar integrative role is given to social relations of production, which are independent of the will of individuals. Conditions are also envisaged, however, in which such relations become characterized by inbuilt conflict, rather than harmony. These are stressed particularly in the 'Manifesto of the Communist Party' in Marx 1973, and analysed at length in Marx 1976, 1978 and 1981. There a consequence of the evolution of capitalism is seen to be the intensification of conflict between classes in society, propelled by economic developments hardly intended for that purpose. In contradistinction to both Durkheim and Marx, the concern of Weber 1977 is not with how a social system 'acts', independently of the conscious intentions of those who belong to it. His interests, rather, lay in how the logic of the rationalia of individual actions could be such that the 'ethic' of Protestant self-denial could unintentionally give rise to the 'spirit' of capitalist accumulation. Even the most resolute of methodological individualists have recognized this feature of social life. So Hayek 1982, chapter 9, argues that the operation of the market cannot be considered unjust because, since no one intended it, no one can be blamed.

Elster 1983 gives a sustained and sophisticated analysis of the mechanisms which subvert and limit the rationality of individual and collective action. These operate both at the level at which individuals frame the beliefs and desires on which their actions rest, and at the level of the systems in which individuals have no choice but to act. Not only do actions have consequences individuals did not intend, but intentions are framed in circumstances individuals fail to understand. The analysis also indicates how remedies may be sought for such a predicament, and that finding remedies must be part of the point of understanding these matters.

Our discussion of the division of labour is rudimentary – sufficient only to make the point concerning its moral and political implications. Durkheim 1982 is the classic contribution to the concern of social science with this issue. For the reasons we gave, it is generally discussed in connection with the phenomenon of social class. Giddens 1971, chapters 3, 5, 7 and 11, provides a good commentary on the formative analyses of

Marx, Durkheim and Weber, and Giddens 1982 offers a useful contemporary perspective on the issue.

The phrase 'the duality of structure', and the central idea employed to resolve the dilemma presented between 'over' and 'undersocialized' conceptions of human nature, are adopted from Giddens 1976, chapter 3, and 1979, chapter 2. Giddens 1984 further articulates the idea of such duality and applies it to a number of substantive fields in the social sciences. In chapter 4 he discusses a number of the issues raised in our discussion above, concluding with an interesting treatment of the 'structure/individual' debate. In chapter 6 he discusses the relationship between the unintended consequences of actions and social function – particularly, the point that the functionality of actions does not explain why people perform them, even though it may explain what they are.

The tension posed for social science generally by the dilemma above is most sharply formulated in Dawe's essay 'The two sociologies' in Thompson and Tunstall 1971. Indeed, this dilemma is the theme of the entire anthology, just as it is one of the main themes of Hollis 1977. The phrase 'the oversocialized conception of man' comes from Wrong's essay in Coser and Rosenburg 1964. The issue is also forcefully put in Homan's essay in Ryan 1973. In Giddens 1984, chapter 6, Willis 1977 is used as an illustration for a discussion of the relevance of his notion of the duality of structure to fields of empirical investigation in sociology. More specifically, in the sociology of education it has become increasingly clear that there is a theoretical problem regarding the relationship of structural accounts of the educational system to explanations of how individuals within the system have been revealed to understand their own actions. This is nowhere clearer than in the two-volume Open University reader, Dale *et al.* 1981. In Barton *et al.* 1981, the main focus of the articles collected is the role of ideology – pupil and teacher self-understanding – in the reproduction of social structure. The sociology of deviance exhibits similar tensions – a revulsion from functionalism towards highly individualistic approaches in the late 1960s and early 1970s, followed by a rapprochement with structural approaches in more recent years. Downes and Rock 1982 give a useful perspective on this development.

The issue of internal relations is raised by Winch 1970, chapter 5, but the clearest account is in Elster 1978, chapter 1. Clearly our view differs from that of Winch, who argues that social relations are internal relations because they are relations of ideas. Napoleon's blunder, we argue, was identifiable as such because of internal relations between circumstances. These only revealed themselves after the event, were wholly objective, and did not consist of ideas that people did or could entertain, by contrast to Winch's analysis of obedience to commands.

The main line of argument in the second part of this chapter derives from Doyal and Gough 1984, which provides many more references than we have space to include here. The idea that human beings need what it takes to be human, and that this entails autonomy as well as survival, is argued at length in Plant *et al.* 1980, chapter 3. The notion that interests are to be defined subjectively was classically argued in 'On Liberty' in Mill 1972, and is staunchly defended, for instance, in Hayek 1982, chapter 7. The opposing view, that 'true' and 'false' needs can be formulated on the basis of human nature, is defended, for example, in Marcuse 1964, chapters 9 and 10.

Both the subjectivist account, and the view that human nature fixes human needs independently of social circumstances, have been the subject of contemporary debates. Within the liberal tradition stemming from Mill, the attempts to escape from subjectivism are reviewed and found wanting in Wall 1975. He argues that only if human interests are objectively determinable can they be employed in the criticism of social, political and economic arrangements. Within the Marxist tradition, Soper 1981 and Geras 1983 take differing views as to Marx's commitment to an underlying notion of a fixed human nature and the centrality of this idea to the continuing relevance of a Marxian perspective upon social and economic problems. Wider-ranging discussions of the variety of possible sources of determination of human nature are to be found in the references given for chapter 3.

For an analysis of health as a basic human need, along with a rejection of the 'minimalist' equation of health with survival, see Doyal and Gough 1984. A discussion of related philosophical issues concerning health and illness can be found in the essay by Doyal and Doyal in Birke and Silvertown 1984. We have merely mentioned education as an indicator of the achievement of autonomy in a society. See Entwhistle 1979, part I, for a fascinating analysis of autonomy in relation to the conventional curriculum of education. The connection between education, autonomy and the needs of individuals in unfavourable social and economic circumstances is discussed in Freire 1972. An immensely readable and vivid plea for the importance of understanding the whole sphere of human need is made in Ignatieff 1984.

The contention that facts do not make value judgments true was classically formulated by Hume, and a good account can be found in Ayer 1980b. This doctrine lies behind the position taken by those philosophers of science who sharply distinguish science from the realm of value judgment. An exemplary statement of this approach can be found in Hempel 1965, chapter 3. An introductory treatment of this question in relation to social science is given in Trigg 1985, chapter 6. A perspective on the debate in ethical theory regarding the independence or otherwise of fact and value can be obtained from the introduction and first eight essays in Foot 1967. A passionate attack on the approach to ethics inherited from Hume is made in Macintyre 1981, chapters 1, 2 and 3.

On the inappropriateness of denying to others rights and capacities you yourself possess, see the excellent discussion in Plant *et al.* 1980, chapter 4. Wolff 1973 gives a good account of the themes from Kant's ethical philosophy which underpin this analysis. As is clear from Plant *et al.* 1980, the argument that people are entitled only to what they themselves produce is a central theme of Nozick 1974.

The contemporary social theorist who has attempted most explicitly to link questions of human liberation with those of satisfying human needs is Habermas. His work is as difficult at times as it is plentiful, however. For a useful introduction, see Bernstein 1979, part IV, and Held 1980, chapters 9-12. Further questions concerning liberation are closely linked to those of social justice. Again the literature is vast, but much contemporary discussion stems from Rawls 1972.

A useful introductory account of Rawls's ideas is contained in Buchanan 1982, chapter 6, in Plant *et al.* 1980, chapters 4 and 6, and in Gutmann 1980, chapters 5-7.

BIBLIOGRAPHY

Achinstein, P., *Law and Explanation: An Essay in the Philosophy of Science*, Oxford University Press, 1971.

Ackerman, R.J., *The Philosophy of Karl Popper*, University of Massachusetts Press, 1976.

Althusser, L., *Lenin and Philosophy and Other Essays*, London, New Left Books, 1971.

Anscombe, G.E.M., *Intention*, Oxford, Blackwell, 1969.

Anscombe, G.E.M., *Metaphysics and the Philosophy of Mind: Collected Philosophical Papers Volume II*, Oxford, Blackwell, 1983.

Armstrong, D.M., *What is a Law of Nature?*, Oxford University Press, 1983.

Ayer, A.J., *Philosophical Essays*, London, Greenwood Press, 1980a.

Ayer, A.J., *Hume*, Oxford University Press, 1980b.

Barnes, B., *Interests and the Growth of Knowledge*, London, Routledge & Kegan Paul, 1977.

Barnes, B., *T.S. Kuhn and Social Science*, London, Macmillan, 1981.

Barnes, B. and Edge, D. (eds), *Science in Context*, Milton Keynes, Open University Press, 1982.

Barton, L. Meighan, R. and Walker, S. (eds), *Schooling, Ideology and the Curriculum*, Lewes, Falmer Press, 1981.

Benton, T., *Philosophical Foundations of the Three Sociologies*, London, Routledge & Kegan Paul, 1977.

Berger, P.L. and Luckmann, T., *The Social Construction of Reality*, London, Allen Lane, 1967.

Berlin, I., 'Two concepts of liberty', in *Four Essays on Liberty*, Oxford University Press, 1969.

Bernstein, R.J., *Praxis and Action*, London, Duckworth, 1972.

Bernstein, R.J., *The Restructuring of Social and Political Theory*, London, Methuen, 1979.

Bernstein, R.J., *Beyond Objectivism and Relativism*, Oxford, Blackwell, 1983.

Berofsky, B. (ed.), *Free Will and Determinism*, New York, Harper & Row, 1966.

Bhaskar, R., *A Realist Theory of Science*, Hassocks, Sussex, Harvester, 1978.

Bilton, T., *et al.*, *Introducing Sociology*, London, Macmillan, 1981.

Birke, L. and Silvertown, J. (eds), *Beyond Reduction: The Politics of Biology*, London, Pluto Press, 1984.

Bloor, D., *Knowledge and Social Imagery*, London, Routledge & Kegan Paul, 1976.

183

Bloor, D., *Wittgenstein: A Social Theory of Knowledge*, London, Macmillan, 1983.

Boden, M.A., *Artificial Intelligence and Natural Man*, Hassocks, Sussex, Harvester, 1977.

Boden, M.A., *Purposive Explanation in Psychology*, Hassocks, Sussex, Harvester, 1978.

Bolton, N. (ed.), *Philosophical Problems in Psychology*, London, Methuen, 1979.

Borger, R. and Cioffi, F. (eds), *Explanation in the Behavioural Sciences*, Cambridge University Press, 1975.

Braybrooke, D. (ed.), *Philosophical Problems of the Social Sciences*, London, Macmillan, 1965.

Brown, S.C. (ed.), *Philosophy and Psychology*, London, Macmillan, 1974.

Brown, S.C. (ed.), *Objectivity and Cultural Divergence*, Cambridge University Press, 1984.

Brown, S., Fauvel, J. and Finnegan, R. (eds), *Conceptions of Enquiry*, London, Methuen, 1981.

Buchanan, A.E., *Marx and Justice*, London, Methuen, 1982.

Buchdahl, G., *Metaphysics and the Philosophy of Science*, Oxford, Blackwell, 1969.

Burtt, E.A., *Metaphysical Foundations of Modern Physical Science*, London, Routledge & Kegan Paul, 1980.

Cartwright, N., *How the Laws of Nature Lie*, Oxford University Press, 1983.

Chalmers, D., *What is this Thing Called Science?*, Milton Keynes, Open University Press, 1978.

Collinson, D., *The Will*, Milton Keynes, Open University Press, 1973.

Collinson, D., *The Free Will Problem*, Milton Keynes, Open University Press, 1976.

Copi, I., *Introduction to Logic*, London, Macmillan, 1982.

Coplestone, F., *A History of Philosophy*, London, Search Press, 1975.

Coser, L. and Rosenburg, B. (eds), *Sociological Theory*, London, Macmillan, 1964.

Currie, G. and Musgrave, A. (eds), *Popper and the Human Sciences*, The Hague, Martinus Nijhoff, 1985.

Dale, R., Esland, G., Fergusson, R. and Macdonald, M. (eds), *Education and the State*, vols. 1 and 2, Lewes, Falmer Press, 1981.

Dallmayr, F. and McCarthy, T. (eds), *Understanding and Social Enquiry*, Notre Dame, Indiana, University of Notre Dame Press, 1977.

Dancy, J., *Contemporary Epistemology*, Oxford, Blackwell, 1985.

Davidson, D., *Essays on Actions and Events*, Oxford University Press, 1984a.

Davidson, D., *Inquiries into Truth and Interpretation*, Oxford University Press, 1984b.

Davidson, D. and Hintikka, S. (eds.), *Words and Objections: Essays on the Work of W.V. Quine*, Dordrecht, Holland, D. Reidel, 1969.

Davis, S., *Philosophy and Language*, New York, Bobbs Merrill, 1976.

Dennett, D.C., *Content and Consciousness*, London, Routledge & Kegan Paul, 1969.

Dennett, D.C., *Brainstorms: Philosophical Essays on Mind and Psychology*, Hassocks, Sussex, Harvester, 1979.

Dennett, D.C., *Elbow Room: The Varieties of Free Will Worth Defending*, Oxford University Press, 1984.

Dijksterhuis, E.J., *The Mechanization of the World Picture*, Oxford University Press, 1961.

Domenos, E.D., *Quine and Analytic Philosophy*, Cambridge, Mass., MIT Press, 1983.

Downes, D. and Rock, P., *Understanding Deviance*, Oxford, Clarendon Press, 1982.

Doyal, L. and Gough, I., 'A theory of human needs', *Critical Social Policy*, no. 10, 1984, pp. 6-38.

Doyal, L. and Harris, R., 'The practical foundations of human understanding', *New Left Review*, no. 139, 1983.

Duhem, P., *The Aim and Structure of Physical Theory*, New York, Atheneum, 1962.

Durkheim, E., *The Rules of Sociological Method*, London, Macmillan, 1982.

Durkheim, E., *The Division of Labour in Society*, London, Macmillan, 1985.

Dyke, C., *Philosophy of Economics*, Englewood Cliffs, New Jersey, Prentice-Hall, 1981.

Easton, S.M., *Humanist Marxism and Wittgensteinian Social Philosophy*, Manchester University Press, 1983.

Ehrenreich, B., *The Hearts of Men: American Dreams and the Flight from Commitment*, London, Pluto Press, 1983.

Eichenbaum, L. and Orbach, S., *What do Women Want?*, London, Fontana, 1983.

Elster, J., *Logic and Society*, Chichester, Wiley, 1978.

Elster, J., *Sour Grapes*, Cambridge University Press, 1983.

Emmet, D. and Macintyre, A. (eds), *Sociological Theory and Philosophical Analysis*, London, Macmillan, 1970.

Entwhistle, H., *Antonio Gramsci – Conservative Schooling for Radical Politics*, London, Routledge & Kegan Paul, 1979.

Evans, M. (ed.), *The Woman Question*, London, Fontana, 1982.

Feyerabend, P.K., *Against Method*, London, New Left Books, 1975.

Feyerabend, P.K., *Science in a Free Society*, London, New Left Books, 1979.

Feyerabend, P.K., *Collected Papers: Vol. I, Realism, Rationalism and Scientific Method; Vol. II, Problems of Empiricism*, Cambridge University Press, 1985.

Filmer, P., Phillipson, M., Silverman, D. and Walsh, D. (eds), *New Directions in Sociological Theory*, London, Macmillan, 1972.

Foot, P. (ed.), *Theories of Ethics*, Oxford University Press, 1967.

Freire, P., *Pedagogy of the Oppressed*, London, Penguin, 1972.

Geras, N., *Marx and Human Nature*, London, Verso, 1983.

Giddens, A., *Capitalism and Modern Social Theory*, Cambridge University Press, 1971.

Giddens, A. (ed.), *Positivism and Sociology*, London, Heinemann, 1974.

Giddens, A., *New Rules of Sociological Method*, London, Hutchinson, 1976.

Giddens, A., *Central Problems in Social Theory*, London, Macmillan, 1979.

Giddens, A., *The Class Structure of Advanced Societies*, London, Hutchinson, 1982.

Giddens, A., *The Constitution of Society*, Cambridge, Polity Press, 1984.

Goff, T.W., *Marx and Mead; Contributions to a Sociology of Knowledge*, London, Routledge & Kegan Paul, 1980.

Goodman, N., *Fact, Fiction and Forecast*, Cambridge, Mass., Harvard University Press, 1983.

Grayling, A.C., *An Introduction to Philosophical Logic*, Brighton, Harvester, 1982.

Gutmann, A., *Liberal Equality*, Cambridge University Press, 1980.

Haak, S., *Philosophy of Logics*, Cambridge University Press, 1978.

Hacker, P.M.S., *Insight and Illusion: Wittgenstein on Philosophy and the*

Metaphysics of Experience, Oxford University Press, 1972.

Hacking, I. (ed.), *Scientific Revolutions*, Oxford University Press, 1981.

Hacking, I., *Representing and Intervening*, Cambridge University Press, 1983.

Hahn, F. and Hollis, M. (eds), *Philosophy and Economic Theory*, Oxford University Press, 1979.

Hampshire, S., *Thought and Action*, London, Chatto & Windus, 1965.

Hanson, N.R., *Patterns of Discovery*, Cambridge University Press, 1965.

Harré, R., *Causal Powers: A Theory of Natural Necessity*, Oxford University Press, 1975.

Harré, R., *Social Being*, Oxford, Blackwell, 1979.

Harré, R., *Personal Being*, Oxford, Blackwell, 1983.

Harrison, B., *An Introduction to the Philosophy of Language*, London, Macmillan, 1979.

Hayek, F.A., *Law, Legislation and Liberty*, London, Routledge & Kegan Paul, 1982.

Held, D., *Introduction to Critical Theory: Horkheimer to Habermas*, London, Hutchinson, 1980.

Hempel, C.E., *Aspects of Scientific Explanation*, New York, Free Press, 1965.

Hempel, C.E., *Philosophy of Natural Science*, New Jersey, Prentice-Hall, 1966.

Hesse, M., *Forces and Fields*, London, Nelson, 1961.

Hindess, B., *Philosophy and Methodology in the Social Sciences*, Hassocks, Sussex, Harvester, 1977.

Hirst, P. and Woolley, P., *Social Relations and Human Attributes*, London, Tavistock, 1982.

Hofstadter, D.R. and Dennett, D.C. (eds), *The Mind's I*, Brighton, Harvester, 1981.

Hollis, M., *Models of Man: Philosophical Thoughts on Social Action*, Cambridge University Press, 1977.

Hollis, M. and Lukes, S. (eds), *Rationality and Relativism*, Oxford, Blackwell, 1982.

Holtzman, S. and Leich, C. (eds), *Wittgenstein: To follow a Rule*, London, Routledge & Kegan Paul, 1981.

Honderich, T. (ed.), *Essays on Freedom of Action*, London, Routledge & Kegan Paul, 1973.

Hook, S. (ed.), *Determinism and Freedom in the Age of Modern Science*, New York University Press, 1958.

Horton, R. and Finnegan, R. (eds), *Modes of Thought*, London, Faber & Faber, 1973.

Hurd, D.L. and Kipling, J.J. (eds), *The Origins and Growth of Physical Science*, vols I and II, London, Penguin, 1964.

Huxley, A., *Brave New World*, London, Penguin, 1955.

Ignatieff, M., *The Needs of Strangers*, London, Chatto & Windus, 1984.

Irvine, J., Miles, I. and Evans, J. (eds), *Demystifying Social Statistics*, London, Pluto Press, 1979.

Joas, H., *G.H. Mead*, Cambridge, Polity Press, 1985.

Jones, W.T., *A History of Western Philosophy*, New York, Harcourt, Brace & World, 1969.

Kearney, H.F. (ed.), *Origins of the Scientific Revolution*, London, Longmans, 1964.

Keat, R. and Urry, S., *Social Theory as Science*, London, Routledge & Kegan Paul, 1982.

Kenny, A., *Wittgenstein*, London, Penguin, 1973.

Kenny, A., *Will, Freedom and Power*, Oxford, Blackwell, 1975.

Koestler, A., *The Sleepwalkers*, London, Penguin, 1970.

Kolakowski, L., *Positivist Philosophy*, London, Pelican, 1972.

Koyré, A., *From the Closed World to the Infinite Universe*, Baltimore, Maryland, Johns Hopkins Press, 1957.

Kripke, S., *Wittgenstein on Rules and Private Language*, Oxford, Blackwell, 1982.

Kuhn, T.S., *The Structure of Scientific Revolutions*, University of Chicago Press, 1970.

Kuhn, T.S., *The Copernican Revolution*, Cambridge, Mass., Harvard University Press, 1972.

Kuhn, T.S., *The Essential Tension*, University of Chicago Press, 1977.

Lakatos, I., *Proofs and Refutations*, Cambridge University Press, 1976.

Lakatos, I., *Collected Papers: Vol I, The Methodology of Scientific Research Programmes; Vol II, Mathematics, Science and Epistemology*, Cambridge University Press, 1980.

Lakatos, I. and Musgrave, A. (eds), *Criticism and the Growth of Knowledge*, Cambridge University Press, 1970.

Larrain, J., *The Concept of Ideology*, London, Hutchinson, 1979.

Larrain, J., *Marxism and Ideology*, London, Macmillan, 1983.

Laudan, L., *Progress and its Problems: Towards a Theory of Scientific Growth*, London, Routledge & Kegan Paul, 1977.

Lemmon, E.J., *Beginning Logic*, London, Nelson, 1965.

Leonard, P., *Personality and Ideology: Towards a Materialist Understanding of the Individual*, London, Macmillan, 1984.

Levy, D., *Realism: An Essay in Interpretation and Social Reality*, Manchester, Carcanet, 1981.

Lichtman, R., *The Production of Desire*, New York, Free Press, 1982.

Losee, J., *A Historical Introduction to the Philosophy of Science*, Oxford University Press, 1980.

Louch, A.R., *Explanation and Human Action*, Oxford, Blackwell, 1966.

Lukács, G., *History and Class Consciousness*, London, Merlin, 1971.

Lukes, S., *Individualism*, Oxford, Blackwell, 1973.

Lukes, S., *Power: A Radical View*, London, Macmillan, 1974.

Macdonald, G. and Pettit, P., *Semantics and Social Science*, London, Routledge & Kegan Paul, 1981.

Macintyre, A., *After Virtue*, London, Duckworth, 1981.

McCarney, J., *The Real World of Ideology*, Brighton, Harvester, 1980.

McGinn, C., *The Character of Mind*, Oxford University Press, 1982.

McGinn, C., *Wittgenstein on Meaning*, Oxford, Blackwell, 1984.

Magee, B., *Popper*, London, Fontana, 1985.

Mannheim, K., *Ideology and Utopia*, London, Routledge & Kegan Paul, 1936.

Marcuse, H., *One Dimensional Man*, London, Routledge & Kegan Paul, 1964.

Marx, K., *The Revolutions of 1848 – Marx*, London, Penguin, 1973.

Marx, K., *Early Writings*, London, Penguin, 1975.

Marx, K., *Capital*, vols I, II and III, London, Penguin, 1976, 1978 and 1981.

Mead, G.H., *Mind, Self and Society*, University of Chicago Press, 1964.

Merton, R.K., *Social Theory and Social Structure*, Glencoe, Ill., Free Press, 1968.

Midgley, M., *Beast and Man*, Hassocks, Sussex, Harvester, 1978.

Miles, I., *Social Indicators for Human Development*, London, Frances Pinter, 1985.

Mill, J.S., 'On Liberty', in *Utilitarianism – John Stuart Mill*, London, Dent, Everyman Library, 1972.

Mill, J.S., *Collected Works*, vols 7 and 8, *A System of Logic*, London, Routledge

& Kegan Paul, 1974.

Mischel, T. (ed.), *The Self*, Oxford, Blackwell, 1977.

Mortimore, G.W. (ed.), *Weakness of Will*, London, Macmillan, 1971.

Mulkay, M., *Science and the Sociology of Knowledge*, London, Allen & Unwin, 1980.

Nagel, E., *The Structure of Science*, New York, Harcourt, Brace & World, 1961.

Newton-Smith, W.H., *The Rationality of Science*, London, Routledge & Kegan Paul, 1981.

Newton-Smith, W.H., *Logic – An Introductory Course*, London, Routledge & Kegan Paul, 1985.

Norman, R., *Reasons for Actions*, Oxford, Blackwell, 1971.

Nozick, R., *Anarchy, State and Utopia*, Oxford, Blackwell, 1974.

O'Connor, D.J., *The Correspondence Theory of Truth*, London, Hutchinson, 1975.

O'Hear, A., *Karl Popper*, London, Routledge & Kegan Paul, 1980.

O'Neill, J. (ed.), *Modes of Individualism and Collectivism*, London, Heinemann, 1973.

Papineau, D., *For Science in the Social Sciences*, London, Macmillan, 1978.

Parfitt, D., *Reasons and Persons*, Oxford University Press, 1984.

Parsons, T., *The Structure of Social Action*, New York, Free Press, 1968.

Pears, D., *Motivated Irrationality*, Oxford University Press, 1984.

Pitcher, G. (ed.), *Wittgenstein*, New York, Macmillan, 1966.

Pitkin, H., *Wittgenstein and Justice*, Berkeley, University of California Press, 1972.

Plant, R., Lesser, H. and Taylor-Gooby, P., *Political Philosophy and Social Welfare*, London, Routledge & Kegan Paul, 1980.

Popper, K., *The Poverty of Historicism*, London, Routledge & Kegan Paul, 1961.

Popper, K., *Conjectures and Refutations*, London, Routledge & Kegan Paul, 1972a.

Popper, K., *Objective Knowledge: An Evolutionary Approach*, Oxford University Press, 1972b.

Popper, K., *Unended Quest: An Intellectual Autobiography*, London, Fontana, 1976.

Popper, K., *The Logic of Scientific Discovery*, London, Hutchinson, 1980.

Pratt, V., *The Philosophy of the Social Sciences*, London, Methuen, 1978.

Quine, W.V., *Word and Object*, Cambridge, Mass., MIT Press, 1960.

Quine, W.V., *Ontological Relativity and Other Essays*, New York, Columbia University Press, 1969.

Quine, W.V., *Philosophy of Logic*, Englewood Cliffs, New Jersey, Prentice-Hall, 1970.

Quine, W.V., *The Roots of Reference*, LaSalle, Illinois, Open Court, 1974.

Quine, W.V., *The Ways of Paradox*, Cambridge, Mass., Harvard University Press, 1976.

Quine, W.V., *From a Logical Point of View*, New York, Harper, 1980.

Quinton, A., *Francis Bacon*, Oxford University Press, 1980.

Raison, T. (ed.), *The Founding Fathers of Social Science*, London, Penguin, 1969.

Ravetz, J.R., *Scientific Knowledge and its Social Problems*, Oxford University Press, 1971.

Rawls, J., *A Theory of Justice*, Oxford, Clarendon Press, 1972.

Rescher, N., *Scientific Explanation*, London, Macmillan, 1970.

Rorty, R., *Philosophy and the Mirror of Nature*, Princeton University Press, 1980.

Rose, S., Kamin, L.S. and Lowontin, R.C., *Not in Our Genes*, London, Penguin,

1984.

Rowland-Pennock, J. and Chapman, J. (eds), *Nomos' Year Book, vol. XIX Anarchism*, New York University Press, 1978.

Royal Institute of Philosophy Lectures vol. I, 1966/7, *The Human Agent*, London, Macmillan, 1968.

Rubinstein, D., *Marx and Wittgenstein*, London, Routledge & Kegan Paul, 1981.

Russell, J., *Explaining Mental Life*, London, Macmillan, 1984.

Ryan, A., *The Philosophy of the Social Sciences*, London, Macmillan, 1970a.

Ryan, A., *The Philosophy of John Stuart Mill*, London, Macmillan, 1970b.

Ryan, A., *The Philosophy of Social Explanation*, Oxford University Press, 1973.

Ryan, A., *John Stuart Mill*, London, Routledge & Kegan Paul, 1974.

Ryan, A., *The Idea of Freedom*, Oxford University Press, 1979.

Ryle, G., *The Concept of Mind*, Harmondsworth, Penguin, 1963.

Salmon, W., *Logic*, Englewood Cliffs, New Jersey, Prentice-Hall, 1963.

Schutz, A., *The Phenomenology of the Social World*, London, Heinemann, 1972.

Searle, J.R., *Intentionality*, Cambridge University Press, 1983.

Searle, J.R., *Minds, Brains and Science*, London, BBC, 1984.

Shaffer, J., *Philosophy of Mind*, Englewood Cliffs, New Jersey, Prentice-Hall, 1968.

Skinner, B.F., *Science and Human Behaviour*, New York, Macmillan, 1953.

Skinner, B.F., *Beyond Freedom and Dignity*, New York, Bantam, 1972.

Skorupski, J., *Symbol and Theory*, Cambridge University Press, 1976.

Sloman, A., *The Computer Revolution in Philosophy*, Hassocks, Sussex, Harvester, 1978.

Smelser, N.J., *Essays in Sociological Explanation*, Englewood Cliffs, New Jersey, Prentice-Hall, 1968.

Soper, K., *On Human Needs*, Brighton, Harvester, 1981.

Sosa, E. (ed.), *Causation and Conditionals*, Oxford University Press, 1975.

Strawson, P.F., *Freedom and Resentment and Other Essays*, London, Methuen, 1974.

Stroud, B., *Hume*, London, Routledge & Kegan Paul, 1977.

Suppe, F., *The Structure of Scientific Theories*, Urbana, University of Illinois Press, 1977.

Taylor, C., *The Explanation of Behaviour*, London, Routledge & Kegan Paul, 1964.

Taylor, C., *Collected Papers: Vol. I, Human Agency and Language; Vol. II, Philosophy and the Human Sciences*, Cambridge University Press, 1985.

Taylor, R., *Action and Purpose*, New York, Prentice-Hall, 1966.

Thompson, J.B., *Studies in the Theory of Ideology*, Oxford, Blackwell, 1984.

Thompson, K. and Tunstall, J. (eds), *Sociological Perspectives*, London, Penguin, 1971.

Timpanaro, S., *On Materialism*, London, New Left Books, 1975.

Torrance, S. (ed.), *The Mind and the Machine*, Chichester, Ellis Harwood, 1984.

Trigg, R., *The Shaping of Man: Philosophical Aspects of Sociobiology*, Oxford, Blackwell, 1982.

Trigg, R., *Understanding Social Science*, Oxford, Blackwell, 1985.

Trusted, J., *Freewill and Responsibility*, Oxford University Press, 1984.

Van Frassen, B., *The Scientific Image*, Oxford University Press, 1980.

Wall, G., 'The concept of interest in politics', *Politics and Society*, vol. 5, 1975, pp. 487-510.

Weber, M., *The Methodology of the Social Sciences*, London, Macmillan, 1950.

Weber, M., *The Theory of Social and Economic Organisation*, New York, Free Press, 1964.

Weber, M., *The Protestant Ethic and the Spirit of Capitalism*, London, Allen & Unwin, 1977.

Wedberg, A., *A History of Philosophy*, Oxford, Blackwell, 1982.

White, A.R. (ed.), *The Philosophy of Action*, Oxford University Press, 1968.

White, A.R., *Truth*, London, Macmillan, 1970.

Willis, P., *Learning to Labour*, Farnborough, Saxon House, 1977.

Wilson, B.R. (ed.), *Rationality*, Oxford, Blackwell, 1970.

Wilson, E.O., *Sociobiology: The New Synthesis*, Cambridge, Mass., Harvard University Press, 1975.

Winch, P., *The Idea of a Social Science*, London, Routledge & Kegan Paul, 1970.

Wittgenstein, L., *Philosophical Investigations*, Oxford, Blackwell, 1973.

Wolff, R.P., *In Defence of Anarchism*, New York, Harper & Row, 1970.

Wolff, R.P., *The Autonomy of Reason*, New York, Harper Torchbooks, 1973.

INDEX

accidental generalizations, as
opposed to causal or law-like
generalizations, *see* coincidence
action: against one's own interests,
103; as attempt, 65; causal
explanation of, 60-70, 94; and
consciousness, 55; deviant, 93,
101, *see also* choice, rules;
distinguished from behaviour,
52-60, 70, 89, 110; intentional
explanation of, 54-8, *see also*
teleological explanation; and
language, 74; practical character
of, 142-51; refraining from, 69;
responsibility for, 55-60; social
character of, 73-80; success in, as
criterion of human need, 171-2
agency: freedom of agency vs.
political freedom, 89-90;
identification with possession of
individual mind, 80-2; not
reducible to cause or reason, 69-
70; social character of, *see also*
social character of action; social
construction of, 73 ff., 82-3; and
social structure, 164-71
agreement: as choosing to think
alike, 81; distinguished from
mere similarity, 151;
evolutionary character of, 151; in
following rules, 85; about
interests, 111-12; in practical

activity, 145, 150-5
aim, in intentional explanation, 54-
60
akrasia, 72
ambiguity: of actions, 62-3, 73, *see
also* imputation of reason; of
observation, 8, *see also*
interpretation, problem of; of
ostensive reference, 142, 146, *see
also* ostensive reference; of
reference, 142
analogies in science, 42-3
analytic/synthetic distinction:
apparently unproblematic, 121-
2; connection with meaning,
122-3; problematic character of,
125-7
anarchism, 91, 105
anthropology, 124, 138, 163
Aristotle, 28-30
artificial intelligence, 71
assessment: of actions, 74; as
general problem of epistemology,
2; of identity of others, 84; of
ideology, 109; of rules, 76
asymmetry between verification
and falsification, 10-11
autonomy of the agent, 164; as
basic need, 171-2, 175-6;
equated with education, 172;
human rational (definition), 100;
limitations upon, 101-14;

necessity
deductive nomological pattern
of, 32-43; contrasted with
intentional explanation, 60-6;
and control of nature, 30-1; *see
also* cause, law of nature
intentional: contrasted with
causal, 60-70, *see also* reasons;
contrasted with deductive
nomological pattern, 60-6;
distinguishing action from
behaviour, 55-60; contrasted
with unintended consequences of
actions, 160-1; necessity of rules
for, *see also* rules, social
character of action
teleological, 28-9
explanatory power, 11, 13

facts: as building blocks for
scientific growth, 4; as distinct
from values, 171, 173; as
necessary for science
notwithstanding critique of
empiricism, 22-4, 26; picture
theory of, 119, 133; as requiring
interpretation, 7-9, 141, 158
fallibility: of methodologies, 170;
of theories, 7, 12; *see also* Popper
false consciousness, 108-14
falsifiability: and intentional
explanation, 65-6; limitations of,
42; role of deduction in, 38-41;
Popper's criterion of, 10
family: as illustrating duality of
structure, 167; as institution of
socialization, 163
feminism, 104; as attempt to
counter ideology, 109
fetishism *see* reification
forbidding: of actions by rules, 75;
of mistakes by rules, 75; necessity
of forbidding mistakes by rules,
83-4; of phenomena by theories,
10; *see also* prohibition
'form of life' (Wittgenstein), 154,
156, 176

freedom, 89-114; of agency,
requiring rules for exercise of,
89-101; and constraint, 166; and
dignity, for and against, 59;
political, distinguished from
freedom of agency, 89-91;
redefined (as 'human rational
autonomy'), 100; social nature
of, 91; *see also* autonomy, liberty
Freud, S., 57-8
function, *see* social function

games, 75; rules in, 91-2, 98;
distinct from social action, 98,
160, 161
geocentrism, 28-30
Giddens, A., 100, 167
goals, 17, 30, 49; *see also* aim,
purpose
growth of science: crude empiricist
view of, 4; as general problem of
epistemology, 2; Kuhn on, 18;
Popper on, 11; *see also* progress
of science

habit: causal beliefs equated with
(Hume), 44; conceptual dividing-
up of world based on (Quine),
125
Hannah, 172
health and autonomy, as needs 171-
3, 175
holism, 164-7
human nature, over- and undersocialized conceptions of, 165,
168
Hume, D., 43-6
Huxley, A., 59

ideology: 89, 102-14; and the claim
to universal validity, 108; critical
nature of, 113; difficulties in
identifying and criticizing, 112-
14; forms of error characteristic
of, 105-7; political character of,

107-14; in relation to power, 104, 107-9

ignorance, 101, 105, 176

imputation: of causal necessity, 45-50; of content to experience, 132; in practical agreements, 152-4; of reasons, 63, 80; of rules, 85

incommensurability, 19, 113, 129; *see also* indeterminacy of meaning and translation

indeterminacy: of descriptions of behaviour with respect to action, 54; of meaning and translation, 127-33

individualism, 76-9, 86-7; contrasted with holism, 164-7; as a moral precept, 174; as objection to notion of ideology, 105; *see also* mentalism, crude

individuality: objections to self-sufficiency of, 76-9, 83-6; as self-sufficient possession of individual person, 80-3; *see also* self-awareness

induction: not deductively valid, 40; definition of, 2-3; Hume on induction and causal necessity, 43-4; Kuhn's use of, 21; Popper's rejection of, 10; *see also* certainty, problem of

innovation: carried on within framework of rules, 92; *see also* creativity, rules

institution, 168; involvement of ideology in, 106-9; as possibly opaque to participants, 98-9; in relation to social character of action, 78-9; *see also* socialization, structuration

institutions: defined as social rules, 78; within explanation of individual action, 74, 78; and patterns of collective action, 96

intention, 81; in intentional explanation of action, 54-60; *see also* explanation

interests: calculated within social

division of labour, 162; falsely represented by ideology, 89, 102-9; to be served by social structure, 173; *see also* needs

interpretation, 24, 114; of actions, social dimension of, 76-9; as a general problem of epistemology, 5, 7-9, 154; of meaning, *see* translation; Popper's solution to, 12; problems with Popper's solution to, 13; *see also* Kuhn

irrationality, 64, 110, 133; acceptance of, as consequence of relativism, 137; *see* autonomy, human rational, *also* ideology, unconscious reason, weakness of will

justification: ideological, 108; of knowledge, 10, *see also* crude empiricism; of actions by reasons, 54-5, 61, 80

Kant, I, 44-6

kinetic theory of gases, 36

Kuhn, T., 14-22, 112-13, 124, 129, 138

language: difference between paradigms in natural science, 20; disanalogy between social action and, 96; identifying alien sounds as, 138-41; in ideological legitimation, 108; likeness between creativity in action and in use of, 92; likeness between repertoire of actions and vocabulary of, 80; practical foundation for use of, 147-55; and relativism in relation to critique of ideology, 113; as a tool, 149; use of, not based on private rule-following, 83-6

law of nature: contrasted with reasons, 66; contrasted with rules, 91, 93; and control of

of knowledge, 10; as viewed by crude empiricism, 4; *see also* experience

signs, arbitrary nature of words as, 122

skill, as part of learning to act, 74-5

Skinner, B.F., 58-9

slavery, 108, 111, 116

Smith, Adam, 159

social action, decisions about causal imputation as components of, 49

social function, 161-3; as missing premise in deriving entitlement from need, 173-4

social process of rule formation, 77

social relations, *see* relations

social science: defined, 176; moral responsibility of, 170

social structure, 158-77; duality of, 164-71; formed by independent rules, 161-3

social system, 158-77; in relation to institutions and social character of action, 78-9, *see also* unintended consequences of actions

socialization, 163; 'under-' vs. 'over-' socialized view, 165-7; *see also* structuration

spectator as episteomological subject, 2, 9, 17-18

statistical laws, *see* laws of nature

structuration, 167-9; techniques for analysing, 169-70

sufficient conditions: causal type of, 67; coincidence of logical and causal types of conditions for action, 66-70; different from necessary conditions, 43, 46; *see also* cause

suicide, 23

superstition, 106

symmetry between explanation and prediction, 52, 61

synchronic-diachronic, 165

synonymy: Quine's attack upon, 125-6; *see also* meaning

synthetic truths, *see* analytic/ synthetic distinction

teleological explanation, 28-9; change from teleological to mechanical model, 30-1

testing of theories: *see* falsifiability, law of nature, prediction

theory-laden character of observation, 9, 13

tools, 152, 161

traditional healer vs. western doctor, 13, 128, 149, 171

translation: apparently unproblematic for crude correspondence theory of truth, 123; bridgeheads, 138-40, 142, 145-6; limits on determinacy achievable via practical agreement, 150; problematic character of, 127-33; *see also* language, incommensurability, indeterminacy

unconscious reasons, 57-8

underdetermination: of belief by experience, 129-33; 141; of meaning by definitions, 125-9; of theory by evidence, 6, 12, 118, *see also* induction, problem of; *see also* disagreement vs. misunderstanding

unintended consequences of action, 99, 105, 110, 158-63, 172-3; understood differently from causal or intentional explanation, 160-1; *see also* opacity of social life

universality: claimed by ideology, 108; as criterion of causal status of law, 46; contrasted with particularity of observation, 6; not required of constitutive activities, 145, 162; of needs, 171

validity, logical, independent of